THE MESSENGER

NAVPRESS
BRINGING TRUTH TO LIFE
P.O. Box 35001, Colorado Springs, Colorado 80935

Our Guarantee to You

We believe so strongly in the message of our books that we are making this quality guarantee to you. If for any reason you are disappointed with the content of this book, return the title page to us with your name and address and we will refund to you the list price of the book. To help us serve you better, please briefly describe why you were disappointed. Mail your refund request to: NavPress, P.O. Box 35002, Colorado Springs, CO 80935.

The Navigators is an international Christian organization. Our mission is to reach, disciple, and equip people to know Christ and to make Him known through successive generations. We envision multitudes of diverse people in the United States and every other nation who have a passionate love for Christ, live a lifestyle of sharing Christ's love, and multiply spiritual laborers among those without Christ.

NavPress is the publishing ministry of The Navigators. NavPress publications help believers learn biblical truth and apply what they learn to their lives and ministries. Our mission is to stimulate spiritual formation among our readers.

ISBN 1-57683-356-9
Cover design by Dan Jamison
Cover illustrations by Albrecht Durer / Planet Art
Creative Team: Sue Geiman, Greg Clouse, Jacqueline Eaton Blakley, Darla Hightower, Glynese Northam

Woodroof, Tim, 1955-
The messenger / Tim Woodroof.
p. cm.
Includes bibliographical references.
ISBN 1-57683-356-9
1. Bible. N.T. Philippians--History of Biblical events--Fiction. 2. Church history--Primitive and early church, ca. 30-600--Fiction. 3. Paul, the Apostle, Saint--Fiction. 4. Philippi (Extinct city)--Fiction. I. Title.
PS3623.067 M47 2002
813'.6--dc21

2002004813

Printed in the United States of America

1 2 3 4 5 6 7 8 9 10 / 06 05 04 03 02

TO MY PARENTS,
JIM AND LOUINE WOODROOF

PAULS TO THIS TIMOTHY

Table of Contents

Prologue

WITH A SOLDIER TO GUARD HIM

(JANUARY, A.D. 62)

THE SINGLE WINDOW OPENING INTO HIS BEDROOM WAS SMALL AND COVERED with oilcloth. Set high in the wall to afford a measure of privacy from the tenants across the way, it watched over the chamber within—a cycloptic eye staring from a masonry face.

As windows go, it had its problems. Rain seeped through the cloth to collect in puddles on the sill and floor. When the wind blew sharply (or neighborhood children threw rocks), the cloth tore and needed replacement. In the cold, it turned the smoke of the stove back into the room but retained none of the heat.

For all its shortcomings, the window did leak a little light and permitted a lonely man to eavesdrop on the noisy city outside. He considered the window a blessing from God.

Morning was breaking, and the first grays of dawn touched the window and crept into the room. Shapes began to emerge from the darkness—indistinct lumps resolving into furnishings and pots and scrolls. In the corner, a man knelt, swaying back and forth to some internal rhythm. He had stripped the blanket from the bed and wrapped it around himself for warmth. A shawl covered his head and shoulders. He mumbled softly, praying in Hebrew, rolling the familiar consonants around in his mouth before releasing them on their journey to God.

Prologue

The man paused and glanced up to note the coming light. The deep lines in his face, accentuated by the shadows, testified to a hard life. The cheeks were hollowed, the eyes sunken. In the morning gray, he looked used up.

But seeing the daylight, he smiled. The unruly mass of wrinkles rearranged themselves into a look of simple pleasure. For a moment, the weariness receded and the joy of a new day animated his face. There was life still in the old man, a strength that could be summoned by an act of will—or by the promise of dawn.

"In the morning, O Lord, you hear my voice," he intoned, borrowing from the Psalms. "In the morning I lay my requests before you and wait in expectation."

He rose slowly from the floor, taking time to stretch his legs and unkink his back. When at last he stood upright, he still stooped noticeably, leaning to the right and canting his head to balance. He was a crooked man, all angles and curves, with hardly a plumb line to his person. He had not always been so—in his youth he'd stood erect enough. But time and injury had bent him beyond straightening.

That, he did not consider a blessing from God.

Shrugging off the prayer shawl and throwing the blanket on the bed, he stepped out of his tunic. His body was compact, narrow in frame. There was no fat on him, though the skin sagged and wrinkled in the way of old people. A mat of gray hair covered his arms and chest, and he stood on strong, well-formed legs. Once, he'd been quite vain about his legs.

Taking up a chamber pot, the old man relieved himself and set down the pot by the door. He moved to the table and dipped his hands into a basin, rinsing his face in the frigid water. Letting the water run down his forearms (in the manner of his countrymen), he dried himself and hurriedly dressed.

It was time to get on with his day.

The adjoining room was larger and lighter than his own, serving as kitchen, meeting area, and bedroom for the rotation of soldiers assigned to guard him. The old man smiled at the snoring figure stretched upon the bed. This particular guard liked his drink in the evening and often slept later than was strictly permitted.

Quietly pouring the wastes from the soldier's chamber pot into his own, the prisoner eased out of the apartment and descended three flights of stairs to the ground floor. Opening the gate leading from the courtyard, he emptied the contents of his pot into the street.

The city was awakening. He paused to drink in the sounds of the morning—the clanking of pots, the strident hawkings of optimistic vendors, the sizzle of cooking fires, the grunts and curses of men carrying burdens, the clip-clop of horses' hooves. Upstairs in the apartment building, he could hear children crying and spouses taking up afresh the arguments of the night before. He felt the rumble of a heavy wagon carrying its load to market.

The old man loved mornings. He loved these sounds.

With a sigh, he turned and went back upstairs to his apartment. The soldier was sitting up in bed, his head held gingerly in his hands.

"It's early for you, isn't it, Rufus? God be with you!" he called softly.

"And the Devil take you," growled the soldier. His head pounded and his mouth tasted stale and dry. He sat very still, hoping a lack of motion would calm his aching temples. Through half-closed eyes, he watched as the old man rebuilt the fire in the stove and set a pot of water to heat. Running a calloused hand over his face and eyes, Rufus swung his feet to the floor and waited for the room to stop moving.

As he did every morning, when his turn to guard this prisoner came up in the rotation, the grizzled soldier told himself how fortunate he was. This was not bad duty. The bed was warm and dry. He could sleep through the night. There was nothing dangerous about the prisoner. Not the worst duty Rufus had ever drawn.

Except the old man talked. Or, rather, he questioned. Strange, probing questions that made the veteran uncomfortable. He had been a man of action all his life, not given to introspection and the deeper issues of life. If it could not be solved with a sword or a swat, he didn't waste his time. Not if he could help it, that is. Not if old men would leave him alone and cease asking questions that had no answers.

The questions bothered his sleep. Deep in the night, Rufus would wake with a start and realize he had been going over their conversations in his dreams. He would lie wide-eyed in the dark, thinking thoughts not proper for a soldier of the empire—a man who had killed and raped—to think. *I've gotten above myself,* he thought bitterly at such times. Angry, he would curse himself a fool for worrying about the gods and whether they cared about the actions of a simple soldier. In the end, he would rise from his bed, grab the wine flask, and drink himself back to dreamless slumber.

Twice in the past month, Rufus had traded duty with another soldier in his squad, choosing to stand watch through the cold of night rather than face this withered Jew with his worrisome questions. Now, warily, he watched as the old man spread sawdust on the floor and began sweeping up the debris of the previous day. *No,* thought the soldier. *He is not a dangerous man. But he sure scares me.*

At that instant, the old man turned from his broom and fixed Rufus with a steady gaze. The eyes gave an illusion of seeing through the soldier, reaching into him and discovering his hidden places. The soldier knew better. He knew the old man could barely see past his own hand, so poor were his eyes. He had to squint hard just to read. Still, Rufus avoided the gaze and looked at his feet, pretending to busy himself with lacing his sandals.

"Are you ready to face the day, Rufus?"

"One day's like another, old man. You either face it or fall on your sword. Given the alternative, even dealing with the likes of you seems bearable." The soldier looked up. "Only, no talk today. Just do your work and leave me alone."

The old man smiled innocently. "As you wish, Rufus. Even Gentiles deserve a Sabbath rest once in a while. So no talk today. We'll declare it a Holy Day, devoted to rest and to prayer." He paused and seemed to consider the terms of his accommodation. "Do you know how to pray, Rufus? Do you think God listens to your prayers?"

The soldier glared hard at Paul and told him emphatically that if he did not shut up, he was likely to meet God with great suddenness and could ask his questions in person.

Section One

TROUBLE IN PHILIPPI

SUMMER, A.D. 60—JANUARY, A.D. 62

Chapter One

YOU SENT HIM TO ME

(LATE JANUARY, A.D. 62)

THE SEA IS A LONELY PLACE WHEN IT STORMS.

On calmer days, the sea draws men into natural community. A ship's crew must work together to trim sails and steer a course. Passengers congregate on deck to share stories and pass the hours in the company of others. There is something about the business of traveling by water that throws men together and binds them in common cause.

But in a storm, every man turns inward and becomes a solitary sailor. Hard winds and high waves drive a man onto the reef of himself. Detached, he must face his own private miseries. Isolated, he must confront his own personal fears. In a storm, though others may be present on the boat, each man faces the tempest alone.

~

It was storming this day. The ashen skies squatted close to the sea—wind and water locked in tight embrace—with the ship, an unwilling partner, caught between. The gale whipped across the gray swells, taking up foam and spray and hurling them angrily at the boat. Rain blew so cruelly it seemed solid, like small nails, needling exposed faces and piercing the most tightly woven cloak.

The ship bucked and rolled, punching her bow into each oncoming wave, then pausing as if to decide whether to plunge to the sea bottom or shed the water from her decks and ride the surface a while longer. She protested audibly in her exertions. The rigging sang a brave working-song, but the timbers of the hull—bearing as they did the brunt of the labor—could manage only an exhausted groan. Staying afloat in this furious sea was killing work.

But the ship was not alone in its misery. Epaphroditus, a Macedonian from the city of Philippi and the descendant of a long line of men who wisely lived on solid ground, knelt on the open deck with his arms wrapped tightly around the railing. Cold, soaked to the bone, and sicker than he had ever been in his life, he was praying—fervently, sincerely—that God would end his suffering and take him home.

Hours before, the first swells of the storm had sent him to the railing in search of relief. Finding none, despite repeated and wrenching efforts, he turned instead to prayer. At first, he prayed for the storm to cease. It raged on. He prayed for some lesser miracle—healing for his stomach or even a momentary lull in the tempest. But God apparently was in no mood for miracles. Finally, with an earnestness only the seasick can muster, he begged for a merciful end.

But the storm blew on and Epaphroditus remained among the living. Leaning as far over the side as his death-grip would allow, the young man made yet another offering to the sea. He felt the rain running down his neck, collecting in every crevice of clothing and body, and filling his boots. He shuddered at the cold. Wiping a wet sleeve across his mouth, he stumbled back to the hatch to plunge below decks again.

A single lantern swung from the ceiling of the cargo hold, throwing shadows around the walls and adding to the sickening sense of motion. It lit, then silhouetted the green faces of his fellow travelers, who looked up as Epaphroditus clambered down the ladder. In his distress, he imagined them to be tortured souls watching another of the damned descend into dark Hades from the gray and stormy world above.

The stench of vomit and urine rose up to greet Epaphroditus, almost persuading him to sit out the storm on deck. But the thought of the rain and wind and plummeting temperatures somehow made the rankness bearable. So Epaphroditus eased himself to the floor, his back firmly against a beam and his hands spread out on the decking to steady himself.

The flickering light showed him to be in his late twenties, of average stature, with a high forehead and strong jaw. His face was framed by a mass of dark hair—that and his nausea made him seem pale. In better light and on better days, he appeared tanned and healthy. But "pale" was the best he could manage under these circumstances. A potter by trade, his shoulders and arms were muscled by long hours throwing pitchers and bowls on his wheel. Behind the eyes, staring dolefully now around the darkened hold, lurked a bright intelligence.

It was not his habit to talk to himself. But there, in the darkness, he began to do so with quiet intensity, lips moving in silent rebuke. *No one in his right mind travels at this time of year. Not by sea. What were you thinking?!*

This was the stormy season, the time when cold winds from the north mixed with warmer air over the Mediterranean, causing sudden and violent tempests. The crossing between Nicopolis and Rhegium was famous for its fury during these late-winter months. Survivors of the crossing at this time of year rarely made the same mistake twice. When next they were required to travel in winter, most chose to go by land. Better to hazard the thieves and bedbugs of the Egnatian Way than risk the Adriatic in January.

Epaphroditus would have preferred to walk from Philippi to Rome. The road was well traveled, even at this season, and he was strong enough to give any bandit second thoughts. But the journey by land required two months of hard marching. Since he was on urgent business, Epaphroditus had gone instead to Nicopolis and booked passage on the first ship for Rome—a grain barge whose captain cared less about the weather than about potential profit.

Unconsciously, his hand felt beneath his tunic for the money belt at his waist. The belt was thick with mail and small purses of coin. The letters were all addressed "To Paul." Some were skillfully scripted, the products of careful thought and patient penmanship. Others, though, had been scratched in haste by people as they stood in his pottery shop. And many of the letters were in Epaphroditus's own hand, words dictated to him by illiterate friends. They all contained warm greetings and bits of personal news, the chatty notes people write to loved ones they have not seen for years. There were words of encouragement and prayers for Paul's quick release. A few of the letters were longer, addressing deeper concerns about the church in Philippi, raising issues only an apostle could resolve.

To anyone else, the letters would have little value. But to Paul, they would be words of life.

The money was a different matter. Epaphroditus carried a considerable sum—larger portions contributed by wealthier members of the Philippian church, smaller amounts given with equal sacrifice by the widows and slaves of the congregation. All of it was for Paul, a gift from people who loved him deeply and wanted to help during a difficult time. There was enough money in the belt to make Epaphroditus nervous and watchful. Perhaps it was better to be on a ship after all, where he could keep his back to a bulkhead and his eyes on his fellow travelers.

In truth, the storm made Epaphroditus feel safer about the money. It would take a very determined thief to master his own nausea, overwhelm Epaphroditus in the crowded hold, and relieve him of his money belt.

And, ironically, the money made Epaphroditus feel safer in the storm. Grasping the belt as if it were a lifeline, he comforted himself by thinking of its contents, as though the financial and spiritual support it contained for the Apostle would guarantee its carrier safe passage through any weather. He would have to suffer out the storm. But Epaphroditus felt confident he would survive.

The young potter slowly loosened his grip on the belt and leaned his head against the beam at his back. Cautiously, he closed his eyes and let his mind drift back to Philippi.

~

The two of them sat on a hill overlooking the city from the north. It was their custom to walk together as frequently as possible. Where their feet carried them mattered little to either man. The walking was an excuse to conduct important business. Clement was shaping the future of his church. Epaphroditus was learning the bittersweet lessons of caring about kingdom matters.

"That was the first time I felt the weight of it all, the burden of being responsible for these people." Clement picked up a twig and broke it into smaller and smaller fragments. "It has been with me ever since. At first, I resented it, fought it. I didn't realize till later what a blessing it was . . . how much I needed it."

Epaphroditus nodded and spoke quietly. "At the shop, I catch myself thinking about our conversations or worrying about someone when I should be attending to customers. I'll sit at the wheel, and my hands take on a life of their own. They're turning the clay, but, in my head, I'm turning the church."

Clement stilled his restless hands and gave himself to the listening.

"Like the other day. I was talking with friends. They were arguing about business and I was bored. I wanted to turn the talk to something that mattered. And then I realized business used to matter to me. I cared about it once. But not anymore. At least, not as much." Epaphroditus rubbed a hand across his face and looked sideways at his companion. "It's getting bad, Clement. I'm even preaching in my dreams. Great sermons. None of those limp lectures I commit in real life! What's happening to me?"

Clement placed his hand on the younger man's shoulder and sat quietly for a few moments. In the plain below them lay the acropolis of Philippi, with its walled defenses and barracks. A spear's throw beyond that, the Egnatian Way divided the city in half. They could see the ribbon of road disappear west toward the setting sun and the distant Adriatic. To the east, they could also see where the road turned south a dozen miles to the Aegean.

Philippi itself sprawled through the narrow valley before them, a haphazard collection of huts and villas and shops and public works. Most of the significant structures—government buildings, temples, guild halls—clustered along the Egnatian Way through the center of town. In the very heart of Philippi, the road opened up into a large square, the agora, where a maze of fountains and shops and public baths crowded together. The two men could see figures scurrying about the marketplace, making the final transactions of the day.

From the vantage of their hilltop, however, nothing in the city caught the eye quite like the theater. In ancient times, the city fathers had cut tiers into a hillside on the eastern edge of Philippi. Since that time, it had served the community as meeting place, concert hall, and sports arena. Now its marble facade and seats glistened in the afternoon sun, catching the late rays and reflecting golds and reds and yellows. It was a sight to make a Philippian proud.

"I know what you're feeling," Clement broke the reverie. "You are in the grip of something larger than yourself. God has placed his hand on you and you cannot shake him off." Epaphroditus nodded almost reluctantly. "You'd think, when God comes knocking, it would be a great joy . . . a satisfaction. But it's also a burden, isn't it? His call leaves you feeling heavy . . . and a little lonely."

"Yes," Epaphroditus agreed quietly. "I can't just enjoy my work and my friends. I can't just live day-to-day. There's a layer to living now that wasn't there before. I feel responsible. I sense that God wants something more of me."

Clement's hand gripped his young companion's shoulder. "Don't push too hard, son. God *does* want something of you. I sense that too. But he will reveal it in his own good time. In the meantime, you must learn joy."

The ship rolled and shuddered, breaking the thread of the potter's thoughts and dragging him back to the present. Epaphroditus spread his hands wider on the decking and pressed his back more firmly into the beam. He urged his thoughts back to Philippi, trying to recapture his conversation with Clement. Instead, he heard himself speaking.

"My old friends tell me that joy is an elusive thing, coming and going with the tides of fate. They blame joy on pleasant circumstance and good fortune. When the gods smile, when all is well, then joy breaks out like the sun after a rain." Epaphroditus looked around at the upturned faces focused on him. He stood against the back wall of the room while the congregation sat, tight-packed, on the floor. "Take pleasure in it while you can, they tell me, for soon enough the rain will return, and joy will fade."

Epaphroditus shook his head slowly, as much from sadness as for effect on his listeners. "Tell me. Is joy the result of good circumstances or good character? Do we find joy because things go well with us or because things are well *in* us? I know people who have every advantage—wealth and power and beauty—who never know joy. And I've seen others who, in the worst of circumstances, are filled with peace and contentment." Many in the audience nodded. They knew people like that as well. They thought of one man in particular, a man who could sing in a dungeon.

"I think my old friends are wrong. Real joy isn't an accident waiting to happen. Real joy doesn't fall on us and then abandon us with changes of fortune. Real joy grows its roots deeper than that. Real joy grows in the soil of contentment and character and commitment. As long as character remains true, as long as faith does not waver, nothing can take away our joy. Not circumstance. Not disappointment. Not adversity." The potter's eyes were shining.

The ship dropped heavily into a trough between the waves, lifting Epaphroditus from the deck and slamming him against the bulkhead. His exhausted body registered the fresh ache and, from some far away place, Epaphroditus became conscious of his stomach again. He tasted a foulness in his mouth and licked dry lips. Resettling himself, he hurried back to the unfinished sermon he had been composing in his dream.

Only this time, it was to another, darker place that he returned.

He could see her lying on a mat pushed into the far corner of the room. His own child-hand rested against the door frame separating her sick room from the work and living quarters of their house. He watched her turn and toss. He heard her moaning. He longed to enter and hold her hand, but was too afraid.

A sour odor washed from her bed, an unpleasant mix of sweat and mold and fever. He could barely stand the stench and had to fight the urge to run from the house to purge his lungs in the clean outdoor air. He resisted, however, and maintained his lonely vigil at the door by breathing shallow, guarded breaths through his mouth. He felt rooted there—afraid to go in, afraid to go away, uncertain and helpless.

Helpless. That was his most powerful memory, a paralyzing impotence that combined with his little-boy dread to sharpen the vision of his mother—wasting and faded—on her mat in the corner. He could watch, but he could not act. He did not know what to do. Long after she was gone, after he had forgotten her face and the touch of her hand, he would remember how it felt to stand in the doorway and do nothing.

In that twilight place between dream and wakefulness, Epaphroditus pondered how the people he loved could cause him such pain.

He lifted his hand to rub his face. He felt the ship jolt and sway beneath him. He became conscious of the choking closeness of the hold, of muffled conversations and timbers creaking.

There were those, he knew, who protected themselves by learning not to love so much. They guarded against the intrusion of other people, careful to avoid an affection that might result in disappointment or loss. Epaphroditus had never learned the trick. He could not keep people at a safe distance, no matter how much he might try. So, early on, he had learned to swallow whatever pain others caused him. But it merely settled in his belly, erupting on occasion in bouts of queasy indigestion. He'd always had a weak stomach.

For the past year, the church in Philippi had been sitting heavy and uneasy in his gut. His affection for these people was causing him as much distress as joy. Sometimes, when lost in thought about the church, Epaphroditus would catch his reflection in a bowl of water or a polished metal surface. And, to his surprise, he would discover he was frowning.

There were problems. And not the kind Epaphroditus had anticipated. Christians weren't being locked up in the Philippian jail or beaten by Roman soldiers. No one's property had been confiscated. It had been a long time since the temple leaders protested this new and vaguely unpatriotic religion. Indeed, the problems faced by the Philippian believers came not from outsiders at all. Their pain was entirely self-inflicted.

After years of relative calm, the church had stumbled over its first real struggle with itself. Not that everything had always been peace and light among the Christians of Philippi. There had been conflicts through the years—hurt feelings and harsh words. But these were isolated cases, involving particular personalities, and the church had always drawn together to restore peace.

This was different. Now the entire congregation was involved. They had all been blown off course by this storm. There were no points of calm, no people who somehow remained above the squall, pointing out safe haven to which the rest could run. As a result, there was no steadying hand on the tiller, no one to steer the church into smooth water.

Words had been spoken, narrow and intolerant words. Longtime companions were at odds, arguing with each other and questioning motives. The leaders of the church—Clement and his fellow elders—had suffered rising criticism and a crisis of confidence. The attentions of the church were consumed with matters that (in Epaphroditus's opinion) were distractions from the real business of God's kingdom.

The Christians of Philippi seemed adrift, isolated from one another, unable or unwilling to connect and reconcile. Each member of the fellowship was so busy bailing his own boat, he had no time to show concern for a foundering brother. Epaphroditus could feel the cold winds blowing through these people, chilling friendships, dampening spirits. He could feel the deck of his stable world lifting and rolling, reacting to the swells of a tempest none of them had expected or prepared for.

It would be easier if the struggle were with unbelievers, if the suffering were physical. They had weathered that kind of persecution before. But this was different, and, in an odd way, more ominous.

So Epaphroditus fretted and worried and tried to calm his roiling stomach. It had punished him for months. Long before he boarded the ship, there'd been a sourness in his belly that tasted foul in his mouth. Whenever he thought too long or too hard about the people with whom he worshiped, he paid for it with spells of dyspeptic suffering.

Worse than his stomach, though, was the rising tide of helplessness, a conviction that he was watching something he was powerless to change. There were times when the frustrating impotence swept over him like a wave, overwhelming his affections and good intentions, dragging him under to a place of dark moods and wordless anger. He wanted to strike something, to be done with paralysis even at the cost of violence. At such moments, he'd make a fist. But his hand would feel small and childlike. And the odor of sweat and mold and fever would sting in his nostrils.

His only hope, he knew, was to find Paul. Paul would understand. The Apostle had been through it all before. This was an enemy he knew well.

Paul would know. He must find Paul. . . .

~

Epaphroditus woke with a start, banging his head against the beam at his back. Disoriented, still half-asleep, he massaged his scalp and tried to remember where he was. It was the nausea that brought him full awake and reminded him of the ship and the storm.

Stumbling to his feet and to the ladder, he made his way up on deck to his station at the railing. Oblivious to the wind and the rain, focused fully on his stomach and its urgent demands, Epaphroditus settled grimly to his lonely battle against the sea and his fears.

Were he in a philosophical mood, he might have reflected that a church, like the sea, can be a lonely place when it is storming. He might have considered how, during calmer times, faith draws people into natural community, binding them together and uniting them in common cause. But when storms come, Christians are as tempted as sailors to turn inward. Hard words and high emotions can drive even the most dedicated disciple onto the lonely reef of self.

But Epaphroditus was not feeling philosophical at the moment. He was too sick to bother with metaphors. He had only enough strength to hold on until the storm passed. When it did, he could worry about Philippi. When his stomach settled, he could go over it all again. Once the storm had blown itself out, he would be that much closer to Rome and to Paul.

Chapter Two

YOU STILL HEAR ABOUT MY TROUBLES

(EARLY JANUARY, A.D. 62)

WHEN WORD OF PAUL REACHED PHILIPPI, IT FELL LIKE RAIN ON PARCHED ground. The long drought of information had left the Philippians weak and fretful. But when they heard at last that Paul was in Rome—even though he was under arrest and awaiting trial—they drank in the news gratefully.

News regarding great events of state—battles and coronations and gossip about the emperor's excesses—traveled quickly to Philippi along Roman roads and sea lanes. Quickly and reliably. But news of more personal consequence—the well-being of distant family or friends long absent—dribbled in by fits and starts. Carried on the lips of road-weary businessmen or transients fresh from the sea, such news was often the victim of poor memory, misunderstood fact, and the natural tendency of messengers everywhere to elaborate. It was almost never timely. It was even less frequently right.

As a result, keeping up with Paul had proven a frustrating and elusive endeavor for the Philippians. Six silent years had passed since his last visit through their city. During those years, every passing missionary, every peripatetic stranger with any connection to the Way was questioned closely and squeezed for the smallest trickle of news: "Have you heard anything about Paul? Do you know where he is?

How goes it with him?" But information was scarce and sketchy.

Most of those questioned knew nothing. They would smile and shrug and change the subject. The few who claimed knowledge gave conflicting reports. Some said Paul had been arrested in Judea and was a prisoner of the Roman governor in Caesarea. Others claimed he was dead, killed by a band of angry fanatics in Jerusalem. One visitor announced with great certainty that Paul had quit preaching entirely and gone back to Tarsus to resume the family business.

For the Philippians it was maddening, all this hearsay and so few hard facts. They were thirsty for some word about their absent friend. But the mix of gossip and secondhand information and sheer fancy passed on by wayfarers served only to deepen their sense of separation from the Apostle. They shared the uneasy suspicion that Paul was in trouble; trouble dogged him like an unwanted companion. If so, they would gladly look after him, take care of him. But first they had to find him. With no idea where Paul might be or what kind of help he most needed, they could only wait for some definite report, clinging in the meantime to every rumor or snippet of news that might connect them to the absent apostle.

For Epaphroditus, though, it was worse than maddening—especially of late. Not knowing was like a canker sore, aching dully when his mind turned to other things and acutely painful whenever he touched the subject directly. More and more, he was convinced he had to find Paul. Paul would know what should be done to heal the body at Philippi. And so, more than most, Epaphroditus reached for any hint, any clue of Paul's whereabouts.

When a brother on his way back to Ephesus told the Philippians he had just seen Paul in Rome, the elders called a special meeting of the church and asked the stranger to tell his news before the congregation.

Epaphroditus was there, weak with relief.

~

"All right, quiet down please!" Clement called the group of one hundred and twenty souls to order. They'd crowded into the central courtyard at the house of Jerome, who, as one of the church's wealthier members, frequently opened his home for their gatherings. It was cold in the open square and the breath of the crowd hung in the air, obscuring the stars and gathering like silver haloes around the torches and lanterns at the perimeter.

"Please, brothers and sisters!" Clement called again, and slowly the conversations died off.

The faces staring up at Clement formed a rough cross section of Philippian society. Rich, poor, old, young, slave, free, male, female, white, black, and most shades between. He looked out over the ruddy faces of fat merchants, the lined and sunburnt faces of farmers, the pinched and pocked faces of those who eked out a meager living by their own wits or by others' mercies. He could see the eager faces of children and the tired faces of their mothers. There were faces marked by privilege and pain, disease and vigor, competence and failure, life in its ebb and in its flow. The slaves in the crowd, drawn from every place and race, showed Spanish, Arabic, African, and even Oriental traits. From the first, the draw of the gospel had been eclectic at Philippi. The church did not play favorites. It could not afford to. It attracted adherents from every segment of the city's diverse population. It welcomed all comers.

Still, there was a unifying reality to the city's life, a boulder of fact that loomed over the rocks and pebbles of daily existence at Philippi. Philippi was a Roman colony, a Rome away from Rome, an outpost of empire culture, politics, and government in a wilderness of rustic provincials. Never mind that Greece had been a center for learning and culture for half a millennium. The Philippians were proud of being *Roman*, governed by Roman law, followers of Roman customs. Though Greek was the language of the marketplace and home at Philippi, the official tongue of the city was Latin.

The crowd in front of Clement showed the signs of Rome's pervasive influence. Several faces looking at him had the brawny, weathered appearance of ex-soldiers; for nearly a century, retired legionnaires had been given land grants in the area. Some faces showed finer features and fair complexions, indicating Italian rather than Greek ancestry. Jerome, who'd made a fortune trading in the gold that was mined to the north and west of the city, always sported the latest Roman fashion and hairstyle. He stood in the crowd this night, in dress and demeanor a testimony to the sway of Roman ways.

While Clement waited for the group to settle, he glanced fondly at Epaphroditus standing at the back of the crowd, leaning against the wall of the courtyard. It was Clement who had shared the gospel with the young potter, browsing through the clay pots and jugs in his shop as he struck up conversations and slowly developed a friendship. He'd purchased enough pottery from Epaphroditus over the course of those first months to meet the needs of his household for three years. *A small price for a soul,* Clement smiled to himself.

Epaphroditus still worked at his wheel to support himself, though the best of his time and energies were now devoted to study and to teaching and sharing good news. He often preached for the church on the Lord's Day. While not exactly eloquent, he was sincere and earnest. People listened well to him. Clement was convinced the future of the Philippian church rested in Epaphroditus's strong hands.

Clearing his throat, the shepherd addressed his sheep. "Brothers and sisters! Welcome! Thank you for gathering on such short notice, but we have great news. We've found Paul. He's in Rome." A ripple spread across the crowd. People stretched and craned to catch a glimpse of the stranger standing beside Clement.

Holding up his hands again for quiet, Clement continued. "Let me introduce you to a brother who worships with the church in Ephesus. He's just come from Rome and brings news of Paul. He asked to meet with us this evening to tell us what he knows and answer our questions. Onesiphorus of Ephesus!"

Shouts of greeting rose from the excited audience. "Welcome, brother!" "God be with you, friend." A knot of boys began to chant, "O-nesi-phorus," earning a stern glance from Clement and a stifled laugh from Epaphroditus. People were so joyous, so eager to hear about Paul. It was almost like old times. For a moment, the church forgot her troubles and united to listen to the word from Rome. Epaphroditus drank in the truce thirstily.

A barrel of a man stepped forward, nearly as broad as he was tall. A thick beard fell down on his chest and thick fingers moved with surprising grace to smooth the unruly curls. His skin was dusky, and the whites of his eyes contrasted starkly with the shadings of his face. He gave an impression of great strength and great humor. Standing there in front of the crowd, he also seemed awkward and self-conscious. He spoke in short, simple sentences.

"Greetings," he began in a soft voice. At once, the crowd fell silent. "I am Onesiphorus of Ephesus. I bring greetings from the church at home. And greetings from Paul. I saw him not more than a month ago." He paused to look around nervously at the uplifted faces.

"First, let me tell you that Paul is well. He has been through some hard times. But he is well. He speaks of you with great fondness. He is anxious to see you again and hopes it will be soon." As Onesiphorus spoke this last sentence, his tone did not seem to match the optimism of his words. "He apologizes for being out of touch for so long. Things have been . . . well . . . difficult for him. He asked me to bring you up to date."

Onesiphorus smiled, took a deep breath, then plunged into a narrative he knew would cause the Philippians worry. He told them of Paul's travels since his last visit to Philippi; the trip back to Jerusalem; the rioting in the temple; his arrest and transport to Caesarea; two years in jail, awaiting trial.

His listeners leaned forward to catch every word. They groaned and grimaced and shook their heads at each turn in the story. They had suspected something like this. "Paul is not exactly a tactful man," Onesiphorus said, explaining the trouble in the temple. And his audience nodded sadly, knowing too well Paul's gift for saying the right thing at the wrong time. "There was a plot on his life," Onesiphorus continued, recounting how Paul was secreted from Jerusalem and sent to Caesarea.

The crowd listened with the attentiveness of the deaf. They listened with eyes and faces and open mouths. They listened like drunks drink, thirsty for the words, knowing full well the ache those words would cause later, but unwilling to deny themselves the intoxication of hearing.

Epaphroditus pressed farther into the wall, feeling the cold of the stone steal into his back and settle in his chest. He closed his eyes to better savor the words. He was impatient to know all the details, fearful for how the story would end.

"And then, when he finally came to trial"—Onesiphorus was warming to his task, speaking with mounting confidence as the story spilled out—"he made an appeal to Caesar."

That surprised them. They knew, of course, that Paul was a citizen of the empire and, like all citizens, had a right to take his case directly to the courts of Rome. But they also knew this right was rarely invoked. Traveling to Rome was expensive and time-consuming. The court system there was notorious for its cumbersome and venal ways. Only people who feared for their lives and were convinced they would not get a fair hearing in the provinces took the desperate step of appealing to Caesar. Things must have been very bleak for Paul in Caesarea.

"Anyway, Paul got to Rome almost two years ago. His case is on the docket. But who knows when he will actually come to trial? He spends his days waiting, and you know how Paul takes to waiting!" Onesiphorus grinned at the audience. They smiled back and some of the anxiety leaked out of both the speaker and his listeners. At least Paul was alive. At least they knew where he was.

"When I was with him, his health seemed good. He was as . . . as . . . " Onesiphorus stammered to find the right word.

"Intense?" someone in the crowd suggested.

Onesiphorus threw his head back and laughed, joined by those in the crowd who knew Paul best. "Yes, yes! That is the exact term! He was as intense as ever. An hour with Paul is like a day chopping wood, I always say! All in all, the news is not so bad. He is under arrest. But he is being held in an apartment, not a dungeon. The Romans are taking their sweet time putting him on trial. But maybe that indicates they have doubts about the case against him. He is guarded around the clock. But he's driving his guards crazy."

"I bet he is!" a hard-looking fellow near the front blurted. The meeting erupted again in laughter, people elbowing their neighbors, finding great humor in the quip. Onesiphorus was a man who appreciated a good joke more than most. But he wasn't sure he understood why this comment should be so funny. It wasn't until later, after the meeting, that he met the jailer Paul had driven to distraction a dozen years earlier.

He waited for the laughter to subside, then continued. "I am concerned, though, about his spirits." The crowd grew still at once. Onesiphorus spoke quietly and slowly, almost to himself. He chose his words with care, wanting to find the right language, trying to understand for himself even as he attempted an explanation for others. The church strained to catch his voice. "He is older now, my brothers. He has lost weight. He looks tired when he thinks no one is watching him. These last years have taken a toll. He seems . . . I don't know . . . lonely, somehow. I think . . . I think he has been disappointed too often. He carries many scars . . . the kind you can't see." Onesiphorus looked from face to face. "From what I saw, Paul is discouraged. I think he needs his friends now as he never has before."

There was a pause, all of them thinking of Paul shut up and cut off. "What can we do for him?" a woman asked softly, and the entire church leaned forward to hear. Onesiphorus fidgeted with his beard and considered his answer.

"Well, he has asked all the churches to pray for him. And prayers are good. I encourage you to pray." Onesiphorus stopped and drew a breath, taking the measure of the people before him. His voice grew stronger. "But forgive me for suggesting that sometimes we pray best with actions, not words. The man is exasperating. There are so many ways we could help. There are so many people wanting to help. But all he would say is, 'Tell them to pray, Onesiphorus. Tell them to pray.'

"So pray! But the old man has more tangible needs as well." Onesiphorus began to list off the items on his thick fingers. "His rent for a two-room apartment is five hundred sesterces a month!" The Philippians gasped. That kind of money would rent a mansion in their city. "But paying the rent is the only thing keeping him out of a dungeon. I gave the landlord what money I had, but it won't last long. Paul needs food and other provisions. I'd like him to have a heavier cloak and another blanket for his bed. He has nothing, brothers, literally nothing!"

Onesiphorus was pleading now, begging for their assistance. But his pleadings were unnecessary. He and all his barrel-chested strength could not keep the Philippians from helping where Paul was concerned.

"But most of all"—here Onesiphorus borrowed a little of the intensity he had charged to Paul—"most of all, Paul needs to know that you remember him, that you still love him, that his work among you was not in vain. Paul needs to know that he has made a difference here—in your lives and in this church. There is nothing you could do for him that would mean more."

Onesiphorus suddenly felt tired. He was not accustomed to public speaking or, for that matter, speaking at all about matters so deeply felt. He looked to Clement for rescue, a private plea to end his part of this meeting. Clement stepped forward and addressed his flock. "That's everything Onesiphorus can tell us. Perhaps you have questions?"

"Shepherd Clement?" A female voice called out from the crowd, though the only part of the woman visible to most was her waving hand. A short, reedlike widow in her forties pushed her way to the front so she could see Clement and be seen by him. She had a sweet face that was now wet with tears. If the report on Paul was "not so bad," it was certainly bad enough for her tastes.

Syntyche looked around at her church family. "We have to do something, and do it quickly. If half of what this man says is true"—she shot Onesiphorus an accusing glance, as if he were personally responsible for Paul's suffering—"Paul is cold and lonely. He is in danger of being thrown into a dungeon. He may not have enough food to eat! I owe him every—" Her voice broke and she stopped to compose herself. It required a moment. "I cannot stand the thought of Paul in such conditions," she continued quietly. "We must send someone to him quickly, someone who can carry a gift from us all."

The crowd murmured agreement. Many spoke up, suggesting things Paul might need. One man volunteered a new cloak. Another offered a pair of sandals.

"Shepherd Clement!" A strong voice carried from the courtyard gate, a familiar voice that hushed the crowd. All eyes turned to the gate, reluctant and apprehensive, like witnesses to an accident who fear to look but cannot help themselves.

The speaker was a man in his early forties. He had a full head of black hair just beginning to show flecks of gray. Of medium height, he was broadly built and growing portly with the years. His dark eyes were piercing, almost fierce. This night, as always, he wore a yarmulke and long black robe—the garb customary to one of his position and race.

His name was Simeon and he had come from Jerusalem to Philippi over a year ago, attaching himself to the church as a believer in the Messiah Jesus. Epaphroditus dated the troubles at Philippi from the moment of his arrival. At the sound of his voice, the potter opened his eyes, pushed away from the wall, and stood on the balls of his feet. *Who invited him to this meeting? How dare he show his face after what he has done!* Simeon made Epaphroditus deeply angry . . . and very nervous.

"Shepherd Clement," Simeon spoke again, now that he had the group's full attention. "With your permission, I have a question or two to put to our visitor. I recognize that many of you are concerned about the condition of Saul—excuse me, *Paul*. But it is important to know what kind of help he requires. May I?"

Clement glanced at Onesiphorus and tried to warn with his look. "Of course, Simeon. I am sure our brother Onesiphorus will do his best to answer your questions."

"Greetings, Onesiphorus." Simeon addressed the stranger directly. "We thank you for bringing us news from Rome."

"You are most welcome. I am only—"

"Tell us, Brother," Simeon interrupted. "What exactly does Paul ask churches to do for him? What request does he make of us?"

"Well, as I said before, he wants you to pray for him. He . . . umm . . . he asks you to remember him to God." Onesiphorus did not understand the question. Like the laughter before, he sensed something was going on he did not fully grasp.

"So it is only you who make the request for monetary support?" Simeon seemed to consider this carefully. "Paul did not request such help. You are making the request for him. Is that correct?"

"Paul would never ask for money. It's not his nature. But I've seen the conditions he lives in. I know his need." Onesiphorus was confused. What did it matter who actually made the request? The need remained, regardless.

"My point, Brother Onesiphorus," Simeon explained patiently, "is that we have poor of our own to care for. These good people before you have families to support and children to feed. Now if Paul himself were asking for money, many here would empty their purses on his behalf. But Paul is not asking. He is expressing no financial need. You are the one asking for money. On his behalf, of course." Simeon stopped and let the point hang over the crowd like the mist of their expended breath.

A red tide began to rise on the neck of Onesiphorus. He was not sure where this was leading. But he was quite sure he did not want to go there. He decided he did not care for Simeon. "Are you suggesting that I am trying to profit myself?" Onesiphorus asked in low and not gentle tones.

Simeon gestured with his hands, stricken that he should be so misinterpreted. "Of course not, Onesiphorus. I am only suggesting that your great love for Paul may have exaggerated in your mind his actual needs. You saw him for a brief period of time. You noticed some things that heightened your concerns. Very well, let's write him a letter. Let's ask Paul straight-out if he needs financial assistance. If he requests the money himself, I'm sure we can call another meeting and raise the necessary funds."

"You've never met Paul, have you, Simeon?" Epaphroditus could stand it no longer. Simeon was parsing the matter of Paul's need with the same patient and killing logic he had used to split hairs over so many other matters of contention within the church over the past year.

"No, I have not had the pleasure, Epaphroditus." Simeon turned slowly to face the young Greek. "But I have heard much about him," he added guardedly.

"I'm sure you have," said Epaphroditus, careful to keep most of the irony from his voice. He moved toward the front of the courtyard as he spoke. "Anyone who knows Paul knows he could never make a request like that. Our brother Onesiphorus is quite right. You can write your letter if you wish, Simeon, but Paul won't ask us for money. He'd sooner go to the dungeon."

A murmur of agreement rose from many in the audience as the group sided squarely with Epaphroditus. Simeon was well aware where the sympathies of the crowd lay. But he had not come to win the crowd's favor. He had come to make a point. He spoke again.

"I realize that many of you feel an emotional attachment to Paul. You like him personally. He is your friend. I am sure that, in other circumstances, I would find him as engaging as you do. However, as I have told you before, Paul is a figure of considerable controversy. Other churches—faithful, God-fearing churches—have serious questions about his methods and his teachings."

Epaphroditus groaned softly. He knew what was coming. He had heard it all before. "Simeon, we've gone over this a hundred times. We know what you think about Paul's methods and his teachings. We know what your friends back in Jerusalem say about him."

"Yes, you do, Epaphroditus. Yet you refuse to take those concerns seriously." Simeon's voice became strident, more confrontational. "You and others in this congregation have allowed your personal affection for this man to brush aside hard realities. He is damaging the cause of the Messiah. He ignores the clear teaching of Scripture. He is leading good people astray—yourselves included!"

"That is your opinion, Simeon." Epaphroditus spoke in a low, barely audible voice. Simeon could make him angrier than any man he knew.

"Not my opinion alone," Simeon insisted. "And, frankly, I resent your dismissing my point as mere opinion. You seem to think that how we view Paul and his twisted teaching is simply a matter of opinion. You opine one way, I'll opine another, but we should all love and accept each other despite our differences on the matter. Well . . . I disagree. This isn't about opinion. It's about truth." Simeon's intensity intimidated the group. People shifted uncomfortably. They looked down at their feet. They looked up at the darkened sky. But they would not look at each other.

"Simeon! That's enough!" Clement spoke firmly. "Epaphroditus is right. We've been over this ground before. Now is not the time to air our differences on this. If you don't want to send support to Paul, don't. But please don't tell us what to do about this."

Simeon changed his approach. Confrontation dissolved into appeal. "Clement, I don't mean to make demands. I simply offer a word of caution." Simeon's voice quavered. His eyes teared. It was obvious that he spoke from a deep reservoir of conviction and concern. Epaphroditus had always believed this quality was what made the man so dangerous. He was no monster. He was quite sincere. But even sincere people could be wrong.

"If you send financial and emotional support to this man, you are encouraging his mistaken ministry. You are becoming his partners in an evil work. People's souls are at stake, Clement! *His* soul is at stake! If you really want to help him, encourage him to repent. Encourage him to undo some of the damage he has done. But do not, *do not* enable him to continue preaching the spineless Christianity he professes!"

"You've gone too far, Simeon!" Clement brought the discussion to a close. "Paul is our friend and brother. Many of us owe our very souls to him. He is in need and we will help him. If you don't like it, you can leave." Clement paused angrily. "Then again, you've already done that, haven't you!"

The crowd stood paralyzed. Even the children were still. A strained, oppressive silence hung over the assembly. For a moment, Simeon worked his jaw, tempted to respond. But then he bowed his head, turned on his heels, and walked into the night.

Epaphroditus searched the crowd. He caught sight of her standing against the far wall, huddled in silent misery. When she looked up, Epaphroditus saw the tears streaming down her face. *Oh, Euodia,* he thought. *How can you listen to him say those things? Knowing Paul, how can you think Simeon might be right?*

Clement broke the mood. "Brothers and sisters. My apologies for that. I didn't know Simeon would be here. Onesiphorus, please forgive this little skirmish. It is a long story, my friend." He paused and seemed physically to shake off a great sadness. "Well, we are here to see how we can help our brother Paul. What should we do now?"

"I have a proposal." Epaphroditus moved to stand beside Clement and face the assembled church. It was getting late. People were tired and cold. They were eager to get back to homes and beds. Now that the tension had broken, children were growing impatient, tugging at their parents' clothes and demanding to be taken to the latrine. It was time to decide on a course of action and call it a night. "If you approve, I will travel to Rome and take whatever gifts you would like to send Paul.

"Today is Tuesday. Give me a few days to make arrangements at the shop. If you would like to help Paul, come by my place and leave your gift. Write him letters and let me carry them to him. I think I can be ready to leave by the Lord's Day. Clement, Jason, Marcion," Epaphroditus made eye contact with each of the elders of the church. "Does this meet with your approval? Will you give your blessing to my journey?"

The three of them consulted one another with a glance and nodded. Jason held up his hands and the crowd quieted. "O Lord," he prayed, "our hearts are with your servant Paul, who sits under guard at this moment because he preaches the good news of your Son. We love him, Lord. We want to help. Bless the gifts that will be entrusted to Epaphroditus. Bless our good brother with safe travel as he carries these gifts to Rome. May his journey result in comfort for Paul and help in his time of need. According to your mercies and your will, we speak this prayer."

An "Amen" burst from almost every person gathered there. But not all. Epaphroditus raised his eyes to look for Euodia. Her spot against the wall was empty. She had already gone.

He knew he could not get to Rome fast enough. The gifts for Paul would simply be his excuse for going.

Chapter Three

THOSE WHO OPPOSE YOU

(SUMMER, A.D. 60—SUMMER, A.D 61)

IT HAD TAKEN EPAPHRODITUS SOME TIME TO APPRECIATE JUST HOW SUBTLE, how complex a man Simeon was.

Simeon had the ability to live on many levels at once. He moved easily among the citizens of Philippi in the marketplace, yet limited his private life to the strict confines of the small Hebrew population. He was amiable and gregarious with all manner of men, but reserved his friendship for those of his own race. He was a loving family man who took obvious pride in his children. But his children were kept at home for schooling and were not permitted to associate with "Gentile" children—even those who belonged to the family of faith. Years before, he had embraced Christianity. Yet in personal habits, he remained a practicing Jew.

An aloofness characterized Simeon in his business dealings and even in his interactions with other Christians, as if some part of himself were hidden away, inaccessible, off-limits. Initially, Epaphroditus had dismissed this as a natural shyness or the reserve displayed by a man living far from home. Increasingly, however, he began to suspect that the aloofness was deliberate, that Simeon intentionally held himself apart. The man's face rarely gave clues to his true feelings and thoughts, and he guarded his words carefully. He was cordial enough at the church's assemblies, but Epaphroditus began to think it was the kind of cordiality a man who knows a secret shows to those not yet informed.

At first, like the rest of the Philippian church, Epaphroditus gratefully welcomed Simeon into the fellowship. After all, Simeon had been a boy in Jerusalem during the years of Jesus' ministry in Galilee and Judea. He remembered vividly how the whole city convulsed during the final days of Jesus' life. He'd actually spoken with eyewitnesses of the resurrection. The stories Simeon told of those who had walked with Jesus and heard him teach fired Epaphroditus's imagination and strengthened his faith. The Philippians were fortunate to have such a man in their fellowship. Weren't they?

Simeon had become a member of the Way during the tumultuous days of the Persecution, not long after Stephen had been stoned. Defying family and friends, he'd confessed his faith in Jesus as the Messiah and joined likeminded Jews who gathered for worship in homes throughout the city. He had weathered that difficult period when the church was forced underground until, with time, believers like himself were tolerated again and allowed to resume their life in the larger Jewish community. Someone with such a background had a great deal to contribute to a small, struggling church in Macedonia. Didn't he?

And Simeon was acquainted with the pillars of the church in Jerusalem. He knew a few of them personally. He had met Peter and spoke of James with an easy familiarity. Naturally, the Philippians bestowed upon him the kind of respectful deference given everywhere to those who had communed with great men. It was an honor to have such a person in their midst. Wasn't it?

Besides everything else, Simeon knew the Scriptures. From childhood, he had memorized the sacred texts. The stories and lessons of the Torah were impressed upon his memory to such a degree that they were as familiar as his own body. Like breathing, they were a natural, almost unconscious extension of his being. To the Philippian Christians, who found it a struggle to master the bare outlines of God's Word, someone so well versed and so deeply read was a godsend.

The Philippian church needed all the mature Christians it could get. So many of her members were brand new to the faith. They came with scars and baggage and broken places in their lives. They huddled together around the faith like shipwreck survivors around a fire. They were glad for the warmth found in the church, but few were in any shape to contribute warmth of their own. No, Philippi was in desperate need of solid, mature, well-grounded, whole people who could care for others and lead them in the Christian walk.

Simeon, with his scrolls and heritage and well-ordered family, reeked of maturity. So when he moved his family to Philippi, he approached the elders about the possibility of worshiping together and they eagerly made a place for him in their fellowship. From the start, Simeon was encouraged to take a prominent role in the preaching and teaching of the congregation.

Only with time did it become clear that Simeon was a man of not only deep learning and firm convictions, but strong opinions. And it was the opinions that proved to be troublesome, for they were at odds with the practices and understanding of the Christians at Philippi. Indeed, those opinions called into question much of what the Philippians had learned from Paul.

~

The first hint of a problem came as the church gathered for a communal meal in the fall of the previous year. It was a beautiful October day, unseasonably warm and bright. They assembled as usual in Jerome's courtyard, with people milling in and out of the house and hovering around the food-laden tables in the middle of the square. Everyone brought something to place on the tables—a loaf of bread, a jar of honey, a flask of wine. Wealthier members brought plates of meat and pots of hearty soup. For the poorest members of the church, these fellowship meals were a lifeline, the most nourishing fare of their week.

Epaphroditus was busy setting up benches around the courtyard when his gaze was drawn to the gateway leading outdoors and to the sight of Simeon and his family spreading a blanket on the ground beyond the gate. Simeon placed a child on each corner of the blanket to anchor it against a gusting fall breeze while his wife busied herself unpacking a food basket. Epaphroditus was puzzled. Why didn't they come into the courtyard with the rest of the church? There was room for them inside.

At the time, Simeon was still new to the congregation. He and his family had moved to Philippi that summer and were hard at work settling into their quarters, establishing a place of business, and getting to know the town. Their contact with the church had been limited to worship assemblies on the Lord's Day. This was the first time that Simeon and his family had attended one of the church's communal meals. Epaphroditus felt a surge of sympathy for this new family. Their eating alone, outside the gate, was probably a measure of their discomfort as strangers to the group. *Well,* thought Epaphroditus. *We can do something about that!*

Jerome rose to welcome the church to his home and prayed God's blessings on the meal. Then someone started a song of thanksgiving ("You set a table before me. You fill it with all good things . . . "). Finally, the line formed to eat.

But Epaphroditus was not watching the line. He was watching Simeon. His family bowed in silent blessing and began to eat from the dishes they had brought with them, isolated from the rest of the church on their blanket just outside the walls. Epaphroditus felt for them. He knew what it was like to be an outsider, to feel excluded and unwelcome. He had been a displaced person himself before discovering Christ. *I hope they know we don't care that they're Hebrews,* he thought. *We welcome all people with open arms in this church.* He walked through the gate toward the family.

"Simeon, Miriam . . . please. There's room inside. Come in and eat with the rest of us." Epaphroditus gestured toward the gate. "We are so glad you've joined our family. There's no need to sit out here." The wife looked embarrassed and glanced at her husband.

"It's Epaphroditus, isn't it?" Simeon inquired. "Thank you for your concern, my brother. I'm grateful for your sensitivity to me and my family." He paused and seemed to weigh his next words carefully. "We are content to eat our meal here. You see, the Law that our Lord Jesus honored is quite clear about the kinds of foods we can eat and the circumstances in which those foods can be eaten. It would be . . . "—again he paused—"it would be *improper* for us to go into the house and eat." Simeon blinked up at Epaphroditus and smiled affably.

Epaphroditus was confused. "Simeon, I know you and your family are new to our city. Some of the food we eat must seem strange to you. But it's all quite good, as long as you stay away from anything Andronica brings. Come on. I'll go through the line with you and steer you away from any food that's inedible!"

But Simeon did not share his humor. Epaphroditus tried again, "Simeon, don't stay out here. Eating *together* is the point of our fellowship meals, not the quality of the cooking. Come inside and join us."

"You don't understand," Simeon explained patiently. "It's not that the food is strange to us or not to our liking. Your food is not kosher. You have not washed your hands properly before eating. And I am not permitted, by conscience or by habit, to break bread with uncircumcised people." He said this without rancor or emphasis. He was simply stating facts. He looked around at his family and smiled.

Epaphroditus stood speechless. "I don't—" he stammered. "I mean, we wouldn't—" He paused, trying to collect himself. Finally, he blurted, "Are you saying that you *won't* eat with us, Simeon?"

"Epaphroditus, please! Don't take offense." Simeon spoke quietly, calmly. "We've come today to support this activity of the church. No doubt, some of our Jewish brothers will be critical that we've gone so far. But you must allow us to give our support in a manner consistent with our custom and our understanding of Torah." Again, Simeon smiled up at the bewildered potter.

Not knowing what to say, Epaphroditus stood awkwardly for a moment, shifting from one foot to another. He mumbled a hurried excuse and retreated into the house where he sat alone in a darkened room and contemplated what had just happened. Though he could not put words to it, he sensed that something significant, something foreboding, had transpired.

~

There were other foreshadowings of impending trouble—indeed, an entire series of them. Simeon was preaching and teaching on a regular basis in the Philippian assembly. Though his lessons were helpful and informative, they all seemed to lead to the same end no matter where he started. Gradually, it became apparent that Simeon had an agenda.

Until his arrival, the teaching diet of the church consisted of a random mix of moral instruction, studies from a few well-known messianic passages in the Psalms and Isaiah, and appeals to the victories and failings of famous characters in the Writings. The church did possess a collection of stories about the life of Jesus, and snippets of these often found their way into sermons and discussions.

So, on any given Lord's Day, the Philippian believers were likely to hear an exhortation to sexual purity (illustrated, perhaps, with the story of David's sin), or a reading and discussion of Psalm 22 or one of the Servant Songs, or the retelling of a parable with an admonition to take its lessons seriously. It was simple teaching, basic and straightforward. It was teaching prompted more by the daily challenges facing Christians in Philippi ("What about my family's idols?" "My husband is not a believer. What should I do?") than by deep knowledge of Scripture. It was baptismal preaching: you have died, you've been buried, you have a new life. It was subsistence teaching. It was bare-bones. It was milk.

And to Simeon, it was appalling. He quickly determined to raise the level of Scripture knowledge within the Philippian church. He spent substantial time teaching from the books of Israel's history. He introduced the Philippians to the Minor Prophets and to Proverbs. His approach to texts was disciplined, detailed, and deliberate.

But it was the books of Law—Torah—that formed the primary grist for Simeon's teaching mill. He loved to camp at the foot of Sinai. He expounded in great detail the worship of the tabernacle. He spoke passionately about things that contaminate and rituals that restore cleanliness. Above all, he taught with conviction about God's covenant and about the everlasting signs of covenant—Sabbath, circumcision, sacrifice.

Epaphroditus found Simeon's teaching exciting and perplexing. It was exciting to know Scripture better. He was eager to learn the ancient stories and grapple more skillfully with the holy texts. Even later, after everything, Epaphroditus felt grateful to Simeon for teaching him so much about God's Testament.

But the teaching was also perplexing. It always seemed to lead to one point that Simeon hammered over and over: "The covenant given by God to Moses is eternal. The signs of the covenant are eternal. Jesus Messiah (blessed be his name!) honored that covenant by submitting to its authority. With his own lips, Jesus Messiah said that he had not come to *abolish* the Law but to *fulfill* it. Brothers, how can we claim to honor our Lord yet fail to keep the Law that he himself honored?"

That was the crux of Simeon's teaching, the place he always ended up. Simeon insisted that all Christians—Jew and Gentile—were required to honor Torah as Jesus did. They had to follow the Law of Moses to live in the kingdom of Christ. At first, he pushed the general principle. Only later did he get down to specifics.

Epaphroditus remembered the Lord's Day when it came crushing home to him just what Simeon was saying. It was early June. Spring had lingered on the Datos Plain, bringing a welcome postponement of the stifling heat and biting flies of summer. The city reveled in the cool evenings and warm days. The air was alive with laughter and music. In the agora, people shopped and gossiped and gambled. The smell of bread and cooking meat wafted from the open doors of homes and temple kitchens.

Simeon preached that spring day from the book of Joshua—the account of the circumcision at Gilgal. In the story, Israel had just crossed over the Jordan to enter the Promised Land. The men of Israel, all of them born during the Exodus journey, had not been circumcised. In a great ceremony of consecration, Joshua circumcised them and "rolled away the reproach of Egypt." It was a powerful passage. And Simeon preached a powerful sermon.

It was at the end of the message that Epaphroditus finally understood where Simeon was leading. "Brothers, the time has come for a second Gilgal. All of us, like the Israelites of old, have come out of the Egypt of sin. We have wandered in the wilderness of ignorance. And now we have entered the Promised Land of Jesus Messiah. It is time to consecrate yourselves. It is time to roll away the reproach of Egypt. It is time for you to be circumcised and to enter fully into covenant with God."

Epaphroditus looked in alarm at the upturned faces of the congregation. They were listening so intently. They had come to hear a word from God. He interrupted. "Forgive me, Brother Simeon, but

I'm confused. When we confessed Jesus and put him on in baptism, wasn't *that* when we were consecrated? Weren't we circumcised in our hearts when we became believers?" He was trying to be helpful, prompting Simeon to correct a misperception he was in danger of leaving with his audience.

Simeon beamed at Epaphroditus as if he were his star pupil. "That is quite right, Epaphroditus. Just as Israel passed through the Jordan to enter the Promised Land, we passed through the water to enter Jesus Messiah. Your hearts have been circumcised through faith. Now, like the Israelites at Gilgal, the time has come for you to circumcise the flesh and complete your obedience to the Law."

Epaphroditus glanced at Clement in dismay. Something was not right. Simeon could not be saying what he seemed to be saying. Clement cleared his throat. "Brother Simeon, surely you are not suggesting that we should be physically circumcised?"

"Of course," Simeon stated bluntly. "That's precisely what I'm saying. To enter fully into the kingdom of Jesus Messiah, God requires that you become obedient to his Law. Jesus was circumcised. All his holy apostles were circumcised. Followers of the Way in Jerusalem still circumcise their children and live in obedience to the Law. So must you."

Suddenly, Epaphroditus felt very thirsty. His mouth turned dry. He could hear the blood pounding in his ears. "But Brother Simeon . . . the people you mention are all Jews. They live under the Law of Moses because that's what they were born to. It's all they've known. But we don't live in Jerusalem. We live in Philippi. Surely Greeks don't have to become Jews in order to be Christians?"

"Certainly not, Epaphroditus." Simeon's gaze was direct; his wry smile pulled at the corner of his lips. "You can never become Jews. You don't have the parents for it!" His eyes invited the group to share his little jest. "But you can become what we call *God-fearers* or *proselytes*. You can live in submission to the Law just as we Jews do. After all, being Greek does not prevent you, or excuse you, from being obedient to God."

They sang a few more songs. Elder Marcion led the assembly in prayer and gave a blessing. Members of the congregation stood and talked and continued the discussion for a while. And one by one, they went home.

Long after they all left, while Jerome's servants put away the tables and swept the courtyard clean, Epaphroditus remained, staring into the far distance, going over and over what he had just heard. His head hurt. And his stomach felt funny.

~

That evening, Epaphroditus knocked on Clement's threshold, pushed aside the heavy curtain that served as a door, and entered the quarters of his spiritual mentor. "Ah, Epaphroditus," the older man smiled. "I thought you might stop by tonight. What's the matter? Simeon bothering you?"

As Clement was sitting on the only stool in the room, Epaphroditus shrugged off his cloak and stretched out on the bed. "You know he is, Clement," the younger man said softly. "And I think he bothers you as well."

Clement had been going over the household books when Epaphroditus interrupted. A tallow lamp hissed and sputtered on the table. Clement put down his pen, closed the account ledger, and looked wearily at his protégé. "He does, my friend. He truly does."

"What happened today, Clement? How could he say such things?" Epaphroditus rubbed his eyes. He picked for a moment at the blanket on which he lay. "Listening to him—he sounds so reasonable, so logical! But he can't be right, Clement. He can't be!" Epaphroditus fell silent. How could he put words to what he was feeling? How could he tell Clement that, listening to Simeon, he feared he was drowning?

Clement looked calmly at his friend. He knew Epaphroditus so well. By the set of the young man's jaw, Clement could tell he was angry. In the furrow of his brow, Clement read struggle and uncertainty. But it was the eyes that spoke to Clement of the deepest feelings. There was worry in those eyes. And fear.

Clement leaned his elbows on the table and clasped his hands together. The light of the lamp played on the planes of his face. Wrinkles and crevices were deepened by shadow. His cheeks and forehead gathered the light and gave a glow to his expression. He spoke at last. "Epaphroditus, I want you to hear me. Simeon is a good man. He believes what he says quite sincerely. He deserves our respect and our patience. But he is wrong, Epaphroditus. He is wrong.

"I remember when Paul was here. Before you became a Christian. Back then, we had problems with our neighbors and with the authorities. They did not understand what a 'Christian' was. I think they were a little afraid of us." Clement paused and smiled to himself, flooded for a moment with memories of those first exciting, terrifying days. "Paul spoke then about troubles he was having with some of his countrymen. He warned me about people who could not let go of Moses. He worried that they would force circumcision on his Gentile converts. Even before he came to Philippi, some nasty battles were fought over this issue.

"I remember that he got in my face one day and shook his finger at me." Clement laughed as he recalled it and then gave a passable imitation of the Apostle at his sternest. "'Clement,' he said, 'you are saved by grace through faith! Jesus saved you by his Cross. Don't believe anyone who tells you something else is needed. You just hold to Jesus. You let him work on your life. Everything else is worthless compared to knowing him.'

"I was just a baby in the faith back then. It shook me that Paul was so insistent about the point. But I do remember what he said. And I want you to remember it as well. Simeon is wrong. I don't care how much of Leviticus he can quote. I don't care how reasonable he sounds. Simeon is wrong. You have Jesus, Epaphroditus, and he is all you need."

Outside, a soft rain began to fall. The two of them sat quietly, listening to the pattering and dripping. They sat for a long time, taking comfort in each other, watching the shadows of the lamp dance on the walls of Clement's room, sharing the absence of words like the good friends they had become.

After a while, Epaphroditus stood and stretched his back. Taking up his cloak, he moved toward the doorway. He stopped beside the stool on which Clement sat. He put his hand on his friend's shoulder. He stood still for a moment. "Thank you, Clement."

He walked to the door and wrapped the cloak tightly around himself, then turned and looked back to the table. "Clement," he asked, "did you see their faces as he spoke? I wonder what they're thinking?" He did not seem to need a response, so Clement said nothing.

Epaphroditus cocked his head to the rain. It had slackened to a drizzle. "Well. Good night then."

"Good night, my son. Sleep well. Things will work out."

Epaphroditus grunted and was gone.

Chapter Four

SUFFERING FOR HIM

(SUMMER—FALL, A.D. 61)

AS A POTTER, EPAPHRODITUS SAW IT HAPPEN WITH UNSETTLING REGULARITY.

For most of his day, when he wasn't waiting on customers or dealing with suppliers, Epaphroditus sat at a kick-wheel and turned the pots and bowls that lined the walls of his shop. One large, heavy wheel of rough stone was set into the floor, balanced on an iron bearing. By sitting over the wheel and moving his feet in opposite directions, Epaphroditus would start the stone moving and then bring it up to speed. A short wooden shaft rose from the center of the kick-wheel to another, smaller disk made of smooth stone. As the lower stone rotated, so did the disk upon which Epaphroditus molded his clay.

A potter's work was monotonous. It involved scooping a lump of clay from a barrel and plunking it in the middle of his wheel. His hands worked the lump, kneading in a little water and softening it to just the right consistency. Then the legs pushed the kick-wheel and the fingers formed the wet clay.

The only variety to this routine involved the particular piece to be "thrown." Epaphroditus would consult his inventory (which meant looking around the shop for bare spots on the shelves) and note that he was running low on pitchers or bowls or cups. He would set to work turning out a dozen long-necked amphorae, or fifty bowls.

Everything would be as it had been a hundred times that day—the same wheel, the same hands, the same clay. Epaphroditus would start the wheel turning and begin forming one more pot in the series. Only this time, something would be different. For reasons he could not name, the clay would begin to wobble, the wheel would shake, and the object between his hands would come apart. He could delay the inevitable—shoving it here, shaping it there. If he were careful, he could bring the wheel to a stop and contemplate the misshapen, unbalanced, half-formed object before pounding it back into a lump and starting again. But he could never seem to correct the problem. Once the clay lost its center, it would not be set right—no matter how hard he kneaded and muscled the mud.

At such times, he tried to blame his tiredness or lack of attention. He would stop to grease the wheel and check the moisture of the clay. He looked for clues in the weather or the time of day. But the truth of it was that sometimes the clay had a mind of its own. It came apart for reasons no one could know, not even the potter. Though Epaphroditus bowed to that reality, he did not like it. It offended his sense of order. He believed that clay should behave predictably. When clay went wrong, there ought to be a reason . . . and a fix.

In the months that followed Simeon's sermon on Gilgal, Epaphroditus thought often of those frustrating moments at the wheel. For with that sermon, he felt the church begin to wobble. Even as he did his best to keep things from coming apart, he worried deep down that the church might not be able to find its center again.

~

After Simeon's call for circumcision, the elders began a series of meetings with him to study the matter. Twice a week, they gathered at Simeon's place of business as the last customers left the shop and evening settled over Philippi. (It would not be "convenient" for them to come to his home, he demurred.)

They listened to Simeon argue that Christians must keep the Law. "Brothers! Jesus Messiah lived under the commands of Moses. It is true that he corrected some misinterpretations of the Law, some abuses my people had allowed to creep into their religious life. But even those corrections showed his respect for Moses. It was the abuses, not the Law itself, Jesus objected to."

They pored over the ancient texts, Simeon translating fluently from his Hebrew scrolls while the elders struggled to keep up in the church's most valued communal possession, the Law and the Prophets in the Greek language.

They met well into the summer. Sweltering, humid air settled over Philippi and turned the city into an oven. Not a breeze blew. Not a relieving raindrop fell. People went about the streets, gasping and sweating from one piece of shade to another. The few who could afford it escaped to the cool of the coast. To the south and east of the city, great bogs baked in the sun and bred flies and mosquitoes by the millions. Like the heat, they too descended upon the city and added to the general discomfort.

Clement and his fellow elders, Jason and Marcion, fought through clouds of them, slapping at hands and neck as they made their way in the evenings to Simeon's shop. There they would sit, sweating in his back room, trying not to drip on the parchments. June passed in this way. And July. And much of August.

~

"But what if he's right, Clement?" Marcion shook his great head and looked gravely at his feet. The three of them were gathered at Clement's place, where they could talk privately and voice fears they dared not speak in front of Simeon.

"How can you even ask that?" Clement was frustrated and worried. He turned on his stool to face the grizzled soldier. "Marcion, you and I go back a long way, back to the very beginning. Think back, Marcion! Think back to Paul! Paul is a Jew. Born and raised! But think about when you first met him. Did he look like Simeon? Did he *talk* like Simeon?"

Marcion's massive hands gripped his knees. Clement had always marveled at those hands, great scarred slabs hanging from heavily-muscled arms and shoulders. What violence those hands were capable of. And what tenderness. Clement was quite sure one of those hands, as a fist, could fell a man with a single blow. Yet Clement had seen those same hands lift laughing children into the air and touch grieving widows with surprising gentleness. Now they kneaded

Marcion's thighs mercilessly, an unconscious symptom of his inner turmoil.

"Paul was different," Marcion acknowledged.

"Did he dress like Simeon?"

"No." Marcion recalled Paul's knee-length tunic and leather leggings. He could have passed for a Philippian laborer.

"Did he ever show any qualms about what he ate?"

"No." Marcion could not remember Paul making an issue of food at all. He ate what he was given. And he shared table with all manner of people.

"Did he ever once make an issue of his race or his own customs?"

"No again, Clement," Marcion answered quickly. He had thought long and hard on these very questions. But something in Clement's manner touched the stubbornness in the old soldier. He raised his head and borrowed language from the only life he knew intimately. "Paul is a recruiter, not a drill sergeant. He signs men up, but he doesn't make soldiers of them. There's a difference, Clement. Paul recruited us for the Christian walk. But then he moved on. Maybe Simeon is just finishing what Paul began. Maybe he's teaching us how to be good soldiers."

Clement could hear echoes of a conversation with Simeon the week before. Marcion had listened closely then, and Clement could tell that he'd taken Simeon's words to heart. As usual, Clement had served as the spokesman for the elders. "We heard that the leaders of the Jerusalem church held a debate about these questions, Simeon. Ten or twelve years ago. Paul told us he was there himself. And they decided that Gentiles did *not* have to be circumcised or keep the Law."

"That is not exactly correct. Forgive me, Brothers, but I believe Paul misled you on that point." Simeon spoke carefully, examining every word before voicing it. "What they decided was that they should not make it difficult for the Gentiles as they were turning to God. They recognized that, in missionary activity, it is sometimes necessary to crawl before running. So they decided not to make circumcision and obedience to the Law *a condition* for turning to Christ. However," Simeon punctuated his words with emphatic gestures, "that does not mean that, as Gentile Christians mature, they shouldn't be encouraged to obey the Law!

"Just look at the practice of Christians in Jerusalem! They are proud of their allegiance to Jesus Messiah. Many of them have suffered greatly for the cause. But all of them are also zealous for the Law." Simeon bore down on the point. "They continue to circumcise their children. They honor the food laws. They make the sacrifices and keep the feasts. If you traveled to Jerusalem, Marcion," Simeon looked at the old soldier intently, "they would insist that you honor Jesus by honoring the Law. If you refused, they would not permit you to join the church. You would defile them with your very presence."

Marcion was making Simeon's argument now. But Clement was still not persuaded. "Marcion, Paul wasn't hiding the bad news so we would enlist—like some of your recruiters do with provincial bumpkins! He wouldn't sign us up for the Faith and simply neglect to mention that obedience to the Law of Moses would also be required!"

"Why not?" Marcion was warming to his subject. "You don't throw raw recruits right into the front line. They need training! They have to learn skills! You have to break 'em in gradually. I've seen my share of fresh-faced kids, Clement. If I told 'em everything about soldiering up front, they'd desert faster than they signed on!"

Jason had listened long enough. "This is all well and good," he interrupted. "But it's beside the point. We've got trouble here and now. Paul is not going to fix this. And neither is the Roman army." He skewered each of them in turn with a withering gaze.

Jason was the pragmatist of the three. The world as he saw it was divided neatly into black and white, problems and solutions. He had little inclination for theological debate or history lessons. He had fidgeted and squirmed his way through their studies with Simeon, anxious for a solution but impatient with the process. For the most part, he had considered their meetings a waste of time.

He numbered off the matters before them. "First, we've got Simeon pushing Moses every Lord's Day and upsetting half the church. Second, we've got a bunch of confused people who don't know what to think anymore. Third, we've got some who are taking sides and digging in. Why, there are members of this church who are barely speaking to each other! And last, but worst of all"—he glared at the other two, daring them to dispute him—"we've got elders who can't make a decision and put this matter to rest! What are we going to do?" His raised eyebrows challenged them both, an imperative call for action.

"What do *you* suggest, Jason?" Clement turned on the younger man. "Start our own little pogrom? Run Simeon out of town? Should we all put our fingers in our ears when he quotes from Scripture? Or are you suggesting that we roll over and let him lead this church straight back to Sinai?"

He caught himself and stopped speaking. He knew he would punish himself later for that outburst. Clement took a deep breath and spoke more calmly. "I'm sorry, Jason. I'm frustrated too. All I'm saying is that when we act, it must be because we know God's will, not because we are reacting to some tensions in the body."

"Rubbish, Clement! Don't use God's will as an excuse to do nothing!" Jason's tone was hard and unbending. "Is it God's will for us to blather on about this until the Lord comes again? Does God want us to tie up the church even longer in arguments over food and circumcision? I'm sick of it! Let's either embrace Simeon and circumcise everyone we can hold down . . . or let's kick him out. I really don't care which. I just want to stop talking it to death!"

"Jason, please!" Clement was weary. He wiped the sweat from his face with the sleeve of his tunic. "Don't be impatient with us. Marcion and I are a little slow. We have to talk things over before we can figure out what to do. Let's be calm. And careful."

Jason stood suddenly and moved to the doorway. "You be calm, Clement. And you be careful, Marcion. I'm going home. When you're ready to act, let me know." He stepped out of the room and into the simmering night, leaving his colleagues to stare at each other in dismay.

~

There was, of course, no confining the debate to back rooms and private discussions. Inevitably, it spilled out into the church at large. Through the summer, Simeon continued to preach and teach at their assemblies. He tried to respect a temporary truce about the issues that troubled him, but those issues were heavy on his heart and sometimes spilled over into his words. After worship, when the visitors were gone and the crowd had thinned and only the core of the congregation remained behind, they would stand around Simeon and worry the matter further. Inexorably, and against their better judgment, the elders were drawn into public debate.

"That's not what Paul told us, Simeon!" And Clement wished once again that Paul were there to speak for himself.

"Oh, I'm quite sure of that, Clement!" Simeon gave no credence to arguments based on the teachings of Paul. "Paul says nothing about circumcision except to disparage it. Unfortunately for him, Torah says a great deal about circumcision. It says that circumcision is the sign of our covenant with God. No circumcision, no covenant! You must decide whom to trust." Simeon looked around at the faces fixed so intently on him. "This self-proclaimed 'apostle'? Or the revealed Word of God!"

Clement winced at Simeon's disdain for Paul. He could not understand his hostility toward Paul, toward someone the rest of them loved deeply. He bit back the temptation to defend Paul's character and answered, instead, with a clear memory of Paul's teaching. "Paul told us that our covenant is based on faith in God's Son. Jesus died for us. We accept his sacrifice. That, and nothing more, is how we have relationship with God."

"How convenient, Clement. I wish it were so simple." Simeon shook his head, as if amazed by the gullibility of some people. "No requirements. No sacrifice. No obligations to submit to the Law. Just call on the name of Jesus and all is forgiven. Is that what you think?" Simeon worked hard to stay polite during these exchanges. But there were times when his convictions overrode his manners and he grew combative.

Epaphroditus stood apart when they talked of these matters. He did not trust himself to keep his tongue under control. By hovering around the periphery, he avoided being drawn into the discussion and saying something he'd regret. But more, Epaphroditus wanted the chance to look at faces and gauge the reactions of those present. So he would orbit the group slowly, listening with his eyes and keeping silent tally.

It was clear that Simeon was not convincing many. Their respect for Clement and the others, their memories of Paul, kept them from taking Simeon too seriously. Even when he was at his most persuasive, when he quoted Scripture and reasoned closely, they filtered what he said through the gospel they had learned from Paul.

But if he was not convincing many, he was convincing some. Epaphroditus could see that two or three of the group hung on Simeon's words and nodded vigorously when he made some telling point. Judging by their expressions, Simeon's appeals were finding a mark.

This concerned Epaphroditus. What concerned him more, though, were the reactions of many others in the group. There were several, Jason among them, whose eyes glazed over whenever talk turned to these matters. Clearly, Simeon's argument left them cold. They weren't lining up to be first for the knife. But neither did they understand Clement's patience. It dawned on Epaphroditus that they simply didn't care. Caught in the middle of a discussion they did not understand or appreciate, they were growing frustrated. Anyone who extended the debate annoyed them. Simeon, with his persistent logic, provoked eye-rolling and pained expressions from this group. But so too did the responses of the elders. Jason had walked out on several of these discussions, voicing his displeasure with his back and his noisy departure. Others were following his example.

"That's not what I think at all," Clement protested. "The Cross *does* obligate you. Salvation makes its own demands. We are different people, Simeon, now that we've met Jesus our Savior. But it's a difference that comes out of gratitude, not rule-keeping."

Simeon looked hard at the faces surrounding him. He spoke past Clement to members of the audience he still hoped to sway. "That's all very mystical, Clement. All very idealistic. I am a more practical man than that. I need to know what God requires of me so that I can live in a way that pleases him."

"Then live like Jesus, Simeon. Do what he would do. What more do you need?"

"Exactly!" Simeon fairly laughed at the opening. "Let's live like Jesus! He lived under the Law. So should we. He was circumcised and respected the customs of God's chosen people. So should we. That's all I'm saying, Clement. Let's live like Jesus."

A murmur of agreement rose from several in the crowd.

Oh, my, Epaphroditus thought to himself. *Like a lamb to the slaughter. Clement walked right into that one.*

~

The two widows shared a long history. They had been friends since before their husbands died. A dozen years ago, they'd sat together at Paul's feet, drinking in the message of the Cross. Together they'd made their decision for Christ. Together they'd shared the good news with others. For the first decade of the church in Philippi, people could hardly mention one name without the other. It was "Syntyche and Euodia," "Euodia and Syntyche"—as if they were one person with a two-part name.

But now, they sat on opposite sides of the room when the church assembled. They barely spoke to one another. When they did, people quickly distanced themselves from the row that was sure to come.

Euodia found Simeon convincing. Syntyche thought him dangerous. At first, the difference in their reactions caught each of them by surprise. They'd talked about it often and intensely—the conversations people have who care deeply about each other and about the subject they are discussing.

In time, however, the intensity turned to heat. And the heat burned away their friendship.

Euodia's alignment with Simeon disturbed many in the church. No one was more devoted to Jesus, more completely converted, than she. Ask members of the congregation to name a model disciple, and Euodia's name would be among the first and most frequently mentioned.

Perhaps it was *because* she was so diligent in her pursuit of Jesus that she found Simeon's message compelling. He offered her a comprehensive and detailed discipleship. He filled in the gaps left by Paul. She started meeting with Simeon for Scripture study and instruction in the ways of Judaism. In dress and habit, she began to model herself after Miriam, his wife. Now, whenever Simeon addressed the church on the Lord's Day, Euodia was quite vocal in her agreement. She would speak the "Amen" loudly when he made a particularly strong (and increasingly confrontational) point.

Meanwhile, Syntyche stewed in silence.

The breach between them surfaced openly the night that, once again, a few core people crowded into Clement's room to hash through the issues.

"Look at us! Who are we to be discussing such questions?" Euodia's face was flushed and her eyes flashed. She looked around at each of them accusingly. Marcion and Jason sat together on the floor, their backs to the wall. A woman named Lydia was seated beside Euodia on the bed. Syntyche perched with crossed arms on Clement's solitary stool. Epaphroditus, Jerome, and Clement stood at the edges of the room, shifting their weight on occasion from one tired leg to the other.

"We're sitting here in this shanty— "

"Now just a minute, Euodia. This *shanty* is what I call home!" Clement forced a laugh, trying to inject a little humor into a discussion that was threatening to turn ugly. But no one was in the mood for levity that evening. They would not be distracted from their anxiety.

Euodia ignored him to press her point. "We're sitting in a slave's shanty. Jason, not so long ago, you worshiped an idol. And Marcion—you're a soldier, not a scholar. That leaves us with"—she went around the room—"a potter, two widows, a merchant, and a cloth seller! A fine group to be deciding the will of Almighty God! Who do we think we are?"

The group cowered under her reproachful gaze. What could they say? Each of them carried a palpable burden of ignorance and inadequacy. They were like blind people, feeling their way around a vast and unfamiliar room. At times they wondered whether they were making up the boundaries of Christian living as they went along. Euodia had hit an exposed and sensitive nerve.

After a few awkward moments, Lydia cleared her throat and leaned forward to speak. She had once been a very beautiful woman. Even now, in her fiftieth year, she remained striking and slender. But her voice had always been her most remarkable feature. When she spoke, Epaphroditus could close his eyes and imagine Lydia, through her lilting and dulcet tones, as she had been in her youth. "Of course, you're right, Euodia. I'm not competent to deal with these matters. None of us is. But who else is there?" She took Euodia's unwilling hand in her own. "God, in his wisdom, has appointed these good men"—she nodded toward Clement, Jason, and Marcion—"as shepherds for this church. He brought each one of us to faith and made us part of this community. Is it too much to believe that he will guide us as we deal with these issues?"

Euodia would not let it go. She withdrew her hand. "But God *is* guiding us, don't you see? He sent Simeon to us!" A collective groan rose in the room. "No, wait! Listen to me! Simeon knows Scripture better than all of us put together. He was there in the beginning, when it all started. Why is it so hard to believe that Simeon is God's instrument to teach us the whole truth?"

"Because what Simeon says contradicts everything Paul taught us, Euodia!" Syntyche could not stand it when Euodia fawned over Simeon. "You remember Paul? Have you forgotten what he told us? Euodia! Look at me! How can you side with Simeon when you owe your very soul to Paul?" She sat only a short distance from Euodia, yet they were an ocean apart. A tremor ran through her body and her arms tightened around herself as if to restrain her emotions.

"Paul?" Euodia's voice was pinched and low. "Don't you talk to me about Paul, Syntyche. Where is Paul?" She used his name like a knife. "We haven't seen or heard from him for six years! Paul doesn't care about us. He abandoned us long ago. I thought he cared . . . once." She spoke bitterly, like a jilted lover. "But we were just another conquest for him. One more church he could boast about. One more church to milk for money. No!" Her voice was barely a whisper. Her words cut more deeply the quieter she grew. "Don't talk to me about Paul, Syntyche. Paul doesn't carry weight with me anymore!"

She seemed to collapse inwardly as she spoke. When she finished, the tears started. But she refused to acknowledge them. She glared with wet cheeks from one person to another, though they would not meet her eyes.

They sat in silence for a long while until, with a dismissive gesture, Euodia stood and stalked out. The rest of them stared at hands and feet for a time. And then, one by one, they rose and made their separate ways home.

~

Clement accepted the invitation to dinner gladly. Jerome always served the very best food and wine. They reclined on couches around the table—Clement, Jerome and his wife Claudia, and their three gangly sons. The food was brought in, blessed, and consumed.

And afterward, Jerome had Clement for dessert.

"I don't care about the theological niceties. I just want an end to it!" Jerome thundered, his open palm smacking the table and causing the plates to jump. Claudia excused herself quickly and retired to her room. The boys also mumbled apologies and fled from the table to play—quietly—in the courtyard.

Clement sat stunned. He had not expected to be ambushed over dinner.

"People have been griping to me for some time now. They're tired of all this wrangling. They don't like what Simeon is preaching, and they don't like it that you keep giving him a platform to preach from. You're losing credibility, Clement. Some of us are wondering whether you have what it takes to lead this church. Shut him down, Clement. Shut him up!" Jerome poked his spoon in Clement's direction for emphasis.

"Who has been complaining to you, Jerome? Who is so upset about this?" Clement stared at his plate, hoping to find in the remnants of his food some augury to guide his responses.

"A large number of people, let me tell you! I could give you names, but they have sworn me to confidence." Jerome spoke more evenly—the calm after his brief verbal storm. "But they are upset. They want it to stop so we can get this church back to normal."

In fairness, Clement reminded himself, this was not like Jerome. Though he was a man of considerable wealth and influence, he usually managed a light touch when it came to matters of the church. Like the chained bear at the Games, Jerome could not be ignored. Everyone in the church respected his wealth and power. But he did not often roar to advertise his strength or get his way.

"Isn't it *normal* for this church to seek God's will, Jerome? Isn't it *normal* to extend love and patience to each other—even, perhaps especially, when we don't deserve it?"

"Clement, I have not asked you here to argue the point. I have asked you here to deliver a message. We're tired of it. Put an end to it."

Clement got up from his couch. When it came to matters of the church, he did not like being dictated to. "I *thought* you had asked me here for dinner, Jerome." He looked hard at his host. "Have you spoken with Jason? Has he prompted this?"

Jerome returned his gaze steadily. He was not a man to be intimidated by a slave, even if that slave was an elder. "You will need to ask Jason that question. As I said, I have certain confidences to protect." But his eyes had already told the story. Clement knew.

"I *will* ask Jason about this. Thank you for dinner." He walked to the door and then turned. "Jerome. Next time? Don't feed me first. I don't need to be fattened for the kill. Just stick the knife straight in. It's kinder that way." He turned on his heel and walked out.

~

Simeon withdrew in the fall. It was harvest time and the fields were thick with men and women cutting grain and carting the sheaves into shelters. The thud of axes and falling trees shook the nearby valleys as families gathered firewood for the winter. Soon the first frost would blanket the plains and freeze the mud in the roads. Snow was already bright on the peak of Mount Pangaion to the southwest—a cold promise of the frigid months ahead.

Jason went to Simeon's office one day and told him he would no longer be preaching or teaching for the church. That, apparently, was the sign Simeon had been waiting for. He never returned to their worship assemblies. He and his family began worshiping in their home, joined by the few women of the church who were willing to conform their ways to Simeon's strict demands. No men went with them. Clement found some wry humor in that. But not much.

In hindsight, Clement could admit that this was the inevitable conclusion to a difficult situation. But the decision to cut off Simeon had been Jason's alone. No one consulted Clement in the matter. Had they done so, Clement would have bowed, however reluctantly, to the hard realities involved. But they did not ask him, and the reproach to his leadership rankled.

Wounded pride, however, is not something a godly man can nurture for long. And Clement, for all his shortcomings, was a godly man. So he bandaged his wounds and gave himself with renewed energy to the people of the church. He hoped that, with the breaking of the summer's heat, the fever that had gripped the congregation would also break.

And it did, to a degree. He and Jason sat down soon after Simeon left and began to repair the rift in their relationship. But it would take a while. Jason remained distrustful of Clement's patient, analytical ways. For his part, Clement found Jason's thirst for action, any action, alarming.

One fall evening, Clement knocked on Jerome's door and offered an apology for his temper and his words. Jerome embraced him and invited him to stay for dinner. Even the dessert was excellent.

But if the fever had broken, in its place came a prolonged lethargy, a heaviness that settled over the church and tempered the joy that had been characteristic of these people for so long. They seemed more withdrawn, less trusting. They felt a vulnerability that chilled them and made them uncertain about the future. Like a fighter who has been knocked senseless for the first time, the church struggled to its feet again. But it moved more carefully now, with less grace and greater vigilance.

Some of their frustration was taken out on the elders. Clement and the others should have protected their sheep better. They should have acted more quickly. Couldn't they recognize a wolf when it was attacking the flock?

But, for the most part, they blamed each other for their shared malaise. They were quieter now, less willing to invest in one another, more cautious in their interactions. They drew into themselves, hiding behind polite and superficial conversations. Their homes, once gathering places for spontaneous and intimate fellowship, were reserved increasingly for family—places of withdrawal and retreat.

To everyone's surprise, Euodia did not leave with Simeon. She had poured too many years, too much effort into the church to just walk away. But her strained presence and the persistent tension between her and Syntyche cast a pall over their gatherings. It made Epaphroditus feel dishonest to sing songs about peace in Christ and the love Christians should feel for one another. Those songs ceased to be celebrations for him. They became indictments.

~

Fall turned to winter. The rains turned to snow. The cold north winds, blowing straight from the mountains, were so cutting they almost made Epaphroditus wish for summer's heat once more. The city filled with the smoke of home-fires, irritating sore noses and catching in throats. The people shivered and coughed their way through the streets. The winter cold seeped through clothing and walls to affect the mood of Philippi's inhabitants. They became grimmer, more abrupt, as though focusing their energies on the single task of enduring until spring.

Epaphroditus spent most of his time in the shop. His wheel was in constant motion, cranking out a surfeit of bowls and pitchers and jugs in a manic effort to distract himself from the struggles of the church. The clay, so cold and cumbersome, fought him at every turn. But that was all right. He fought it back, pounding and kneading it into submission. The truth of it was that he found the contest therapeutic.

He was at the wheel, working the clay with cracked and cold hands, when it happened again. The foreboding wobble. The clay bucking and heaving under his hands. He brought the wheel to an abrupt stop and stared at the deformed object before him.

A wave of anger surprised him and then swept him away. He beat the clay with his fists as if it were a living thing and he could make it bleed. He swept the lump from the wheel with a forearm, stomping and kicking at it where it fell to the floor. He threw it against the wall and stood over it, fists clenched and breathing heavily. It was cold in the shop, but the sweat poured from his forehead.

He sat down then . . . and stared at his trembling hands . . . and realized that he was afraid.

Chapter Five

YOU CAME ALONGSIDE ME IN MY TROUBLES

(MID-JANUARY, A.D. 62)

SLOWLY, FITFULLY, THROUGH THE DAYS BEFORE HIS DEPARTURE FOR ROME, the Christians of Philippi straggled into Epaphroditus's shop. They came as he was opening in the morning. They waited in the afternoon, examining his pottery while he finished with customers. They interrupted him as he sat at the wheel. They caught him just before he closed up in the evening.

And all of them brought something for him to take to Paul. A purse of coin. A personal letter, tied and sealed. A hand-woven blanket. Paul's sons and daughters sending comfort to their absent father.

~

Jerome and Claudia were the first to stop by. Epaphroditus was not surprised. As the wealthiest members of the congregation they had the easiest access to surplus coin. The couple appeared at midmorning, while the potter was concluding his first sale of the day.

"Good morning, Jerome . . . Claudia. I'll be with you in a moment." He counted out change for his customer, sent him on his way, and then turned his full attention to the pair.

"Good morning, Epaphroditus." Jerome looked around the shop approvingly. "You keep a neat shop, young man. I hope business is going well for you." The economy of Philippi was never far from the merchant's mind.

"Well, Jerome, if you would stop by more often, you would see that I keep pretty busy," Epaphroditus chided gently. He winked at Claudia. "Fortunately, your wife comes in regularly and purchases some of my wares. You two must have a butterfingered dish washer around your house!" They laughed together. With three active boys chasing each other through the kitchen, pottery had a short life expectancy in their household.

"We have brought a little something for you to take to Paul." Jerome came right to the point of their visit. He drew out a purse filled to bursting with coin, and handed it to Epaphroditus.

The potter hefted its weight. "You're very generous, Jerome. Thank you."

But Jerome waved the thanks aside. "It's nothing. Each of us does what he can. I happen to have the curse for making money. It is an easy thing for me to give." He paused and then added seriously, "Epaphroditus, keep your eyes open while you're in Rome. If there is something else I can do—" He let the promise of additional support linger, unspoken, between them.

He fixed the younger man with an appraising look. "Now, Epaphroditus. About yourself. I would like to help you with the expenses of your journey." He drew out another purse and extended it.

But Epaphroditus held up a hand. "That's not really necessary, Jerome. Thank you, but I can cover my own costs."

"Young man, you are already making a considerable sacrifice to volunteer for this journey. Will you close up the shop while you are gone?" He was curious.

"No. I've built up enough inventory to last while I'm away and I've hired someone to look after the customers for me."

"Excellent." Jerome approved of good business practices. "Still, a shop like this can't bring in enough income to pay for an employee *and* a trip to Rome." He fixed Epaphroditus with a businessman's eye and held out the purse again. "I want you to take this money and use it for your journey." He shook the purse gently until Epaphroditus relieved him of it.

"Thank you, Jerome. It will be a help." It embarrassed him to need the money so badly. In truth, the shop brought in barely enough income to keep Epaphroditus fed and clothed.

Claudia stepped closer and handed him a sealed letter. On the outside, in her neat and careful hand, were the words *From Jerome's Household*. "We sat down last night and wrote a letter to Paul. We intended to make it encouraging." She glanced down quickly, a little ashamed. "We couldn't help telling him a bit of what has happened in the church here. There are so many questions we want to ask him." She looked at Epaphroditus, hoping he would forgive this imposition on a prisoner.

He smiled and put his hand on her shoulder. "Claudia. You're not the only one who wants to ask Paul some questions. I'm planning to ask a few myself."

They stood for a moment, thinking of Paul and better days. And then, suddenly, it was time for Jerome to get on with his schedule. "Take care of yourself, young man. Watch your back. Don't let some thief bang you on the head and make off with my money!"

"I'll be careful, Jerome." He walked them to the door.

"By the way," Claudia paused before leaving, turning to lay her hand on Epaphroditus's arm, "your sermon this Lord's Day was really quite good. I've thought about it all week." She smiled, squeezed his arm, and left.

Epaphroditus watched their backs as they walked through the cold toward home. Clement had warned him about loving the praises of men. Was it a sin that he loved it so when someone complimented his preaching?

~

Lucian was waiting for him the next morning when Epaphroditus came downstairs to open the shop. He stood, frail and shivering in the crisp morning air, a thin cloak wrapped around his frame.

"Ah, Lucian!" Epaphroditus greeted him with an embrace. He felt like cold stone. "How long have you been standing here?" He ushered his visitor into the shop and out of the wind.

"Not so long. It is a cold morning though." He gummed a grin at Epaphroditus. Lucian had not a tooth in his head.

"Here." Epaphroditus pulled up a stool beside the small stove that heated the shop and sat Lucian down. He threw a few pieces of coal on the smoldering ashes from the previous day and blew the flame to life again. Taking an iron pot, he poured in some wine, added a little honey and water, and set the mixture to warm on the stove. "Give it a few minutes, Lucian. A cup of mulled wine and a little time by the fire will take the chill off." He pulled up another stool and looked fondly at the old man.

Lucian was another ex-soldier. A lifetime ago, in a battle far away, he had taken a spear to the side that left him tilted and in constant pain. The army retired him early and gave him a plot of land east of Philippi. There he crabbed out a bare existence, tending a few olive trees and raising a little grain, running a small flock of sheep. His life was hard and subsistent. Always a bachelor, he had no family to look after him. When his health failed entirely, as it threatened to at any moment, Lucian would have nowhere to turn.

Except for the church, Epaphroditus consoled himself. Lucian could rely on the church to take care of him when that time came.

He was a fixture in the Philippian congregation. On the Lord's Day, he always started walking before first light, arriving at Jerome's house early enough to stand at the gate and greet those who came for worship. How many times had Epaphroditus walked up to find Lucian's angled figure at the entrance and received his toothless welcome? He was a particular favorite with the children. During the week, as he watched his sheep or after the day's work was done, he carved little wooden figures that bore an uncanny resemblance to adult members of the congregation. On the Lord's Day, he distributed his creations to his young friends and was rewarded by their delighted shrieks.

After Lucian warmed himself a bit, Epaphroditus asked, "What are you doing here so early, my friend?"

"I've brought something for Paul," Lucian said, reaching into his tunic. He pulled out a shiny gold aureus and handed it proudly to Epaphroditus.

Epaphroditus took the coin, but then had to turn away. It required a moment to control his emotions. That coin must have represented a year's income for Lucian. "Where did you come by this?" he managed to ask.

"Oh, I can put a little aside once in a while. I sold some sheep in the fall and did a bit of work for a neighbor last summer." Lucian spoke as if it were a small thing. He leaned forward and extended his hands to the growing heat of the stove.

Taking a cup, Epaphroditus ladled some wine from the pot and handed it to Lucian. They sat for a moment, enjoying the warmth and the comfortable companionship. Epaphroditus spoke up finally. "I'm sorry, Lucian, but I can't take this to Paul." He held up the coin and looked at it thoughtfully. "Paul would never forgive me if he knew I got this from you."

Lucian glanced sideways at Epaphroditus and then back down to his cup. "I was hoping we could keep this between the two of us, Epaphroditus." He looked up and winked. "A secret between two friends."

Epaphroditus laughed. "You old scoundrel," he said fondly. "So you came looking for an accomplice?"

"I was thinking we might partner up. Yeah."

Epaphroditus considered it for a moment. "Tell you what I'll do. I won't tell Paul you sent him any money. But you can't send all of this. You have to keep some of it."

"I'm doing fine, Epaphroditus, just fine," the old man objected. "Paul needs this money more than me. Besides, you can't cut that coin in half!"

"I'll make change, Lucian." He took one of the donated purses from his belt and counted out fifteen denarii. Dropping the aureus into the purse, he handed the denarii to Lucian.

"Aw, Epaphroditus. That's too much! What am I gonna do with that kind of money?" And Lucian tried to hand ten of the coins back.

"You'll find some way to put that money to use, old man. Enough now. Do you want me to take something to Paul or not?"

Lucian nodded reluctantly and put away his change. "Um . . . there's one more thing, Epaphroditus. I was thinking you might help me . . . ahh . . . send a note to Paul. I'm not much good with the writing." Epaphroditus knew Lucian could barely scratch his name.

"Of course, Lucian. Just a moment." Epaphroditus ducked under his counter and brought out his writing utensils. He spread a sheet of fresh parchment on the counter, uncorked the ink pot, and submerged his quill. "What would you like to say?"

Lucian cocked his head and narrowed his eyes in concentration. "Ahhh, start with 'Lucian the Shepherd, to Paul in Rome.'" He paused, as Epaphroditus wrote, to compose his next words. "I was sorry to hear you're in prison again." Pause. "I hope you are staying warm and have plenty to eat." Pause. "Things are good with me. I still get around, and my old wound don't bother me too much." His expression saddened. He stared into his cup as though reading his message from its contents. "I was wondering if you could pray for the brothers here, Paul. We are a little wounded ourselves just now." Pause. "Nothing for you to worry about, but we could sure use your prayers."

He stopped for a long while and went somewhere deep within himself. "I want to thank you for telling me about Jesus." He reached up and rubbed at his eyes. "It's the best thing that ever happened to me." Epaphroditus ducked his head and continued to write, though the words swam on the page.

Lucian consulted his cup a while longer. "I reckon that's all. End with 'I salute you—one old soldier to another.'"

He waited for Epaphroditus to finish writing. They sat together in silence for a while, each lost in private reverie. At last, Epaphroditus stood and went to his shelves, taking down a cup and bowl to send home with Lucian. Lucian thanked him—for the pottery and for helping with the letter. Finishing his wine, he cinched his cloak about himself, said his goodbyes, stepped back out into the frigid morning, and limped his way toward home.

Long after Lucian left, Epaphroditus sat at the counter, reading and rereading the letter, pondering old soldiers and new hope, broken lives and healing love. He did not think Paul would mind if the page had a few stains.

~

Lydia came by in the afternoon. She handed another full purse to Epaphroditus and a letter of several pages, carefully sealed. She had written *From Lydia* on the outside. Like everything about her, her script was exquisite.

He asked her to sit for a while and tell him stories from the early days. Lydia was always good for at least one tale Epaphroditus had not heard before.

"Paul was absolutely shameless." She laughed as the memories crowded around her. "He would talk about Jesus to anyone, anytime, anywhere. Did you know that he used to stand up in the agora and start telling stories about his travels? He'd spin grand, exotic tales about faraway places he had been and strange customs he had seen. Paul is a wonderful storyteller, you know. And then, once he gathered a crowd, he'd say, 'Nothing I have learned in all my journeys is so wonderful, so amazing as the story I want to tell you now.' They would all lean forward." She mimicked the crowd, face up, eyes bright. "And he would tell them the story of Jesus." Lydia glowed as she spoke. "By the time they figured out that this wasn't just another strange tale, that Paul believed it with all his heart, they were hooked. I've seen him baptize three people at a time after one of his 'travelogues.'" She smiled and shook her head at Paul's audacity.

There was a persistent rumor in the Philippian church that Lydia had fallen in love with Paul. Epaphroditus never gave it much credence. Frankly, he found it hard to imagine the graceful and distinguished Lydia being drawn to Paul. Paul was many things—forceful, intense, intelligent—but no one would accuse him of being attractive. When she spoke of Paul like this, though, he wondered if there might be truth to the rumors.

"Why did you never marry?" The question came out before Epaphroditus realized his thoughts had formed words. Lydia arched an eyebrow at him and he flushed with embarrassment.

"You haven't married yet, Epaphroditus," she noted. "I've never asked *your* reasons." Her tone was reproachful, but her eyes seemed to enjoy his discomfort.

"I . . . well, I—" he stammered. "I'm not sure I'm the marrying type." He reddened even more deeply.

Lydia reached over and patted his knee. "You just haven't found the right girl yet. You will." She spoke with confidence. "Now, let's find something else to talk about, shall we?"

Later, when she rose to leave, she hesitated for a moment. "Epaphroditus." She stood directly before him, looking closely into his face. "We are all two people. The public and the private. The person we share with others and the one we keep to ourselves." He thought she was chiding him again for prying into her personal life. But he was wrong. "While you're with Paul, you must do your best to listen for both of him. He will try hard to put his best face on. You must listen past that." She put her hand on his cheek and watched him intently. "Do you understand?"

"Yes, Lydia. I'll try."

"When you return, I'll want to know how the private man is doing." She continued to stare into his eyes, willing him to understand. Then, abruptly, she leaned in and planted a kiss on the side of his face. "You take care of yourself, Epaphroditus. It's a long and dangerous journey to Rome. It would cause me pain if something happened to either of *you* on the way." She poked his chest and turned away, laughing at her little joke.

~

He slipped out of the shop several times, when business was slow, to visit with merchants who traveled regularly. He knew a grain buyer who journeyed to Corinth and Nicopolis every few months to sign contracts. There was an iron trader who carted large wagons of Philippian ore to smelters in Thessalonica and Athens. He called on a ceramics exporter who purchased delicate painted vases from Greek artisans (quality stuff, not the simple and utilitarian wares Epaphroditus produced) and shipped them to an eager Roman market.

Each man made the same recommendation. "So you need to get to Rome. And in a hurry!" Aristias, the exporter, contemplated Epaphroditus gravely. "You know, this is not the best time to travel. Roads are terrible. Snow in the passes. And ships!" He rolled his eyes. "Can't you wait a couple of months?"

"No, I have to go now. What do you recommend?"

"Well." Aristias scratched his beard. "Take the Egnatian Way to Nicopolis on the coast. That's a week's walk. From there you have your choice." He held up the back of his hand to Epaphroditus and raised a thumb into the air, counting off the options. "Keep on the road and go north. You'll have to deal with snow in the mountains. And it'll take you a good six weeks to make the trip—if you have perfect weather! Will you have money for inns?" Epaphroditus shook his head no. "So you'll be sleeping in the open. Not a good idea!"

Aristias stuck out his index finger next. "You can book passage on a ship from Nicopolis to Brundisium. Sail up the coast a ways, dash across the Adriatic, and then follow the Italian coastline to port. *If* you don't get blown to Africa and *if* the captain doesn't get drunk and run you aground in the dark, you're looking at four or five days on board. Of course, you'll still have a long walk to get to Rome." Aristias bit his lower lip and thought a while. "The main problem with that plan is you might have to camp out in Nicopolis for a month until you find a ship that'll risk the passage. Sailing this time of year is a fool's bet. Most captains won't try it unless there's a pot of gold to be made. Which brings us to your third option."

Another finger shot out. "Get yourself on a grain barge making the run between Alexandria and Porta. They stop at Nicopolis before making the final run around the boot of Italy and up the coast to Rome. They're always willing to take on passengers, especially this time of year. Once you make port, there's a day of hard walking and you're seeing the sights of Rome!"

Epaphroditus groaned inside. There were no good options. "So what would you do, Aristias?"

"Me?" He laughed. "I'd stay home 'til spring!" Epaphroditus gave him a pained look. Aristias studied him and then spoke seriously. "If I had to get to Rome in a hurry, I'd probably take the grain ship. It's dangerous, no question. But it's also fast. And it sure beats sleeping in the snow for two months!"

Epaphroditus extended his hand. "Thank you, Aristias. You've been very depressing."

Aristias chortled and shook the proffered hand. "Glad to be of service, Epaphroditus. Think of me as you're going under for the third time."

~

When he returned to the shop, Euodia was waiting for him.

"Good day, Euodia."

"Good day to you, Epaphroditus." She smiled a nervous smile. "So you're off to Rome tomorrow!"

"That's the plan. Unfortunately, I'll need a wheelbarrow to cart all the stuff people have brought me for Paul." He laughed until he saw the struggle between relief and disapproval pass across Euodia's face.

They looked at each other for a moment, Paul hanging between them, until Euodia held out a letter to Epaphroditus. He took it and questioned her with a look.

"That's for Paul, if you'd be good enough to carry it."

He turned the letter over in his hand, studying it as he thought. "I'm surprised, Euodia. I didn't expect you to send anything."

"There's no money in it, if that's what you mean," she retorted. "But I had some things I needed to tell Paul. Some questions for him to answer. Simeon helped me put together a list."

"Oh. I see." Epaphroditus spoke softly, tapping the letter against his chin. It felt warm to his touch. "Euodia, Paul is under arrest. His life could be on the line. Is this the right time to argue theology with him?"

"Why don't we let him make that decision?" She looked up, challenging him. "Will you take the letter or not?"

He tapped the letter for a while longer and then said, "Of course." He moved behind the counter to place it with the stack of other letters he would carry to Rome. "Euodia?" How could he broach the subject without breaching the dam? He started again. "Euodia, I am so sad about what has happened. These past few months must have been very difficult for you."

"Humph." She smiled, but not with her eyes. "You have no idea."

"We love you, Euodia."

"And I love you . . . all of you!" She said it fiercely, and he saw she was trying to fight back tears. "But this isn't about love. It's about truth. Can you understand that?"

"I understand that you want very much to do the right thing." He reached over the counter to touch her shoulder, but she drew back.

"If you would be kind enough to take my letter to Paul, I would be grateful. Be safe on your journey, Epaphroditus."

"Thank you. I'll try."

She turned and walked out.

Epaphroditus reached for the letter and turned it over and over in his hands. He thought about throwing it away. Why cause Paul needless pain? He was severely tempted to break the seal and read what she (and Simeon) had written. In the end, he bolted the door to his shop, gathered up all the letters, and climbed the stairs to his sleeping quarters to pack.

Chapter Six

YOUR MESSENGER TO HELP ME

(MID-JANUARY, A.D. 62)

CLEMENT HUNCHED OVER THE TABLE, BLOWING ON HIS HANDS TO WARM them for the task ahead. It was cold in the room and a mist rose with his every breath. He had wrapped himself in his cloak and taken the blanket from the bed to cover his legs and feet. Still, he shivered in the damp night air.

As long as he kept moving, the chill did not affect him greatly. Only in the evenings, while reading or mending clothing, did he feel the cold seeping into his bones. Occasionally, he would stand a small brazier in the middle of the room, lighting it to throw a little warmth into his quarters. But it filled the room with smoke and belched a thin layer of ash over every surface. Most of the time, he preferred the cold to the coughing and wheezing brought on by the fumes and cinders.

On the table before him burned an oil lamp and a tallow candle, throwing two fitful haloes of light onto the table's surface. Spread between them were several pages of blank parchment and Clement's writing utensils. Clement stared at the empty pages. They seemed to stare back, accusing him of procrastination and indecision with their chaste whiteness.

Epaphroditus was set to leave in the morning, and Clement could no longer put off writing his letter to Paul.

As he blew on his hands, the burdened elder formed and discarded sentences in his head. How should he begin? What tone should he strike? How could he offer encouragement and at the same time enlist Paul's help? With a grunt, he reached for the ink pot, shook its contents, and uncorked it. He took up a fresh quill and sharpened a nib with quick, familiar strokes of his knife. Dipping the quill into the ink, Clement placed it against one of those blank, reproachful pages and began a letter to his old friend.

Clement the Shepherd, to Paul, my brother and father in the faith. Greetings and grace to you, my friend—from myself and from all the brothers at Philippi.

I pray for you daily, asking God to protect you and bless you with every good thing in Jesus Christ. For many months, I prayed blindly, not knowing where you were or how things were with you. Now we have heard you are in Rome. So I pray even more fervently, asking God to watch over you in your imprisonment and to permit this difficult circumstance to result in a wider audience for the gospel.

He paused every few words to dip quill into ink, blotting the page with a cloth in an attempt to mend the stains and smudges that inevitably marred the crisp letters and white paper. Writing was a messy process. The coarse paper caught the quill, leaving an unsightly stain or sending a fine spray of ink ahead of Clement's hand. After a lifetime of committing words to paper, Clement still found himself exasperated by the mechanics of penmanship. And the more exasperated he became, the more he blotched and smudged. Often, by the time he finished, the page would be pockmarked with stains, his fingers black, and his tunic front covered in long stripes of ink where he had unconsciously wiped his hand.

We speak of you often here and recall with great joy the times you spent among us, the impact you have had on our lives. Even though you have been absent from us for so long, you still hold an important place in our hearts and are honored among us.

We are eager to hear how things are for you and to receive some word from you about your situation and needs. Our constant prayer is that God will deliver you and bring you to us again soon. I beg you to make every effort to defend yourself well before the court, but not to give offense in doing so. The Romans are as willing to condemn you for being irritating as for being guilty. Think of us as you stand before the judge and speak softly so that you can win your release and join us again in the near future. I say this because I know you, my friend. Sometimes your zeal can overwhelm your manners. I would be most upset to learn that you deprived us of your presence through a fit of immoderate rhetoric!

The words came easily to Clement once the actual writing began. He was an educated man, fluent in several languages, well read, and skilled in the art of communication. That he was also a slave proved only that bad fortune, like grace, fell in mysterious ways and had nothing to do with merit or attainment.

He'd begun life in Philippi, some sixty years before, as the pampered son of a wealthy merchant. His father provided the best tutors and finest schooling he could afford. As a young man, Clement traveled widely, learning mathematics and a little medicine, and studying with a series of philosophers.

Recalled years later by a desperate letter, he returned to Philippi to find the family business bankrupt, his parents impoverished, and a mountain of debt charged against his father. For days, he wrestled with the family finances. He pored over ledgers filled with his father's precise script. He studied contracts and loan agreements. He spoke to creditors. He examined options.

In the end, Clement approached a prosperous friend of the family, offering to sell himself and his services in exchange for relief from debt. His offer was accepted and the necessary papers were drawn up and witnessed. He entered his new household as tutor for the children and domestic manager—overseeing the details of a large and busy residence. Technically, he was a slave. But, in time, Clement attained an honored position in the home and was gratified to discover that his hard-won learning was being put to good use.

Over the many years that followed, he served the household to the best of his considerable abilities. The family came to look upon him as a trusted uncle; and after the death of his own parents, Clement bestowed upon his adopted home all his familial affections. Twice he was offered his freedom. But the boys he had taught and loved grew into young men who continued to need his skills and guidance. Now, he taught the sons of the sons and watched over the interests of the extended family with a patriarch's eye. The timing had never seemed right to detach himself from the household. Leaving would cause more pain than relief. He came to regard emancipation as he did his own funeral—a sad thing, to be avoided if possible and, if not, postponed for as long as he was able.

Besides, there was the church to consider. Though his masters had expressed grave concerns when he first became a Christian, they eventually accepted his conversion, allowing him considerable freedom in his dealings with the congregation and tolerating the steady stream of visitors flowing to and from his quarters. His duties in the household permitted him ample time for mentoring and teaching and meeting his other responsibilities as a leader of the church. It always made Clement smile to think that only great wealth or slavery could afford such freedom.

When Clement regarded the future, he did so with a strong sense of purpose and contentment. The rest of his life would be devoted to his two families—the home he had adopted and the church that had adopted him. In protecting their health and well-being, he found a responsibility worthy of his best skills and most persistent efforts.

Clement laid down the quill and blew again into his hands. He flexed his back and reread what he had written. Now for the hard part. Now to write about the brothers. Clement was not eager to burden an imprisoned man with the details of their struggles at Philippi. He knew Paul well enough to know that news of trouble would weigh on him. Paul had a mother's protectiveness for his churches. When one was hurting, he worried and fretted over it.

But, in truth, it was not concern about Paul's anxiety that made the writing so difficult. Clement found the task distasteful because it forced him to face the struggles at Philippi fully, systematically. It was one thing to run from this crisis to that, smoothing ruffled feathers here, calming fears there. It was quite another to summarize those struggles in writing, to list them in black ink on white paper, to reach around them with words and offer them to someone else for inspection and comment.

Clement feared that writing about the struggles of the past months would give them a reality and significance he preferred to avoid. Isolated events could become patterns when linked together with verbs and nouns. Individual people might add up to sides and cliques in the cold light of lettered logic.

With a sigh, he picked up his quill again and resharpened the nib. He rearranged the pages on the table. He reread his words, remixed the ink, restretched his knotted back. He stood and paced the tight confines of his room, his head bent in concentration. The silence of the night surrounded him, insulated him, wrapped around him like the cloak he held so tightly about his shoulders.

He snorted and shook himself, willing his body to sit again on the stool, his hand to take up the quill, and his mind to form the words that needed to be said.

Yes, speak softly, my friend, for we need you back in Philippi. I beg you to do whatever is in your power to win your release and then travel to be with us again. This church is struggling, Paul. We need you here.

Epaphroditus will fill you in about recent events here. No doubt, some of the letters he carries will also speak to our situation and give you additional insights into what is happening. I leave it to him, and to them, to inform you about a Hebrew named Simeon and the trouble his teachings have caused. Epaphroditus can tell you about the debate it has provoked among us. I'm eager to hear your response to Simeon's message—though I know already what you will say.

My main concern, however, lies in another direction, my friend. Frankly, it is not Simeon and his teachings that bother me. He has done us no great damage himself. It is how we have reacted to him that concerns me . . . and how we have damaged ourselves.

I remember something you told us at the end of your first stay in Philippi—on the day you had to leave us. You spoke then of troubles ahead. And you told us that the danger lay not in the troubles but in how we handled them. You said that at such times we must hold on to Jesus and to each other. Well, the troubles are here. And though our faith remains strong, our family has been shaken deeply.

When you were forced to leave Philippi, all we had was each other. We held on for dear life, caring for one another, encouraging and defending one another. It was hard—everyone suspicious of us, rumors flying, rejection by old friends and even relatives. But it was also a wonderful time! I have never felt closer to my brothers and sisters. I have never been prouder of the way we all conducted ourselves.

Things are very different now. We are suspicious of ourselves. The rumors we deal with are coming from inside our fellowship. We're pushing each other away when we ought to be holding on most tightly. I'm not sure what has changed. But hard times are bringing out the worst in us rather than the best.

Clement paused to rub his stiff fingers and stare absently at the leaves of parchment before him. He did not want to do this. In writing about their struggles, he was indicting himself and his leadership of the church. In asking for advice, he was confessing his own inadequacy. With reluctance, he fashioned a fresh nib on the quill and dipped it into the ink once again.

It's the way we talk to each other that worries me. We speak past each other these days. Everyone has an opinion to share, but no one is really listening. Everyone has an answer for our troubles, but no one is willing to try someone else's solution.

And we've grown tired of the whole mess. But, in our fatigue, we excuse ourselves to gripe and grumble. We condone gossip and unkind words. People are being impatient with each other. I see us withdrawing, cautious about each other, fearful that we may be hurt if we stay too close. It breaks my heart, Paul.

Sadly, I am in no position to address this directly. There are those in the church who blame me for causing this situation. They say I did not act decisively, that I talked and prayed and studied when I should have been dealing firmly with Simeon. Part of me agrees with them.

Clement poured out the story of his conflict with Jason, of Jason's impatience with the pace of their discussions, of the way he gathered support from others in the congregation to put an end to the debate and reach a decision. He wrote of the dinner with Jerome. He told Paul about Euodia and Syntyche and the rift in their relationship. He shared his worries about Epaphroditus and the discouragement, the burden, his young protégé was feeling.

The words tumbled onto the pages, words on top of words. They piled up—more than Clement intended to say but, somehow, less than was adequate to convey his concern. He wrote and crossed out and blotted and wiped his ink-stained hands. He wrote until deep in the night, each word a wound. It cut him to tell the story.

But there was healing in the writing as well, comfort in sharing his burden with the one man he trusted to understand and help. The letter was his confession. And Paul was his priest.

I know we will survive this challenge. Our faith in Jesus is too strong to let this destroy us. But it is our faith in each other that worries me. We have seen a darker side of our fellowship. We have learned that our love for each other is more fragile than we imagined. We've been hurt and disappointed by people we thought we could trust.

The question is, can we forgive each other and regain what we once had? Now that we've behaved badly and selfishly, can we trust each other to act like Jesus again? We still have faith in our Lord, Paul. What we are missing is joy. We still look forward to his return. What we lack is peace in the meantime. It's not our hope of heaven that is failing. It is our confidence in each other. Unless we can recover that, I fear it will be a long and lonely wait until Jesus comes again.

It is late and I need to close. In the morning, Epaphroditus will begin his journey to Rome. When he arrives, listen carefully to what he tells you. As you know, he is a good man who loves the church. I would be grateful if you could pay some attention to him. He needs your encouragement and teaching, for he will play an important role in our future.

Come to us quickly, Paul. Pray for us in the meantime. And if you are delayed, could you send a letter? Could you write some advice for an old elder at the end of his wits? I would be grateful.

I have you in my heart, my brother. My prayers are with you daily. May the grace of God be yours.

Clement set down his quill and stretched his neck. He was shaking now; whether from the cold or from the strain of his writing, he could not tell. Pulling the blanket around himself more tightly, he picked up the pages of his letter and reread them a final time. Satisfied, he folded and sealed them with the dripping wax of the candle. He tied a string around them and wrote *From Clement* on the packet.

Rubbing tired eyes, he blew out the lamp and candle and stumbled his way in the dark to the bed. He stretched out fully clothed, covering himself with the blanket and waiting for the shivering to stop. As his body heat slowly warmed his hands and feet, Clement closed his eyes and began his evening prayers. He thanked God for his mercies. He confessed his sins. He asked for the gift of another day. He prayed for Epaphroditus and for his safety on the journey to Rome. He prayed for Paul.

At some point in his prayers, half-asleep, he threw off the blanket and groped for the letter on the table. Clutching it to his chest, he lay again on the bed and begged God to use his letter to convey to Paul what was needed. He asked that Paul might see in his words, between his words, a clear picture of the situation at Philippi.

He prayed like that much of the night. He prayed and slept fitfully and awoke to pray again. He held to the letter for warmth. A talisman against his fears. A portent that he was not alone. A promise that help was coming.

In the dark hours before dawn, he finally fell into a deep and dreamless sleep. Even so, the letter kept its place against his chest.

~

While Clement wrote, Epaphroditus packed.

In the end, it came down to how much he could carry. The money belt was heavy with coin and bulky with the folded letters. It rubbed and chafed under his tunic. He was determined to make everything else fit into a leather knapsack he could sling across his shoulders. Other than a stout walking staff that would double as a weapon, Epaphroditus wanted his hands free. A traveler had to keep his eyes sharp and his hands at the ready.

He studied the mass of donated articles piled on his bed and shook his head. Blankets, cloaks, boots, tunics, writing supplies, a flint striker, a vial of salve, and sundry other items spilled over the bed. The Philippians had been generous but not very realistic. There was no way Epaphroditus could carry it all to Rome.

He opened the knapsack on the floor. Into it went a square of oilcloth that would serve both as a cloak in wet weather and as a ground sheet for sleeping. He rolled up two of the donated blankets and placed them in the pack. Into a bronze pot, he put a wooden cup and the flint striker, a small bag of grain, strips of dried beef, and a block of salt. He paused, surveying the pile on the bed, and then nestled the vial of medicinal salve between the grain and the beef. It took up little space and Paul might welcome it. Wrapping the pot in a cloth, Epaphroditus found room for it in his knapsack.

By the time he packed a few other personal items, he could carry little else. He folded one of the tunics from the bed and placed it in the knapsack for Paul, chiding himself even as he did so. Clothing could be purchased cheaply enough in Rome. With the money Epaphroditus was bringing, Paul could buy whatever he needed. But the tunic had been given by Syntyche, a relic of her long-dead husband, and Epaphroditus knew it would mean a great deal to Paul.

On impulse, he unrolled the pouch containing writing supplies. The leather sheath was rich and supple, and the supplies, he noted, were of the finest quality. Sheets of expensive parchment, smooth and polished, rested inside the pouch. Bottles of various colored ink were tied to the side. Epaphroditus pulled a slender leather sheath from a loop sewn into the pouch and shook out a beautifully crafted bronze pen. He stared at it and thought how Clement would love to have such an instrument.

After a few moments, he returned the pen to its sheath, rolled up the writing kit, and placed it into his knapsack. He knew Paul would complain that it was all a needless luxury. But he also knew that, after the grumbling was done, Paul would take great joy in using it.

Closing the pack, Epaphroditus hefted its weight and grunted at the thought of the miles before him. He cleared the bed, carefully stacking the gifts he could not take in a corner of the room. Removing his boots and blowing out the lantern, Epaphroditus knelt beside his bed to offer up a prayer for his journey.

In moments, he was fast asleep. He slept the heavy slumber that is God's gift to the young and the clear-conscienced and the labor-weary. He slept as if his body knew it would be weeks before he would lie on a mattress again. He slept and dreamt of Rome.

If Clement, tossing and turning on his own bed, could have seen Epaphroditus sleeping so soundly, he would have been sorely tempted to shout, "Fire!"

~

Both men were up before the first light of dawn filtered through the gray skies.

Epaphroditus threw cold water on his face, laced his boots, and shouldered the knapsack. Taking up his staff, he picked his way down the stairs to the shop. At the door he turned, pausing for a moment to survey the room and his handiwork . . . thinking of the years he had spent in this place . . . wondering if he would return.

He closed the door and walked briskly through the gathering light to Clement's quarters. The old man greeted him and, together, they walked across a courtyard to the household kitchen. It was warm there, heated by the cooking stove and the bustle of servants preparing the day's meals, and the two cold men grinned at each other in relief. Clement went over to the stove, reaching around a mountainous Nubian woman to sample the dishes simmering on the stove top.

She slapped at his hand and wagged a finger in his face. "Stop it, Clement! You want I should tell the master that a hungry old reprobate stuck his dirty finger in the oats?"

"Why, Flavia!" Clement answered, all innocence. "You wound me! An old reprobate? I'm not so old!" There was only the slightest crack in her stern demeanor. "I am hungry though. And I've brought a friend to share in the morning meal."

Now the facade dropped away entirely as Flavia greeted Epaphroditus. She enveloped him in her ample arms and smothered him to her more-than-ample bosom. She cooed over Epaphroditus as if she had not seen him in months, though it had been only days since his last visit.

Epaphroditus blushed red and choked out a greeting to Flavia. She and Clement winked at each other, taking great delight in the younger man's discomfort.

She sat the two men on stools and ladled a mixture of warm oats and fresh milk into bowls. Setting the bowls and wooden spoons before them, she rested her hands briefly on their shoulders, looking from one to the other, and then returned to her work.

The two of them fell hungrily to their meal. After Epaphroditus had wiped the last of his oats from the bowl with his finger, Clement reached into his cloak and slid his letter across the table. "This is for Paul."

Epaphroditus picked up the letter and noticed its bulk. He cocked an eyebrow at Clement and shook his head. "Clement. You write like you preach—long! Did you say everything you wanted? Looks like you didn't leave anything out!" His words were taunting but his tone was gentle. He could imagine the effort that letter had cost Clement.

He lifted his knapsack to the table and placed the letter inside. "Don't worry, Clement. I'll get to Paul and tell him how things are here. Maybe I can bring him back with me." He reached across the table to place his hand on top of Clement's. "It'll be all right, Clement. A good friend of mine told me that just recently."

Clement smiled at him. "Are you ready? Do you have everything you need?"

"Humph! I have everything I can carry! There's a pile of stuff in my room—odds and ends people wanted me to take to Paul. Would you see that it's all returned?"

"Certainly. You have money? A warm blanket?"

"Yes, Clement! Stop mothering me. I'll be fine."

They stared at each other in silence for a time, a chasm of unspoken affection yawning between them. Suddenly Clement leaned across the table and caught Epaphroditus's sleeve in his grip. "You be careful, son," he whispered with surprising fervor. "Watch yourself. Don't break an old man's heart, hear? You come back as quick as you can!"

He loosened his grip, embarrassed, and stood to leave. Epaphroditus swung the heavy pack onto his back. They thanked Flavia, who waved them away, and walked into the crisp of the morning.

~

The church gathered on the Egnatian Way, just on the outskirts of Philippi. People clumped in groups, standing close for warmth and stamping their feet against the cold. They were there to bid Epaphroditus God's blessings on his journey.

The two men crested a hill, catching sight of the waiting crowd before the crowd spotted them. Clement rested his hand on the younger man's arm and they stopped momentarily to observe the group. The low murmur of their conversations rose toward them in the quiet morning air. At this distance, the figures were indistinguishable, wrapped in heavy hooded cloaks against the frigid morning. Still, they radiated something deeply familiar to the watching pair. By noting the way they stood, the gestures they made, or the tilt of a head, Clement began putting familiar faces to the anonymous figures. He knew them well.

"This is what your journey is about, my son." Clement gripped Epaphroditus's arm. "These people are worth the risks. Oh, how I love them!" He said it fiercely, protectively, as if his commitment to them were in doubt and the intensity of his statement would set the matter straight.

"I know," Epaphroditus agreed, trying to ease the old man's grasp. "I love them too, Clement."

At that moment, a shout rose from the group and arms pointed up the hill toward the pair. They walked toward one another, embracing as they met and exchanging the customary greetings.

"God be with you, Clement!"

"And with you, Alexander."

"Blessings on you, Epaphroditus."

"And on you, Claudia!"

They gathered in a tight circle, Epaphroditus in the center. As many as could reach laid a hand on his shoulder or head. Jason spoke. "Well, Epaphroditus, the adventure begins!" The crowd laughed nervously. "Go with God, young man. We commit you to his care, believing he will watch over you on the journey and bring you safely to us again." Amens rose from the group. Hands squeezed his shoulders and arms and patted his head.

In her high, clear voice, Syntyche started a song that the others picked up.

This is his command, that we love one another.
He has loved us, and called us his friends.
A friend of his is a friend of ours.
And so we love like he loved us.

The group fell silent for a moment. Then Marcion raised his hands above the assembly and offered a prayer of blessing.

And, suddenly, it was time to go.

He hugged each of them, listening to their urgent goodbyes and their last hurried messages to Paul. Stepping back from the group, he waved to them all, then turned and walked away quickly to cover his emotions. Their shouted blessings followed him as he tramped down the road. He strode purposefully westward, buoyed by their words and thinking of his journey's end.

A few days walking. A few days on the sea. And he would be with Paul.

Epaphroditus marched over a hill and the shouts faded away. Soon, the rhythms of his stride, the rise and fall of the road, the warming of the day numbed him to all thoughts of past and future. He walked. And, for the moment, walking was enough.

Section Two

PAUL AND THE PHILIPPIANS

SUMMER, A.D. 49

Chapter Seven

COME OVER TO MACEDONIA

(LATE SPRING, A.D. 49)

PAUL POKED AT THE FIRE IN A DISTANT, DISTRACTED MANNER. HIS MIND wasn't on the sparking embers or dancing flames. He did not hear the crack and hiss of green limbs burning. He stared absently into the coals, his thoughts elsewhere.

Above him, the sky was black and dense with stars. A waxing moon peeked over the mountains of Phrygia, promising soon to flood the night with her reflected glory. But, for the moment, the dark was so profound it felt like silence.

Below Paul, on a narrow plain caught between the hills on which he and his companions were camped and the moody waters of the Great Sea, lay the port city of Troas. Even it was dark and quiet. The last of its cooking fires had winked out hours before. No candles glowed from windows or open doors. Though the moon would soon catch the waving masts of boats at anchor and the marbled columns of its public buildings, for now Troas slept, wrapped in the black blanket of night.

The inky darkness matched Paul's mood precisely. He sat silent before the fire, hunched over and brooding, poking at the flames with angry jabs. His face, framed in the flarings of the fire, showed his irritation and fatigue. He did not know what to do next, and the not knowing weighed heavy on him, like time on a prisoner. No one was better than Paul at enduring hardships or keeping a calm head under pressure. But Paul could not abide waiting or aimless activity.

To the best of his ability, Paul stayed on the move, always thinking, always looking ahead. He wanted to know what needed doing today and tomorrow and next month. He arose each morning with a clear sense of purpose and the anticipation of useful work.

But, on occasion, fate intervened to disrupt his careful plans and require of him a period of waiting and listening—a doldrums of the soul, a reminder that God's will was not bound by the plans of men. When such times were forced upon him, Paul tried to be gracious. He told himself these reminders were good for him, a needed counterpoint to the heady melody of apostolic calling. But in truth, these waiting times ate like a fungus at the Apostle. After a few days, sometimes after only a few hours, the waiting eroded his genial demeanor and exposed the streak of impatience and melancholy he was prone to.

It had been weeks now, not days. Progress and retreat. Advance and delay. Movement and inertia. Paul had reached his limit. He sat and abused the fire—jab, poke—working to keep his frustrations from spilling over onto his companions.

~

The conference in Jerusalem had gone as well as could be expected. The conservative element of the Jerusalem church—an odd coalition of Pharisees, priests, and rabid Zealots—argued strongly against a Gentile ministry, particularly Paul's Gentile ministry. They complained about the disregard of Torah. They lamented that Gentile believers refused to be circumcised and keep a kosher table. They worried aloud where this Antioch Christianity might lead.

"If we don't root these Gentiles in Torah now," one speaker argued, "it will only be a matter of time before Moses is thrown out entirely. How can we preach Messiah and not preach the Law he himself observed? How can we convert Gentiles to the Way without teaching them how to walk in it?" He paused, warming to his theme.

"Brothers, I myself traveled to Antioch. I saw the people they were baptizing there. I know what kind of lives they used to live. They were idol worshipers! They were rank sinners! They are the proof of everything we Jews have said about the Gentiles for centuries! And now we're supposed to call them 'brother'? Now we're supposed to be one big happy family in the Lord? A little confession and a little water, and we are asked to receive them with open arms?" A murmur spread through the sympathetic crowd.

The speaker drew a breath, calming himself to make his reasoned conclusion. "For myself, I am willing to meet the Gentiles halfway. We will overlook their godless past. We will extend fellowship, though it goes beyond the bounds of any concession we have made in all Israel's history. But they also have a duty. Let them be circumcised. Let them observe the Law. Let them enter the house of Israel in order to share in Israel's Messiah!" He finished to enthusiastic stomping of feet and shouts of approval. He may not have spoken for all, but he certainly spoke for many.

Fortunately, he did not speak for God's leaders in Jerusalem. So clear was Peter's statement, so ringing was James's endorsement of his ministry, Paul set out from Jerusalem invigorated and eager to get among Gentiles again. He traveled up to Antioch with a clear sense of God's will for the coming months: a new foray into Asia Minor, encouraging the churches he'd already established in Syria and Galatia, pushing into fresh territory along the northern boundaries.

The relief, though, was short-lived. As soon as they put Antioch behind them—and then all through the spring—Paul and his traveling companions kept running into stone walls.

His decision to visit the fledgling churches along the Asian coast cost him dearly, both in time and patience. He knew, to be fair, they needed an apostle's teaching and steadying influence. There were problems only he could resolve, questions only he could answer. Each morning, they brought yet another reason why Paul should stay just one more day, maybe two.

Yet all the while, Paul burned for new territory. Fresh from Jerusalem, he was weary of church problems—the personality conflicts, the leadership issues, the grind of debate and tension. So, even as he worked with the disciples in Derbe and Iconium, he was looking past them toward the ungospeled lands that lay to the north.

Finally, having encouraged as much as he could stand, Paul and his companions broke away to continue the journey. But a late snow caught them in the high country and blocked their way. A sudden warming melted the snow but washed out the roads. They made crabbing movements to the west, probing for better weather and other access into Bithynia and Mysia. One miserable day, a gang of bandits took the travelers by surprise, stealing their pack mule and meager travel funds. Soon after, Timothy fell ill, forcing them even farther west to the more moderate climate of the coast.

Now destitute, worn out from the road, and convinced that God had no business for them in Asia Minor, Paul and his partners camped above Troas and contemplated their next move. As he had done more anxiously each evening, Paul brooded before the fire, aching with impatience, not knowing what God wanted of him.

It was Paul's custom to pray for guidance by throwing out to God a series of "yes" and "no" questions and awaiting some sign, some answer that would lead him to a decision. He thought of his questions as a kind of internal *urim* and *thummim*. He would lay the issues before God. And God, by whispered proddings, would make his will known to Paul. Perhaps it was nothing more than thinking through options in the guise of prayer. But often Paul found a great sense of peace in this process. And on occasion, he was granted a panoramic view of God's will.

This night, as he stared into the fire, he laid his questions before God one at a time . . . and listened intently for any response. *Is my duty with the churches we've just left?* Silence. *Should I return to Jerusalem?* Only the wind and the insects spoke up. *Do you want me backtracking to Cyprus to reconcile with Barnabas?* The branches hissed and sparked, but no voice spoke from the burning bush.

His companions sprawled around the fire with him, but, taking their cue from the Apostle, they said nothing to break his concentration. They knew better than to attempt polite conversation or offer opinions as to their destination. When these black moods fell on Paul, his friends offered him the compliment of their silence, knowing that eventually the mood would lift and a new plan would form. Tonight, they counted stars. They gazed at the dark outlines of the city. They drank in the cool breezes and sweet smells of the sea. But they did it quietly so Paul could think and pray.

Silas lay on a blanket, a fresh stalk of spring grass clenched between his teeth, staring up at the sky. Younger than Paul, he was built like a Greek wrestler—short legs, long and powerful arms, thick neck. He even had a wrestler's temperament—solid and strong and patiently persistent. But Silas was not Greek. Nor would he ever discard his clothing, coat himself with oil, and enter the arena. He was a Jew, a follower of the Way for many years, and an esteemed member of the Jerusalem church. He was not a longtime companion of Paul's. Indeed, he had known *of* Paul far longer than he had actually known him. But Silas had seen with his own eyes the miracle of Antioch (the thriving, vigorous community of Gentile Christians Paul and Barnabas had built there) and was a fervent defender of Paul's work and understanding of the gospel. Already he had learned to take in stride whatever direction Paul's passions drove him—toward ecstasy or despair.

Luke sat opposite the fire from the Apostle. This was appropriate because, in almost every way, the two men formed a study in contrasts. Paul was Jewish, Luke was Gentile. Paul was short, Luke tall and painfully thin. Paul was balding while Luke's head sprouted a mass of thick and unruly hair. Paul already intimated the tilt that would later become so characteristic of his posture. Luke sat with straight back and square shoulders. Paul (usually) was voluble and articulate. But Luke was a watcher, more comfortable observing, listening, and storing away. When Paul fell into despondent silence, it was Luke, more than the others, who understood the mysterious healing power of withdrawal.

Timothy lay with his back to the fire, wrapped in his bedroll, snoring softly in exhausted slumber. He was young, too young to have yet developed the pacing and endurance of his older companions. With a puppy's eagerness he would bound awake each morning, rushing through the rituals of cooking and packing, doubling the miles on the road by running ahead to peer over the next rise and running back to report what he'd seen to the others. He was so eager to please, so glad to have been included. But he was ill equipped, physically, for the hardships of travel. Slight, almost frail, he ended each day's walk in numb exhaustion, choking down a little food before turning his back to the campfire and falling, at once, to sleep.

To the surprise of his two wakeful companions, Paul spoke, although he seemed to address himself rather than them. "Perhaps we should go down to the harbor tomorrow and see if any boat is sailing toward home." He found a new stick and resumed his torment of the fire. "We have no money, we have no place to preach, we . . . have . . . no . . . plan." With each word, he stabbed at the fire. Running a hand across his balding pate, Paul looked at his companions and confessed, "I don't know what God is trying to tell us. It seems clear enough he doesn't want us here."

At that moment, Timothy mumbled in his sleep and edged closer to the fire. Paul gazed fondly at the blanketed figure for a while. Then, shrugging off his doubts for the night, he announced, "I guess we can wait till the morning to decide what to do. Nothing we can accomplish now. Let's all get some rest."

Luke grunted his agreement, wrapped himself in his bedroll, and committed his bony hips and shoulders to the hard ground. Silas rose to gather more wood and stoked the fire for another hour of warmth against the evening's chill. Then he, too, rolled himself in a blanket, spoke a "good night" to his companions, and closed his eyes.

Paul collected his bedding and moved away from the fire and the camp. When the sky was clear, as it was this evening, he preferred to lay out his blanket where the light of the flames did not interfere with the display of stars. He needed the advantage, for the stars were less vivid than in his childhood. Even when he squinted, they resolved not into distinct points of light but blurred smudges of blue-white. Deep in the night, he would awaken to stare into the heavens, covering one eye and then the other, squinting and straining, wondering how rapidly his eyes were failing.

Paul spread his blanket a stone's throw from the camp and sat heavily upon it. The ground was so hard and unforgiving. He dreaded another night without a mattress. "I'm getting too old for this, Father!" A strange way to begin evening prayers, perhaps, but Paul believed in speaking truth, even to God. And since he'd begun in candor, he decided to continue. "It was your idea for me to carry good news to the Gentiles. You put this burden on my heart. You called me your chosen instrument. Well, if you're going to use me, use me! Tell me what you want me to do. Show me where to go. Lord Jesus, help me! You spoke to me on the road to Damascus. You've sent me dreams and visions. Talk to me now. Talk to me now, Lord. I'm listening."

But the night was silent. Paul rolled to his back and pulled the blanket around him. He lay still and quiet . . . waiting . . . listening. After a while, his concentration slipped. His knotted shoulders relaxed. His breathing deepened. Paul slept.

And all that night, until early the next morning, not a sound, not a dream disturbed Paul's rest. Not even the hard ground or the cold of night interrupted his slumber. He slept the rejuvenating, invigorating sleep of childhood.

Though he did not know it yet, Paul would need the rest.

~

"Up! Get up! Everyone, let's get moving!" Paul walked from figure to sleeping figure, kicking at the blankets and rousing his companions to reluctant wakefulness.

Timothy sat up, looked at the still-dark sky, and promptly lay down again with an impatient grunt. Luke raised to his elbow and rubbed the sleep from his eyes. Silas regarded Paul with a weary expression and complained, "It's still the middle of the night."

In truth, it was already morning. The first harbingers of dawn stood above the mountains, turning the sky from black to dark blue. In an hour, the sun would be above the horizon and the day would be upon them.

But Paul was not concerned about the hour. He was engaged in a frenzy of manic activity. He threw twigs on the ashes of their campfire and blew it back to life again. He set a pot next to the fire, heating water for their morning ablutions. He rolled his bedding into a tight bundle and began to pack up his knapsack.

And all the while, he talked. "Get up, I tell you! We've got places to go and things to do. Come on! We've got a ship to catch—first boat out this morning if we hurry. Wake up, men! I know where God wants us to go. I see what he's been trying to tell us."

That got the others out of their blankets. They came to the fire, warming their hands and scratching their tousled heads. In their sleepy way, they tried to comprehend this transformed figure before them. Gone was the fatigue and frustration of the night before. No moody silence now. No distracted demeanor.

Paul beamed triumphantly at each of his companions in turn and announced, "I've had a vision. We're going to Macedonia!"

~

Three days later, just past midday, the travelers topped a rise to find Philippi spread before them and, beyond that, the Datos Plain stretching away to the west. The day was bright and growing hot. Already, summer had come to the Macedonian interior, and beads of sweat gathered on their foreheads and darkened their clothing at chest and back.

Paul led the group to the shade of a nearby tree, where they sat to rest and contemplate the city below. A sense of gravity, of destiny, sobered the quartet. For a while, they lost themselves in thought about the work ahead.

"We can't be sure, of course," said Paul, breaking the reverie, "but the people of this city have probably never heard the name of Jesus. In all this land"—Paul swept a hand to take in the plain before them—"not one person knows about the Cross and the hope we have because of it." He fell silent again as the four of them pondered that fact and the immensity of their challenge.

Silas looked at Paul and cocked his head in question. "What were Isaiah's words? 'Give thanks to the Lord, call on his name; make known among the nations what he has done.'"

"'The Lord has done glorious things,'" Paul took up the quotation. "'Let this be known to all the world.'" He looked at his companions, the weight of the moment heavy on him. "That's why we are here, to tell these people what God has done. He's already prepared them to hear our message. We just need to find the ones who are ready to listen."

Turning his attentions again to the city, Paul spoke in a whisper to himself. "This is what the Jerusalem conference was about. This is where God has been leading us for weeks. This is why we've slept on the ground and walked so many miles. This city . . . these people."

Timothy jumped to his feet, eager to finish the journey and start the work he'd been recruited for. But Paul reached up and put a restraining hand on his arm, pulling him back down and drawing the group close. "Before we go, a reminder, my friends. We are about to enter a strange city, so keep your eyes open. These people"—he looked particularly at Silas—"will be different from us. Open your hearts to them. Hold nothing back. And one more thing." His voice hardened. "There will be people here who oppose us. They won't understand what we preach. They may try to harm us. The Spirit has promised many people here. But he has also promised suffering. We must be ready to take the bad with the good." His eyes rested on each of them in turn, watchful for any hint of fear or doubt.

Timothy nodded impatiently, ready to get on with it. Paul could only smile and pray that God would spare the boy from the worst of what might lie ahead. Luke and Silas, who already carried scars for their convictions, looked at each other and then at Paul. If it came to it, they knew how to suffer.

Silas raised his hands in blessing over the small group. "Father, we are your servants. Use us as you see fit. Help us to be bold in our witness. Give us courage in rejection. May your kingdom grow through our work in this city. We pray in Jesus' name."

They spoke the "Amen" together and stood up. "It's time," Paul announced, and turned down the hill for the final approach to Philippi.

~

The sounds of the city reached them first. The clang of a blacksmith's hammer. The rumble of wagons and horses' hooves. The raucous cries of street vendors. The murmur of a thousand conversations. The tramp of soldiers marching. The laughter of children. Though the travelers were in a strange land, there was something comforting about the city's sounds. *Life makes familiar music no matter how far from home you wander,* Paul thought to himself.

Next came the smells—again familiar and welcoming. The perfumes of community: wood burning, meat cooking, soap and sawdust and smoking incense. And the odors of community, less pleasant but still familiar: tanning hides, rotting garbage, sweating bodies, sewers, and horse manure. The pungent aroma of human activity washed over the travelers and ushered them through the gates of the city.

And then, all at once, the sights of the city overwhelmed every other sense.

For Luke, of course, the sights were as familiar and comforting as the sounds and smells. He was Greek, after all, and this was for him a homecoming of sorts. He was returning to the land of his birth, the wandering son home at last.

But for the other three, there was little of comfort to be seen in Philippi. Their ears had fooled them. Their noses had lied. Nothing was familiar about this place. They were walking on alien ground. Paul, Timothy, and Silas stared at the smooth-faced men and unveiled women. They gazed in wonder at the columned temples and marbled theater and public bathhouses—sights they had seen before, to be sure, but never so many and so closely woven into the fabric of a city. They looked at and quickly looked away from the statues and frescoes and vase-paintings that depicted naked figures engaged in war and sport and the business of daily life. Images of the human figure (much less, images of the *naked* human figure) were forbidden in Israel, infrequent in Asia, but sprouted like weeds among the fountains and temples of Philippi.

While the usually subdued physician took on the role of guide—pointing, explaining, educating—his companions wandered, slack-jawed, about the streets. They stood, overwhelmed, in the agora, watching these alien creatures buy pottery, sell vegetables, and drink wine in open-air bars. They sat in the lower tiers of the empty theater, intensely uncomfortable with thoughts of the pagan entertainment conducted there. They paused briefly before the temple of Dionysus and watched the hooded priests dart to and fro among the shadows. They looked in wonder as women walked about unaccompanied, stopping to converse with members of either sex, looking men brazenly in the eye and speaking as if equals.

At the end of the day, Luke sat them at a bench facing a fountain where they rested before leaving the city to make camp for the night. Energized by the tour, Luke droned on about the government of Greek cities, their mode of education, the way they conscripted armies. The others listened dully, hypnotized by the play of water, welcoming the momentary distraction from the wash of revulsion and astonishment and confusion that threatened to engulf each of them.

When he had gathered some strength, Paul motioned to the others that it was time to leave. They shouldered their packs, walked through the city gates, and took a path northward, toward the mountains.

Paul set the pace now, walking out in front to keep his own company. He was in no mood to talk. The day in Philippi had shaken him.

The Apostle was certainly no bumpkin. He had been in cities larger than Philippi. He had been far from home and among strangers before. But his time in Tarsus, his journeys to Syria and Asia, had not prepared him for what he had seen this day.

There, he had been among people at least distantly related in culture and sensibilities. They may have worshiped different gods and eaten different foods. But even in that diversity, a core of common customs remained. Men and women acted in particular ways. Public decorum was strictly regulated. Entertainment and frivolous art were condemned. People knew their place and kept to it. The notion of the "secular" was absurd, for every activity was deeply and profoundly "religious."

But here it was as if, in crossing the Aegean, he was confronting an entirely different breed of human. Paul had dealt with Greeks all his life. But they had been travelers on his home turf, strangers painted against a familiar backdrop.

Now *he* was the stranger, and the strange was the norm. Paul marveled that he had spoken their language for as long as he could remember, yet never really understood the people behind the words. How could he communicate with such people? Where was the common ground on which they could meet?

He glanced behind to see Timothy in lively conversation with Luke. *Ah,* Paul thought to himself. *How quickly the young recover!*

But lagging behind them was Silas, wearing the vacant look of a soldier after battle. Paul almost stumbled as he realized how Philippi must have appeared to his Jewish colleague. Paul, at least, had the advantage of years in Cilicia, of his many travels, to parry the blow of so alien a place.

But Silas! Poor Silas. He was a product of Jerusalem, born and reared in the backyard of his own people. It had been a stretch for

Silas to wrap himself around the Antioch experience. Only six months before, he had tasted his first nonkosher food. Now, thought Paul, he was walking away from Philippi in his shawl and side curls, trying to make sense of a city that was farther from Jerusalem, geographically and culturally, than anything he had ever encountered.

The absurdity of it all suddenly bubbled up in Paul and spilled out in laughter. First a chuckle. Then a guffaw. Finally, he had to stop in the middle of the road, bending over and holding his stomach, as the laughter racked him. He thought about poor Silas and could not catch his breath. He thought about himself, how far the good Pharisee and zealous Jew had fallen, and the tears poured down his cheeks. He laughed until he was red-faced and gasping. He laughed until his sides ached and he wanted to stop. Then another wave would catch him until he sat down, helpless, in the road. He looked through tears at his bewildered companions gathering around their fallen leader, and roared uncontrollably. He felt a sudden urge to urinate. And the thought of an apostle lying in the road, incapacitated, tear- and piss-stained, struck him as so funny ("What would Jerusalem think?") that the laughter rolled over him in convulsions, leaving him—finally—whimpering and weak, a victim of epileptic hilarity.

Chapter Eight

ON THE SABBATH

(LATE SPRING, A.D. 49)

THEY TRAVELED INTO PHILIPPI ON EACH OF THE NEXT THREE DAYS . . . WATCHing . . . listening . . . becoming acquainted with the rhythms and routines of Philippian life. They tuned their ears to the cadences and nuances of the Greek they overheard in the agora. They cautiously tasted the food offered for sale by the vendors. They made discreet inquiries about the Jewish population (there was no synagogue in the city) and the temples (some dedicated to emperor cults, some to Greek divinities like Dionysus, and some to foreign gods from Egypt and Asia) and the prevalence of Latin signage (Philippi, they learned, was a Roman colony and proud of it).

They heard spouses arguing and merchants fighting and surly youths yelling profanities. They saw a funeral procession winding its sad way through the streets of Philippi to the burial ground outside the walls. They heard the prostitutes, standing on street corners, brazenly drumming up business. They watched a soldier steal fruit from a shopkeeper's counter, raising an eyebrow at his victim, daring him to make a fuss. They saw the hunger of the poor, the loneliness of the old, the worry etched in the eyes of mothers.

And the more Paul saw, the more familiar the city became to him. These were people after all, with human feelings and questions and foibles and concerns. They grew old and died just like people in Jerusalem. They fell in love and then grew cold to each other, like so many couples he knew elsewhere. They gave birth to children and then spent the rest of their lives worrying over them—like Jewish parents or, for that matter, parents in every place.

Paul began to see how he could communicate with the Philippians. He realized there was common ground after all. Not common custom, perhaps, or culture, but common humanity. Common hopes and worries. Peel the different habits off a Jew or a Syrian or even a Greek, and beneath beat the heart of a person created by a common God.

With that realization, Paul started to enjoy the excursions into Philippi. He learned to relax and blend into the flow of life as it meandered through the city. He engaged strangers in conversation, testing his Greek while he pumped them for information. He smiled at the children. He joined in the chorus of reprimands when gangs of youths tore through the narrow streets, endangering everyone in their path. He listened to musicians playing in the forum, and to politicians who came there to speak.

On the third day, Paul did something extraordinary. With the last of their coin, he purchased a razor. That evening, he put a pot on the fire and heated water. Taking a bar of soap from his pack, he lathered his beard and, to the horror of Silas, cut that badge of Semitic honor from his face.

Years before, while working with Gentiles in Antioch, Paul had dispensed with the side curls he'd worn since childhood. Most men boasted beards in Syria but only Jews wore the distinctive locks at their ears. Convicted that he was a representative of the Lord of all people, Paul refused to let the way he looked and dressed become a barrier between himself and his prospective audience.

So off the curls had come. Besides, many Jews living among the nations had abandoned the *payos*. They were a luxury only Jews in the homeland could afford.

The beard was different. Paul had never been clean-shaven in his postpubescent life. It was as if he were undressing with each scrape and stroke, baring himself as the facial hair fell from his cheeks and chin. When, at last, the deed was done, he felt naked. And wounded.

Unaccustomed to the razor, he had managed to take off as much skin as whisker.

Dipping his hands into the warm water, he washed away the last wisps of beard and blood, and presented himself for the others' inspection. Luke grunted approval, understanding at once the decision Paul had reached. Timothy, barely able to shave at all, looked with envy at the curling whiskers lying on the ground. Silas could only stare, wide-eyed, at the bleeding cheeks and throat of his mentor.

And then Paul offered the razor to him.

"Oh, no!" Silas shouted, grasping his beard in a protective, defensive way. "I'm not shaving for anybody!"

"Yes you are, Silas," Paul spoke in a level, calming tone. "You're shaving for them." He nodded over his shoulder toward the darkening city. "How many beards did you see in the city today? Only foreigners had facial hair. Even the beggars find a way to scrape the hair from their chins."

"But we *are* foreigners, Paul. We're Hebrews, and Hebrews wear beards." Silas was pleading now.

"True enough, my brother. But we are also emissaries of our Lord Jesus. How many of those people will immediately dismiss us as Jews and refuse to listen to our message?" Paul was insistent. "How many will see us only as foreigners and walk away before we have a chance to talk? We can't do anything about the color of our skin or our accents. But we can dress like these people. We can eat like them. We can become like them in every way possible." Again, Paul held up the razor to his companion.

Silas swallowed hard and fingered his beard frantically. "I'll cut off my *payos,*" he offered, desperate to make a deal. He reached for the razor and sawed off the locks of hair at his temples. Throwing the curls at Paul, he demanded, "There! Does that satisfy you? Look at me. I'm almost a Gentile!" He was near tears, the habits and thinking of a lifetime dying hard.

"No, Silas, that does *not* satisfy." Paul kept talking in that level, killing tone. "The beard must go too." He ran an exploratory hand over his own chin. "It does feel strange. I wonder why they go to all the trouble."

"For cleanliness," Luke spoke up. "Most Greeks are fanatics for personal hygiene. They bathe regularly, daily if possible. They consider beards dirty and unhealthy." He pointed to his own smooth-shaved cheeks and cocked his eyebrows at Silas.

"There you are," said Paul, the matter concluded. Motioning to the razor in Silas's hand, Paul smiled thinly. "Come on, Silas. It's only a beard. It will grow back."

Silas stared at the razor and then let it fall to the ground. "I won't do it, Paul. I can't." He dropped sullenly to his blanket, wrapping himself and turning his back to the fire, no longer willing to discuss the issue.

Paul sighed and stood for a moment, wondering whether to push things further. In the end, he relented. "Tomorrow is Sabbath. I heard in the city today that a small band of worshipers meets for prayer at the river. If we make an early start of it, we can join them and see where God leads."

Luke and Timothy nodded their agreement and prepared for sleep. Silas made no sound at all, his back a silent rebuke. Paul looked over at his friend, praying for him to understand, to adapt. Then, stretching out on the ground himself, Paul closed his eyes to see what sleep might come.

~

Paul awoke the next morning to a soft moaning. Disoriented, he was not sure at first what to make of the noise. He bolted up to find Silas sitting before the fire, holding the shreds of his beard in his hands. His cheeks glistened with water and blood and tears. He turned doleful eyes on Paul, neither accusing nor questioning, but mourning.

Paul knew only too well why Silas suffered.

Being the product of an excellent Jewish upbringing, Silas was knowledgeable, dedicated, zealous, and obedient. But he was also limited. Within the confines of his homeland and the faith of his fathers, Silas flourished. Set down in a foreign land, however, and challenged to think beyond Moses, Silas struggled. What he lacked was flexibility . . . adaptability . . . the capacity to identify what was at the core of his faith and the willingness to jettison anything peripheral.

He lacked the certainty that faithfulness required more of a man than reflexive obedience. Judaism made rocks of its adherents. Christ required changelings.

Paul could read the evidence of his friend's inner turmoil, written across the slump of his shoulders, the crease of his brow, and—particularly—the clumps of hair in his hands. Like Paul himself, Silas had once been so certain, so confident and sure. Life laid out neatly before him. He knew who he was and what was expected of him.

Then came the word of the Cross. The messiness of a crucified Messiah left him stunned and disoriented. His world had tilted precariously when familiar passages from the prophets took on new and unexpected meaning, when questions about the sacrifices and the Gentiles threatened to swamp him. The journey to Antioch had left him drunk with implications, reeling in front of doors that opened to unimagined horizons.

Now he sat in a strange country, on the outskirts of an alien city, preparing to champion an impossible Messiah to people he would not have touched or spoken to in a prior life. He sat with his beard in his hands and the ashes of his *payos* still fresh in the fire. He sat and moaned softly, the stifled sound of a man who needed to scream but lacked the strength.

Paul knew what Silas was going through. It was familiar territory to him. He had covered that ground himself and done his own share of grieving. He arose to embrace Silas, one fellow sufferer offering comfort and empathy to another. They stood that way for a long time, awkwardly, until Luke cleared his throat and, from his bedroll, wondered aloud whether they might be going too far in their adoption of Greek ways.

~

The mists of the morning were clearing from the river by the time Paul's band approached the huddled figures standing at the water's edge. It was a small group, only a dozen, comprised entirely of women.

Three older women wore the veiled and heavy garments of Hebrews. Paul guessed they were widows, stranded on the banks of the Gangites River by entrepreneurial husbands who'd shown the bad manners to die without leaving sufficient funds for their wives to return home.

The rest of the women were younger, dressed in the linen tunics and wool *himatia* and delicate sandals of Greeks. In deference to their older companions and out of respect for the worship conventions they had adopted, the Greek women wore head coverings, though Paul could not help smiling at the brightly colored scarves, and the curls and ribbons that strayed from beneath them. They were obviously trying, but any rabbi would have been scandalized by such an immodest display.

The women stood together, hand-in-hand, eyes raised to heaven, united in the posture of prayer in spite of differences in dress and background. Their whispered murmurings were magnified by the water and drifted down the riverbank to the four men who waited respectfully for a break in the group's devotions. As he waited, Paul closed his eyes—the better to hear—and drank in the sounds of faith that echoed, in fits and snatches, from their huddle to his. His own lips began to move in low accompaniment.

When the prayer ended, Paul opened his eyes and called out, "Greetings!" The women, still lost in meditation, started at the interruption. "Forgive me. But we are Jews from Jerusalem and have only recently arrived at Philippi. We are told there is no synagogue in the city, but that a group meets for prayer at this place. It is Sabbath, and we come to worship the Blessed One." Paul canted his head to one side, putting a request to join them in his bearing rather than in words.

One of the "widows" stepped forward—a mother hen protecting her vulnerable chicks—and fixed Paul with a practiced and world-weary gaze. "You don't look very Jewish. Where is your yarmulke? Where is your beard?" She took in his workman's clothes and leather boots, the sheen on his chin and his closely trimmed hair, and dismissed him at once as a fraud.

"My sister," Paul addressed her in Aramaic, "I am Saul, a student of Gamaliel. I know that I do not look the part"—he spread his hands in frank confession—"but I am a Hebrew, born of Hebrews, just as you are."

The older woman thawed visibly, the familiar sounds of her native tongue chasing the suspicion from her eyes. "Saul," she answered, returning Aramaic for Aramaic. "Welcome! I am called Deborah.

How wonderful to hear the language of my parents again!" She took a step forward, averting her eyes as was proper for Jewish women to do with Jewish males. But not for long. She had lived too many years in Philippi and dealt with too many men. Her downcast eyes signaled her acceptance of Paul. But they quickly found his face again and signaled further that she would not be trifled with.

Paul and his group approached the women. "We have come to worship." Paul continued as spokesman, switching to Greek so that all the women could understand. "May we join you?"

Deborah polled her companions with her eyes and spoke for the rest. "We have just begun our prayers. Please." And she led the two groups to a grassy bank at the riverside. They sat, the women clinging together and the men, in deference to ancient tradition, sitting apart. After a few moments of silence, Deborah motioned at Paul to indicate that, as the eldest male, he should lead the devotions of the group.

Paul sat for a moment longer, allowing the familiar words and rhythms of the synagogue service to fill him. He would speak the Scriptures and prayers in Greek, but in his heart, the ancient Hebrew liturgy would swell and roll—an eternal tide of faith moving beneath the foam and flotsam of circumstance. He pulled his cloak up around his head, surveyed the small assembly, and began.

"Bless the Lord, O my soul; all my inmost being, bless his holy name. Bless the Lord, O my soul, and forget not all his benefits—who forgives all your sins and heals all your diseases."

The men and older women, more familiar with the rituals of the synagogue, immediately responded with the "Amen." The younger women, less sure of themselves and following the lead of the others, watched carefully and murmured quietly.

"Hear, O Israel: The Lord our God, the Lord is one." Paul launched at once into the *Shema.* The entire group, even the Gentiles, quoted the Scriptures together. Paul noted with delight that the Greek women knew these pivotal passages by heart and nodded his approval at them.

"These commandments that I give you today are to be upon your hearts." Silas recited the words with quiet intensity, glad for the comfort of the familiar after the disorienting strangeness of the city. He fingered his bare chin as he recited. Somehow, the *Shema* made even the lack of whiskers seem endurable.

"To love the Lord your God and to serve him with all your heart and with all your soul." Deborah looked around at her small flock. She was relieved to have this strange Jew, so oddly dressed, leading the worship. He spoke the service with authority and precision. Deborah quickly recognized him as a man of learning, someone accustomed to leading Sabbath worship—a traveling rabbi, perhaps, or a renegade priest. She'd seen all types in her time. This one would bear watching. But, for the moment, she lost herself in the beauty of his words and the relief of not having to stumble through them herself.

"You are to make tassels on the corners of your garments." As Lydia recited the *Shema,* she examined Paul with her characteristic thoroughness. She listened past his words to the tone of voice, the care with which the words were spoken, the demeanor of the man. She watched his hands move and noted the calluses and cuts that marked his fingers and palms. A scholar with scars! She measured what she could of the man behind the scars and words, sensing in him an utter lack of pride—yet, at the same time, an aura of authority. He treated his companions as equals, but they obviously deferred to his leadership. From what she had seen of his interaction with Deborah, he displayed none of the condescension toward women Lydia had come to expect of Hebrew men. His manner was frank and open. Lydia thought she might trust this man.

As the *Shema* came to a close, Paul stood to speak the Benedictions. "Blessed are you, O Lord, our God and the God of our fathers. . . . Holy are you and your name is to be feared. . . . Favor us with the knowledge of yourself. . . . Forgive us for we have sinned. . . . Heal us from the pain of our heart. . . . Accept us, O Lord, and live in Zion." The prayer flowed from Paul and washed over his listeners, who sat like rocks in a river, allowing the wonder of the words to pour around, between, over, and through them. The words scrubbed them clean. The words brought nourishment and healing and hope. The words, by some strange alchemy, bound them together and marked out common ground. The world dissolved, worries receded, wounds ceased to ache. For a brief time, all that existed were the words—streams of living water for thirsty men and women.

"Blessed are you, O Lord, who makes peace." Paul found himself at the end of the Benedictions but unwilling to break the reverie. He sat down once more and allowed the moment to unwind at its own leisurely pace. Something holy was happening: Ancient Hebrew rites had been spoken on the banks of a Macedonian river and shared by Diaspora widows, Philippian God-fearers, a youth with a Jewish mother and Greek father, and one ex-Pharisee. Paul lowered his head and marveled at a God who could perform such wonders.

Raising his eyes to Deborah, Paul asked, "Do you have scrolls?" He knew before she shook her head that they would have no Scriptures. "We carry none ourselves," he acknowledged. To the Greek women, Paul explained, "It is customary at this point to read a selection from the Torah and the Prophets. I have no scrolls"—he opened his palms in apology—"but I do carry much of God's Word in my heart. Perhaps you will permit me to recite a passage or two."

He closed his eyes and willed the appropriate passages to mind. Then, drawing himself as upright as his bent back would allow, he announced, "Hear the words of the Lord to Moses." His eyes opened and fixed on the seated women. "I will raise up for them a prophet like you from among their brothers; I will put my words in his mouth, and he will tell them everything I command him. If anyone does not listen to my words that the prophet speaks in my name, I myself will call him to account."

Paul looked over his small audience and allowed the words to hang in the air between them for a moment. "Now hear the words of the Lord to Isaiah: 'Here is my servant, whom I uphold, my chosen one in whom I delight; I will put my Spirit on him and he will bring justice to the nations.'"

As Paul quoted the Scripture, Silas prayed silently. Were they hearing what Moses promised so long ago? Would they understand the message of Isaiah? This "prophet," this "servant"—would the women wonder whom was meant? Paul had chosen these particular passages with great care—Silas knew that. Now, with his whole being, Silas prayed that God would use these Scriptures to open the hearts of the women.

Paul continued, throwing each phrase, each sentence, at his listeners like well-aimed darts, hoping that—with one or two of them—the words would stick. "This is what God the Lord says to his servant: 'I, the Lord, have called you in righteousness; I will take hold of your hand. I will keep you and will make you to be a covenant for the people and a light for the Gentiles, to open eyes that are blind, to free captives from prison and to release from the dungeon those who sit in darkness.'"

He could see the eyes of several women light up at the mention of "the Gentiles." Two of them exchanged curious glances. One woman—in her late thirties, Paul judged—would not take her eyes off his face. For a moment, Paul felt uncomfortable. Even citing Scripture, he could not help noticing how beautiful the woman was. But the discomfort ran deeper. Her gaze seemed to be peeling him back, layer by layer, to examine his core. Perhaps, he told himself, he had not yet acclimated himself to the direct and unembarrassed manner of Greek women. But it was more than that. Paul sensed that here was a woman who could take his measure, someone who would not be fooled.

"'I am the Lord; that is my name! See, the former things have taken place, and new things I declare; before they spring into being I announce them to you.'"

Paul, finishing the quotation, looked around the knot of women and spoke directly . . . simply. "I am Saul—or Paul, if you prefer. These men with me are Timothy, Luke, and Silas." Each nodded in turn, identifying himself and greeting the women silently. "As I said before, we are from Jerusalem. We have traveled a long distance. But we made that journey because we have great news to share, both with the scattered people of Israel"—he looked at Deborah—"and the God-fearing Gentiles." He returned Lydia's steady gaze.

His voice grew stronger, more formal. "I announce today that Israel's Messiah has come. The Scriptures I just quoted have been fulfilled. The 'prophet like Moses' has appeared. The Servant of God has arrived."

The reaction to Paul's announcement was mixed. The Jewish women looked at one another with wide eyes, obviously aware of the announcement's import and equally excited to hear this long-awaited news. The Gentile women took the news differently. Some were confused, too new to Judaism to understand "Messiah." Others recognized the name but missed its significance.

"'The Anointed,'" Paul explained, "is the name we Jews give to the One who will save the world. Our prophets speak of a man who will come and teach us God's ways again, and call us to repentance and righteousness. He will sit on David's throne and rule over all people. He will make peace throughout the earth and welcome all nations into his kingdom."

"This is remarkable news, Brother Saul!" Deborah spoke up—although, in doing so, she broke the rule of silence for women during synagogue services. Paul suppressed a smile at her excitement, reckoning that rules did not apply so strictly when sitting on the grass by a river in Greece. "And we are grateful you've traveled so far to spread the word. Ladies," she spoke to the women seated around her, "this is an event my people have long prayed for."

Turning once again to Paul, Deborah asked the inevitable question. "Has Messiah already established his throne? When will the arrogance of Rome be broken?"

Paul spoke softly. "Deborah. The work of Messiah is not what we thought it would be. Everything about him is different from what we expected. He has already established his throne, but his kingdom is in the hearts of men. He reigns in our lives, not in Jerusalem or Rome. He has no intention of defeating Roman armies. He intends to conquer their minds and souls."

Deborah listened, her brow wrinkling in question. "But the rabbis always said Messiah would throw the Romans into the sea."

"I know, my sister. I used to teach that myself." Paul tried to put her at ease, to prepare her for the shock still to come. "But Messiah's enemy is not Rome. It's Satan. It's not the power of armies he came to battle, but the power of sin."

"Oh, my," Deborah worried. "That must have come as quite a shock to our leaders. They've been counting on him for so long, for so much. How did Messiah . . . what did he say to make them understand?"

Paul studied the grass at his feet, wishing he had a script for this next part. Silas's silent prayer intensified. This was the critical moment. "Well, Deborah," Paul said as gently as he could, "they did not understand. Messiah could not persuade most of them. Most of our leaders in Jerusalem do not accept that Jesus of Nazareth is Messiah. But," he hastened to add, "many of the people believe. There are thousands in Jerusalem who name Jesus as Lord."

Poor Deborah was completely confused. "But Saul, if they won't believe, why doesn't Messiah simply remove them? Why doesn't he throw them from the temple and exile them from the Lord's people? Yahweh has never permitted a few rebellious priests to hinder his plans!"

"Well, my sister, that leads us to the hardest part of all." Even as he prepared to say it, Paul marveled that anyone believed. On the surface, it sounded so ludicrous, so absurd. "Our leaders in Jerusalem rejected Messiah. They plotted against him and handed him over to the Romans. The Romans crucified him. But, after three days, God raised him from the dead! He died for our sins, you see. God raised him as a promise that we, too, could have new life!"

Deborah stared at Paul in utter disbelief. And then she laughed.

"You have crossed land and sea to tell us that Messiah has come! But when he arrived, the very people who have spent their lives looking for him didn't recognize him? He won't defeat the Romans and he can't even persuade his own people to believe him? And then you suggest that God would allow his Messiah to be crucified?" She looked at Paul as though his skin were crawling with worms, the laughter still on her lips turning to anger and contempt. She struggled to her feet, shaking her robes to dislodge the grass and any stray lies that might have clung to her clothes. "Let's go, ladies." She fixed Paul with one more cold stare. "This madman has disrupted our worship and wasted enough of our time."

Deborah marched off, leaving her bewildered brood to gather themselves and hurry after her. Only Lydia remained seated—and the two women who turned out to be her household servants.

"Lydia!" Deborah commanded over her shoulder as she hurried back toward the city. "We are leaving!"

Lydia still had not moved her eyes from Paul's face. When she spoke it was not to Deborah, but to him. "'He was pierced for our transgressions, he was crushed for our iniquities; the punishment that brought us peace was upon him, and by his wounds we are healed.' Isn't that what the prophet said?"

Who was this woman? How did she learn the Scriptures? "Yes. That is what the prophet said. And much more besides." Paul returned her gaze, trying to put into his face every bit of sincerity and trustworthiness he could muster. Silas was praying so intensely, he felt lightheaded.

"Lydia!" Deborah had stopped and turned to insist that Lydia follow. "Come along right now! That man is dangerous! I won't allow you to stay another moment! Do you hear me?"

Still, her eyes searched his face. Was he lying? Was he insane? She graced Paul with a smile and spoke to Deborah. Though she did not raise her voice, her words carried the distance that now separated them. "Thank you, Deborah. I wish to stay awhile. I have a few questions."

"I will not leave you here with this lunatic! Come back with us at once." Deborah took a few paces toward Lydia as if to physically compel her obedience.

Only then did Lydia take her eyes from Paul. Turning to Deborah, the younger woman said, "It's all right. I'll be fine." She spoke politely, but there was no mistaking the firmness, the stubbornness in her voice.

Deborah stood glowering at Paul, trying to think of something to say. Finally, with an exasperated "Bah!" she turned on her heel and hurried off.

"What is your name?" Paul asked, when Deborah's parting invectives could no longer be heard.

"I am called Lydia," the woman responded. "I am a seller of fine cloth. And I have long been an admirer of the Jewish faith."

"You know your Scriptures," Paul acknowledged. "More important, you seem to understand them."

Lydia dismissed the compliment with a wave of her hand—the practiced habit of a frequently flattered woman who had learned what most compliments were worth. "What does the prophet mean? Who is he talking about?"

Paul glanced at his companions in relief. Silas positively beamed.

"Lydia," Paul started over. "Let me tell you a story."

~

A patient observer, perched on the hillside overlooking that bend in the river, would have watched the conversation continue as the sun climbed high in the sky. He would have seen Paul's hands moving, punctuating his words with broad gestures and pointed finger. He might have guessed, from the stillness of the women and their attentive posture, how engrossed they were in the lessons of their teacher.

If he was very patient, and completely lacking in any demands on his time, such a spectator might have remained through the hours of the afternoon, as the heat of the day settled into the valley and the shadows started to lengthen.

And just when even the most diligent observer could be excused for quitting his lonely vigil and returning to the city, he would have been rewarded with a sight as perplexing as it was novel: Paul extending his hand to Lydia, leading her and the members of her household to the edge of the river; Paul wading into the river with the women while his companions gathered at the shoreline to watch; Paul raising his hands above each woman in turn, moving his lips briefly, and then lowering them beneath the water's surface.

He would have seen, but not understood, the embraces that followed. He might have heard, but not comprehended, the laughter rising up from the river, the exclamations of joy. He would have watched the group raise their eyes to heaven in prayer, but could not have guessed what they were praying or to which god their prayer was addressed.

The watcher on the hill would know he had witnessed something unusual. What he could not know was that he had seen the end of the world as he knew it and the dawn of a new era for the land of the Greeks.

~

"Where are you staying, Paul?" Lydia stood, dripping, at the edge of the river, reluctant to end the day by watching this remarkable man walk away. She had so many questions. What now? What next? Her life had been turned inside out. After the story she'd heard, after the commitment she'd made, Lydia was not about to let Paul wander off.

"Don't worry, Lydia." Paul smiled reassurance. "We're not going anywhere. Our camp is to the north." He pointed vaguely at the sun-speckled foothills rising above the walls of Philippi. "We'll be back in the city every day. Let's arrange a place where we can meet."

Lydia examined the four of them, their worn sandals and frayed clothing. They had the gaunt look of men who were not eating regularly. "How much money do you have?" It was a challenge in the guise of a question.

Paul raised his hands in defense. "We are doing fine. I will find work in the city. We don't want your money, Lydia. You have already given us the one thing we want most."

She continued her scrutiny for another moment, then came to a decision. "You're coming home with me. I have a large house with comfortable beds and plenty of food. These Macedonians can't get enough purple cloth. They all want to dress like kings. Which is fine with me. It has made me a very rich woman."

Paul almost groaned at the thought of a clean and dry mattress. Timothy looked at him pleading, his mouth watering at the mention of food. Luke and Silas were certainly not falling over themselves to refuse her offer.

Still Paul hesitated. "Perhaps your husband will object to your dragging home four strangers."

A shadow passed over Lydia's lovely face. "I have no husband." She turned and began to walk quickly toward the walls of Philippi. "Are you coming?" But her back made it clear the words were a command, not a request.

Chapter Nine

I HAVE YOU IN MY HEART

(SUMMER, A.D. 49)

"I'LL GRANT THAT YOU TELL A GOOD STORY. I THINK IT'S FASCINATING. Really, I do." The young man, who had appointed himself spokesman for the crowd, shook his head in amusement. "But you're asking us to take this fable for fact!"

He looked around at the gathering—a random assortment of searchers, curiosity seekers, and the merely bored—and raised his voice to reach the back of the throng. "We Greeks tell a few good stories ourselves—about the gods and their bumbling ways. Don't we, my friends!" The crowd laughed and nodded its agreement. "Nobody tells better god-stories than Greeks, Paul. But we don't actually believe them! Oh, there might be a few superstitious women who still hold to the old tales— "

"Now hold on there, young man," an old woman bristled. "Just because you don't believe in the gods doesn't mean those who do are simple or superstitious!"

A third member of the crowd, middle-aged and well dressed, spoke up. "The gods—and the stories we tell about them—serve useful purposes in our city. They teach important lessons to our children. They warn us about the danger of pride and the power of fate." He shot a warning of his own at Paul. "But they are our gods. Our stories.

And our purposes. We don't need some imported deity to teach us the meaning of life! We've got enough home-grown ones to do that!"

Paul flashed his crooked, disarming smile at the crowd surrounding him. "I'm not telling you about an 'imported' god at all. God doesn't belong to a particular place or people. The whole world is his. He is as much the God of Philippi as he is of Ephesus or Jerusalem—or Rome, for that matter. He is the God of all and, because of that, all people have a place in his heart."

"Bah!" The young man blurted derisively. "And that's another thing about your story! Even if the gods do exist, they keep their distance. They don't care about us. They may use us. They certainly bully us from time to time. They may even bless us on occasion—when it suits their purposes. But, mostly, they ignore us."

Paul looked around at the faces in the crowd. He could see that they did not like what the young man said. But neither did they disagree with him. They wanted him to be wrong about the gods. But they were afraid he merely spoke the truth.

"And that's why the stories we tell ourselves about the gods are so important." Paul spoke more intensely now, his eyes searching for the people who were listening, for the telltale signs of concentration and interest. "You say there are many gods. But I tell you there is only one." His tone was challenging. "You say the gods couldn't care less about you. But I say that God cares about you deeply. He loves you! You wonder what the gods want of you? Well, the God I'm telling you about has come to earth to tell you exactly what he wants. He wants your hearts. He wants to live inside you."

"Why should we believe that?" The young skeptic spoke up again. "We've never heard of such a god." He scanned the crowd to invite its agreement.

Paul took a deep breath and looked straight at the speaker. "You may not have heard of him, but that doesn't mean he's a fable. I'd never heard of you until today. But you're certainly real enough—and irritating!" Paul rolled his eyes, clowning for the crowd, and they responded with sympathetic laughter. Even the young man joined in. The Apostle tried again. "Not every story you've heard about the gods is true. And not every new story is a fairy tale. I know I'm telling you a different god-story than you've ever heard. But the good news is, this story also has a different ending, a better ending!"

"The gods I know are good enough for me," said the well-dressed man, throwing up his hands in rejection and turning to elbow his way through the crowd. "Don't you people have anything better to do than stand here and argue about religion?"

Apparently, they did not. The crowd pressed closer to Paul, and someone shouted over the heads of those in front, "Talk on, stranger!"

Directly behind Paul, sited in the middle of Philippi's agora, was a fountain, dribbling water from the mouth of a stone lion into a shallow pool. Grasping the shoulders of the men at either side, Paul lifted himself to the edge of the pool so that he stood just above the crowd. He began the story again.

"Imagine that there are not many gods, but only one. Imagine a God so powerful that he could create everything you see around you—the land and the rivers and the mountains and the sky. That God is Lord of all. He gives breath to all living things. He makes the sun rise and set. He establishes nations and governs the seasons." Paul paused to survey his audience. "Can you imagine that kind of God?"

"What does he look like?" someone called from the crowd. "Where does he live?"

Paul smiled and motioned with his hand. "I can't tell you what he looks like. God is invisible. He isn't made of flesh like you and me. He doesn't eat or drink or marry. And he is spirit. He is everywhere and in everything."

They were trying. Paul could tell by the focused eyes and furrowed brows that many in his audience were working to conjure up such a God. But it was a stretch for them. This was not the way they had learned to think about deity.

"Now imagine that this God is also good." Paul let the word sink in for a moment. "Not just powerful, but holy. He doesn't throw temper tantrums. He doesn't steal women. He doesn't get drunk. He is good. Every virtue, all that is excellent and noble, is found in him."

An old man near the front of the crowd asked softly, "Do you mean he never does wrong?"

"What's the good of being a god if you can't bend the rules every once in a while!" The young spokesman laughed, winking at the crowd.

Paul just shook his head. "I know your gods are both good and bad. They can be merciful and they can also be lazy. They are powerful. But they are also petty and impulsive. That's not the way it is with my God. He is holy to the bone."

"I thought you said he didn't have flesh like us!" The young man was quick.

Paul chuckled. "A figure of speech." He was enjoying himself. "Above all, think about a God who is not just powerful and good. He is loving. Imagine a God who loves us." Now the crowd grew still, caught by the thought of a god who might actually care. "He loves us like a father loves his children. In fact, he loves us so much, he became one of us. He was born of a woman. He lived and walked on the earth."

"Wait, wait!" objected one of the listeners. "You just said he isn't flesh . . . that he is invisible. Now you say he was born of a woman. Well, which is it?"

Paul pursed his lips in frustration. There were so many things he took for granted, raised as he was in the rich tradition of Judaism. He had grown up with the notion of one holy and transcendent God who wanted covenant relationship with men and women. With mother's milk, he had imbibed the idea of an invisible God who revealed himself through words. How could he expect a Philippian crowd to grasp in moments what his own people had taken centuries to understand? The more he tried to bridge the gap between himself and other cultures, the more grateful Paul was he had been born a Jew.

"God is spirit. But he wants us to know him. He wants us to live like him. What better way to show that than to become one of us? God became a man to teach us about himself and to show us how he wants us to live."

"Where did this happen?" called another voice. "Where did God choose to live?"

"He was born in Bethlehem of Judea. He was born among the Jewish people."

A murmur spread through the crowd. The young critic gave voice to the doubts of those around him. "Of all the places a god could choose to live, why become a Jew? Now a Roman—that would make sense. I could see a god growing up in Caesar's household. He wouldn't be the first!" He cocked an eyebrow at his neighbors and they shared a cynical laugh. "Or maybe a palace in Athens. Those philosophers all think they're a gift of the gods as it is! But a Jew? God might as well have been born a pig!" He was enjoying himself immensely, and the crowd along with him.

Paul felt the hairs on his neck rise, the prejudice of his audience ugly even when disguised with laughter. How could he make them understand? How could he break through? The Apostle spoke quietly, forcing the crowd into stillness, making them crane to catch his words. "God wasn't born in a palace. Not even a Jewish palace. He was born in poverty. He made a living as a carpenter. He knew what it meant to go hungry and pay taxes and sleep on the ground."

The words hung over the crowd, too improbable to be received. Paul could see the heads starting to shake, the mouths working to voice disbelief, when a shout from the perimeter cut through the crowd.

"You'd better listen to him! He speaks for God Most High!"

Like the Red Sea, the crowd parted to make way for a tall, reed-like girl. She was dressed in tatters, her bare feet dangling at the end of thin and dirty legs. At the top of her head sprouted a mass of matted hair. And out of her grime-smeared face, two feverish, haunted eyes wandered restlessly over the assembly. "He is telling you the way to be saved!" she said in a singsong voice, and began a strange, jerking dance—turning and turning as the crowd backed away.

Paul stared at this odd creature, overwhelmed by the wash of hurt and desperation that radiated from her. He found it physically painful to watch her. The abuses and cruelties she had suffered in her young life were written in her every move. Who was this poor girl? What kind of evil spirit possessed and tormented her? And how could such a confused child know who he was?

The girl stopped her dance and planted herself firmly before Paul. She looked hard at him. He returned her gaze evenly, entering into a brief and intimate contest between the two of them—his calm against her turmoil, his compassion battling her torment. They stayed there for a time—locked in silent struggle, matching wills, taking the measure of one another. The crowd, transfixed, looked from the Jew to the child and back again—spectators to a spiritual standoff they could not comprehend.

Suddenly, the child threw back her head and screamed—a high, keening shriek—and bolted from the crowd, down the street, and out of sight. Every eye followed her and remained fixed on the corner around which the girl disappeared.

When, finally, Paul cleared his throat and tried to pick up the thread of his narrative, he knew the cause was lost. He was too troubled, and the people were too distracted, to keep the dialogue going. Slowly, though the girl had warned them to listen, his crowd melted away until Paul stood alone, perched on the edge of the fountain, staring across the forum in the direction of the child's flight.

"Sad, isn't it?" The Apostle started at the unexpected voice and turned in its direction. A solitary figure stood to his right, the last vestige of the ebbing crowd. He was about Paul's age and size. Like the Apostle, he was balding. His clothes were not expensive, but they were clean and neat. Paul noticed at once the contradiction in the man—the eyes that glowed with confident intelligence, the ear pierced with the sign of slavery.

"Sad about the girl." He nodded in the direction Paul had been staring without taking his eyes off the Apostle. "She can be . . . unsettling."

"Yes," Paul agreed. "Poor child. What's her story?"

"Tell you what," the man countered with a smile. "Come with me and share some wine and bread. I will tell you her story. And, in fair exchange, you can finish the story you began here."

Paul walked over to stand in front of the stranger. "I accept," he said simply. "I am Paul of Tarsus." And he reached out his hand.

"Good," the stranger grunted, and grasped Paul's outstretched hand. "I am Clement, of the household of Gaius. Come this way."

~

They sat in the relative cool of Clement's quarters, the curtain pulled back from the doorway to allow any stray breeze to blow through the room. On the table lay the remains of their meal—a half-empty pot of wine, a bowl of hummus and ripe olives, hard crusts of bread. Clement sat on the bed and faced Paul, his full attention concentrated on the strange figure perched atop the stool.

Paul was talking. And as his lips moved, his hands beat accompanying time, punctuating his story with emphatic gestures and broad sweeps. Paul could never be a thief, Clement thought to himself. Thieves, when caught, frequently lost their hands. For Paul, such a loss would leave him mute as well as maimed. His hands were as necessary for speaking as his tongue.

"That's why the Cross was needed. That's why Jesus had to die." Paul jabbed an insistent finger at Clement. "One life for many. The holy for the sinful. The innocent in place of the guilty. It was the greatest, the most profound act of love the world has ever witnessed."

He sat back on his stool, astonished by the wonder of it all once again. Paul had told about the Cross a thousand times, in hovels and marketplaces and synagogues. He had shared the Cross with kings and paupers and slaves like Clement. But he never tired of telling the story. And he never lost the sense of awe that overwhelmed him afresh with the telling.

"And you say your prophets predicted all this would happen? Hundreds of years before this Jesus appeared on the scene?" The question was not a challenge. Clement was merely getting his facts straight, focusing on the details while the enormity of the story he'd just heard sank in.

"Yes, yes!" Paul beamed with excitement. "Isaiah was speaking of the Christ when he said—" He closed his eyes and quoted the passage as though it were written on the inside of his eyelids. "He poured out his life unto death, and was numbered with the transgressors. For he bore the sin of many, and made intercession for the transgressors.

"And our father David, speaking by the Spirit of God, foresaw the exact events of Calvary: 'A band of evil men has encircled me, they have pierced my hands and my feet. I can count all my bones; people stare and gloat over me. They divide my garments among them and cast lots for my clothing.'"

"That is remarkable." Clement shook his head. "So this Messiah, promised by God and predicted by the prophets, was rejected when he finally appeared. His own people handed him over to the Romans to be crucified. Is that right?" Clement waited for Paul to give a sad nod. "And he did this deliberately, knowing all along this is how it would end?"

"But three days later, God raised him from the dead." Paul retold the end of the story. "The victory of life over death and good over evil; a pledge of hope for all who believe in his name. We can live again, Clement!" Paul leaned forward, the teacher in his most persuasive mode. "Finally, after death. But right now as well!" Paul's fist pounded his open palm, driving his point home. "No more dead ends and dead hearts and dead dreams. No more sins that enslave us and mistakes from which we never recover. Forgiveness, Clement! Second chances! Starting over with God!"

Clement listened with shining eyes and then sat back on the bed, trying to place some distance between himself and his companion. Paul's intensity made Clement nervous. He feared being overwhelmed, swallowed up, by the passion of this strange Hebrew.

But it was more than that. He wanted some distance between himself and the peculiar story he'd just been told. He needed breathing room, a chance to hold the story at arm's length and examine it objectively. Already, he felt himself drawn to the power of the story, to the beauty of a God who loved that much. And the paradoxes of the Cross! God dying, life out of death, the Son for the sinners—it set his head swimming.

He needed time. He had to keep Paul quiet long enough to make sense of the impossible. Should he ask him to leave? Should he make some excuse that would let him escape this stifling room and Paul's disturbing story?

At that moment, Clement made a decision that would change the course of his life. He decided not to run. He decided to stand and fight. He decided to tell Paul a story of his own.

"All my life, I have been a student." He began quietly, his voice even and matter-of-fact, his eyes focused on a crack in the far wall. "It didn't matter much what the subject was. If there was something to be learned, I wanted to know about it.

"In my youth, I wanted to know how things worked. I would stand and watch the blacksmith for hours. I was fascinated with potters and tanners and the artisans in the agora."

Paul sensed that Clement was walking into territory he did not often visit and rarely shared with others. He clasped his hands in his lap and willed his body into stillness. He had done his best with his words. Now it was time to do his best with his ears. Paul opened himself to the story Clement needed to tell.

"As I grew older, 'how' questions lost their appeal. I became much more interested in knowing 'why.' I studied science and mathematics and rhetoric. I traveled through Greece and attached myself to various teachers. I learned quite a bit." Clement smiled to himself, recalling those heady, word-filled days. "But one of the things I learned is that you can be quite brilliant and quite miserable. One of my brightest teachers beat his wife. Another sank into deep melancholy from time to time. I heard later that he drank the cup." He dragged his eyes from the wall to look coldly at Paul. "I discovered that knowing Pythagorus and having joy were not the same thing.

"So I narrowed my studies even more. I concentrated on philosophy. I spent time with the Stoics and the Peripatetics and the school of Socrates. I read what they said about the soul and morality and religion and public order. Again, I learned a great deal. Those were the happiest days of my life." He paused, and Paul could see the shadow cross his face. "I would be at it still, no doubt. Learned lectures on noble subjects in the company of the best and brightest." A note of self-mockery, of self-loathing, crept into Clement's voice. Paul heard it immediately. He grew more still. He tried not to breathe. He wanted nothing to distract him from the listening, or Clement from the telling. There was something here, close to the surface now, and it might prove to be the key.

"That's when the letter came." And again, Clement smiled. But it was not the smile of happy memories or fond thoughts. It was the smile one bestows on an unfaithful wife or a stupid son—the bitter, disappointed smile of a wound too deep for tears.

"My father's business was in trouble, the letter said. I was needed at home." Clement stared at his feet now, unable to look up, unable to meet Paul's eyes, pretending perhaps that Paul was not there, that he was telling this story to himself. "Of course, I rushed home. And things were as bad as the letter said. All the savings gone. All the assets sold or hocked. We were wiped out. Worse! We had debts that—" his voice trailed off, the rest of the sentence unnecessary and too painful to speak.

"It took me several days to discover what had happened. I didn't see the discrepancies at first—the double entries, the debits disguised as expenses. He hid it so well." Clement spoke softly, as if he were afraid to be heard.

And then he raised his eyes to Paul. And Paul saw in them the fury, the red-rimmed rage that Clement could barely restrain. His fist came crashing down on the table and his voice shook with emotion. "He'd gambled it all away! He wasted a fortune on games and horses! He put my mother in rags and made a slave of me because he never met odds he didn't like."

Paul was confused. "Who? Who are you talking about, Clement?"

"My father—may he rot in Hades!" Clement spit out the words as though they were too distasteful to hold any longer in his mouth. "My own dear papa. It's been fifteen years and I still hate him for it." He slumped against the wall, rubbing his hands over his eyes and fighting to gain control of himself again. After a moment, his breathing slowed and his voice regained its quiet, composed quality. He glanced at Paul, a wry smile playing on grim lips. "Imagine my surprise to discover that my carefully cultivated Stoic calm went straight out the window. Everything in my training taught me to bow to fate, to accept my destiny with grace. But it counted little. All that study, all those years of debate and reading, had not changed my heart. I had the best education money and talent could obtain. And I would have traded it all for a sanction to kill my father."

He sat on the bed, knees drawn up, an elbow on each kneecap. He let his head fall back against the wall and closed his eyes for so long Paul wondered if he were asleep. "Well?" When he spoke, his voice was marked with great weariness. "Can your Christ do anything for me? I gave up on the gods the day I discovered what my father had

Chapter Ten

THE OTHER VETERANS

(SUMMER, A.D. 49)

WHEN THE CEILING OF THE NEWLY CONSTRUCTED TEMPLE COLLAPSED, ONLY ten people were inside. Perhaps the builders had used rotten marble. Perhaps the masons had been careless when fitting the great slabs together. Or, perhaps, the god honored by the temple was not worthy of such veneration. Temples falling on the heads of the faithful did little for a deity's popularity.

Whatever the cause, the resulting shower of stone and beams took off three legs and two arms of the worshipers who survived. Four others did not survive, leaving this life to pass on to the underworld, where, presumably, they intended to lodge complaints against the carelessness of their adopted divinity. Of the four, two were figures of influence in Philippi, requiring the city to mark their passing with a procession.

~

News of the temple collapse and the deaths of Cleisthenes the politician and Severus the commander spread rapidly through Philippi. Paul heard of it within moments of the bodies being recovered from the rubble. Passing gossips, eager to show how much they knew about the two prominent victims, filled Paul's willing ears with unofficial obituary—careers, financial holdings, surviving family members.

The more he heard, the more intrigued Paul became.

Both men had enjoyed successful careers in their respective fields. Cleisthenes had served several terms on the Philippian council and even represented Philippian interests to the Senate at Rome. Severus had been posted to Philippi years before and placed in command of the three legions scattered through Macedonia. From the day the two men met (according to Paul's sources), they had struck up a close friendship.

Perhaps the friendship was inevitable, since the two men had so much in common. Both were educated and respected. Neither, though hardworking and ambitious, was particularly wealthy. Both had married well, though certainly not above their stations. And both, to their great and oft-expressed sorrow, were childless.

But it was the story of the wives that most interested Paul. At first (again, according to his street sources), the wives tolerated their husbands' friendship. Then begrudged and resented it. Then actively campaigned to destroy it. What did they find in each other that a good wife could not provide? Were they lacking conversation at home? Surely the attraction was not sexual!

Finally, in desperation, the wives arranged a meeting, a strategy session aimed at accomplishing together what they had been unable to achieve apart. It was at that meeting (so the story went) that the two women, like their husbands, struck up an immediate and close friendship. From that day on, the two were inseparable and had remained so for more than five years now.

That the two men were together when they died surprised no one who knew them well. And that their wives should seek out each other's comfort and companionship in that moment of tragedy was equally predictable.

The news was carried throughout the city by hired criers. Tomorrow's funeral would be a joint one. The procession would begin at first light, pause at the forum for a few fitting tributes, and proceed on to the burial site. The widows, Euodia and Syntyche, expressed gratitude to the citizens of Philippi for every expression of condolence.

~

As they had done in joy, so they did now in sorrow. The two women clung to each other, their friendship their solace. Together, they stumbled after the funeral biers and listened numbly to the tributes offered in their husbands' memories. Together, erect and dignified in their mutual grief, they watched as the fire consumed their past and scarred their future. Leaning on each other, and surrounded by a knot of friends and mourners, they picked their tearful way home after the ashes had been committed to the grave. And when the last of the city officials and army officers and guild representatives and neighbors left, the two of them sat together, exhausted, wondering how they would survive the nine days of mourning, so closely regulated by custom and religion, that lay ahead.

It was then that the first of the messages arrived by courier. Euodia broke the wax, read the message, read it again, and then called to Syntyche. "What do you make of this?" And she read it a third time, aloud.

The Lord is my shepherd, I shall not be in want.
He makes me lie down in green pastures,
he leads me beside quiet waters,
he restores my soul.
He guides me in paths of righteousness for his name's sake.
Even though I walk through the valley of the shadow of death,
I will fear no evil,
for you are with me.

As she listened, the tears pooled again in Syntyche's eyes, surprising her because she had thought there were no more tears left. "How beautiful," she said at last, reaching for the note. "Who is it from?"

"There's no name." Euodia carried the note to her friend, and the two of them sat together to examine the words more carefully—a welcome distraction from the prison of their own pressing memories. They read and reread the message. "It must be a passage from one of the poets," Euodia pronounced at last. "But I have never heard it quoted before."

"Neither have I. But how appropriate! 'The valley of the shadow of death.' 'Quiet waters.' Grief and comfort, do you see it? The poet is mourning. But he trusts someone to soothe him."

The two women embraced each other and cried softly for a few moments.

When their eyes dried, they took up the note again, reading the words once more, feeling strangely comforted and strengthened by the poem. Before putting it away with the rest of her correspondence, Euodia looked at Syntyche and asked, "I wonder who the 'shepherd' is?"

~

The next day, according to custom, was set aside as a day of rest—a time for the grief-stricken to recover from the graveside ordeal. Of course, Euodia and Syntyche passed the day together. In the afternoon, the second note arrived, delivered by the same courier, written on the same cheap paper, sealed with the same nondescript wax stamp.

> *The people walking in darkness have seen a great light; on those living in the land of the shadow of death a light has dawned.*
>
> *He will swallow up death forever. The Sovereign Lord will wipe away the tears from all faces.*

"There it is again." Syntyche pointed to the line. "'The shadow of death.'"

"Yes," mused Euodia, turning the paper over, examining it for any clue as to the sender. Again, there was no name. "Another beautiful poem. But what does it mean? Look at this. 'The Lord will swallow up death forever.' And then he will wipe away tears." The two women looked at each other.

"He's talking about hope!" Syntyche exclaimed, reaching for the note and tracing the lines with her finger. "Look, Euodia! Light out of darkness. A dawn from the shadows." She paused and thought for a moment. "By the gods! This is wonderful verse. Who wrote it?"

Euodia examined her friend thoughtfully. "It's not poetry, Syntyche." She fingered the fourth line. "It's a prayer."

~

On the third day, custom dictated that the bereaved visit a temple to begin the purification process—a series of sacrifices and ritual washings necessary to clean away the contamination of death. Euodia and Syntyche endured the ceremonies and made the sacrifices, all the while keeping a watchful eye on the ceiling above their heads.

When they returned home, a third note awaited them.

The cords of death entangled me,
the anguish of the grave came upon me;
I was overcome by trouble and sorrow.
Then I called on the name of the Lord:
"O Lord, save me!"

Euodia watched the tears well up in her friend's eyes. She saw that the words pained her and made the anguish, the still-fresh sorrow, rise to the surface. She threw the note on the floor. "This is intolerable! Who is sending these letters? Who could be so insensitive?"

But Syntyche stooped quickly to retrieve the letter. "No, Euodia. Don't say that. Someone is trying to comfort us. I know it. What I don't know is how he can write exactly what I'm feeling." She read the lines again, shaking her head in wonder. And then the hand fell to her side and the tears came again. "I would cry 'Save me!' if I thought any god would listen."

~

The notes came daily through the prescribed period of mourning. The same courier. The same paper and seal. A few brief lines.

There is no god besides me.
I put to death and I bring to life,
I have wounded and I will heal.

They began to anticipate the letters, waiting for the courier's knock at the gate, reading the messages hungrily, talking about the words and marveling at how appropriate, how healing they were.

For men are not cast off by the Lord forever.
Though he brings grief, he will show
compassion,

so great is his unfailing love.
For he does not willingly bring affliction
or grief to the children of men.

They asked the courier to linger, filling him with cakes and fruits while they probed for the sender's identity. An older gentleman, he said. A foreigner, he thought. No, he did not know a name. And could he please have another piece of sweet bread?

On the last day of the bereavement period, the two women waited together for the courier to appear. During the morning, they spread the messages on a table and read them through yet again. They served as impatient hosts to the friends and hangers-on who gathered in Syntyche's home to eat the feast that officially closed the nine days of mourning. They hurried (as much as the priests would permit) through the final temple sacrifices and ceremonies that declared them clean from the impurities of death. They rushed back to Euodia's house in the late afternoon, only to find that the courier had not come.

"Perhaps that's it," Syntyche said wistfully, hoping Euodia would contradict her. "Maybe our mystery writer feels he has done his duty and offered what comfort he can."

"You're probably right," Euodia agreed, much to Syntyche's disappointment. "It was kind of him to be so thoughtful. But we are through the worst of it now. At least, I certainly hope so! Perhaps he knows that." She smiled at her friend.

They sat awkwardly in the silence, each with an ear tuned to the front gate, pretending not to be waiting. When the knock came, they exchanged a look of relief and triumph, and rushed into the courtyard to greet the courier.

There he stood, letter in hand as usual—a sight, Euodia realized, they had come to depend on. Euodia took the note and invited the young man inside for refreshment and interrogation. But the courier excused himself, pointing to a satchel bulging with packages and correspondence still to be delivered.

There in the courtyard, by the fading light, they tore open the seal and read:

If the only home I hope for is the grave,
if I spread out my bed in darkness,
if I say to corruption, "You are my destiny,"
and to the worm, "You are my end,"
where then is my hope?
Who can see any hope for me?

They stood there while the last of the light died, chewing on the words. Euodia started to say something, but then lapsed into silence. Syntyche took the note and held it up in the gathering darkness, trying to read it again.

Finally, Euodia blurted out, "Well, if that was meant to be comforting, it failed miserably! Corruption and worms? Not exactly what women who've just buried their husbands need to hear!"

Syntyche did not respond at first. She kept peering at the note, though it was unreadable now that night had come. "It isn't meant to comfort, Euodia. It's meant to provoke. Don't you see?" She turned to face her friend. "We've been so focused on death and funeral arrangements and processions, we haven't even asked the really important question. Is this all there is? Do we have nothing more to look forward to than a few more years of life before we join our husbands in their graves?" Syntyche thought of the note and laughed in appreciation. "He knew we'd come to it eventually. He's been leading us there all along."

"Where? What are you talking about Syntyche?" Euodia was starting to get concerned.

"Perhaps I can answer that," a man's voice responded from the shadows at the gate. "Forgive me for eavesdropping, ladies. I don't mean to startle you." A small man, balding and thin, stepped into the courtyard with his palms held open to show that he posed no threat. In the dark, he was little more than a silhouette. But even in the dark, his eyes glowed as if lit by some inner light. "Syntyche is right. Permit me to introduce myself. I am Paul of Tarsus. The letters are from me. Can we talk?"

Chapter Eleven

THE ONE WHO BEGAN THIS GOOD WORK IN YOU

(SUMMER, A.D. 49)

FIRST THE FISH MUST BE CAUGHT.

To that end, in all but the worst winter months, thousands of boats launched into the Aegean Sea each morning. The men who manned these boats were hard and weathered and sea-wise. And they attacked their work with a variety of tools. For the largest fish, baited metal hooks were lowered into deep water on hand lines. For the smallest, casting nets were used in shallow waters close to shore. For everything between, seine nets hundreds of yards long were trailed behind boats to encircle and trap their prey.

Rushed back to port while still fresh, the day's catch would be sold and offloaded to an entrepreneur responsible for cleaning and preparing the fish for market. Though fishing itself involved hard work, the truly dirty work took place on the docks. Here, fish were graded, scaled, gutted, salted, boiled, dried, filleted, fermented, ground into paste—various treatments applied as appropriate to the wide variety of species harvested from the waters of the Aegean.

The final step was the most important. At least, it was the most lucrative—making all the hard and dirty work worthwhile. While it is true that all fish are taken from water and processed near water, it is also true that most fish are consumed away from water. The largest market for a fisherman's catch has always been inland, far from the smells of the sea and the docks.

Getting the catch to those markets involved a complex network of buyers, haulers, wholesalers, retailers, and street hawkers. But the network was necessary to squeeze real value from the flesh and bones of red mullet and mackerel. For until the fish made the journey inland to cities like Philippi, until they were distributed to the stalls and shops of the agora, and until they (finally) were sold to housewives and domestic slaves shopping for the evening meal, they remained fish. But when everything worked right—when the fish were biting and the knives were sharp and the roads were passable and the shops were open—a marvelous alchemy occurred.

Fish were turned into coin.

Paul thought of his work at Philippi as a fishing enterprise. The city was his sea. Its citizens were his fish. However, as with the salted fillets he could purchase at the agora, certain steps were necessary to turn flesh and bones into something even more precious.

First, the Philippians had to be caught. And so, every day for his first month in Philippi, Paul launched himself into various parts of the city: trolling through its markets and buildings and streets; telling travel stories and striking up conversations and speaking about an invisible God to anyone who would listen; casting his nets wherever he could to see what he might find.

In this, Paul was uniquely gifted. Timothy was too young and unsure of himself to engage in the kind of rough-and-tumble, quick-on-your-feet dialogue required of street debaters. By personality, Luke was not suited for striking up conversations with strangers. And Silas, though progressing, still found it difficult to carry on a sustained discussion with some woman who insisted on staring him full in the eye or a man who dropped curses and blasphemies into every other sentence.

But Paul was made for this. The longer he lingered in Philippi, the more he loved its people. There was an energy in the Philippians, a curiosity and ambition, that Paul admired. He loved the give-and-take with the crowds in the agora. He enjoyed their questions. He even found in their appalling ignorance of spiritual things an opportunity; the gospel and the God it talked about seemed so fresh and appealing to their ears. As much as anything, he enjoyed the challenge involved in catching the hearts of his hearers. What "bait" should he use? How should it be presented? Did this one require a long line and a light touch, or should he be brought to the boat quickly?

Like every good fisherman, Paul refused to be discouraged on those days when, in spite of his hard and long labor, he returned to port empty-handed. He would recline, exhausted, at Lydia's table, finding refreshment and renewed energy in the food he consumed and the company he enjoyed. By the time supper was over, the sparkle had returned to his eye as a growing band of believers gathered in the evening hours to hear stories about Jesus and learn what it meant to be his follower.

Paul excelled at the catching. But for the "dirty work"—for the methodical, arduous, patient toil of preparing people once they'd been landed—Paul relied heavily on his companions.

~

"I am Clement," the older man said by way of introduction. He shifted nervously on his feet. Patting the door post (he'd been told to look for the fresh-carved silhouette of a fish), he continued, "I think I have the right house. A friend of mine told me that if I came here most any evening, I could learn . . . that is, someone would be teaching about —"

"Ah, Clement! Welcome. I was told you might drop in. I'm Lydia. This is my home." She opened the gate and ushered him into the courtyard. "At least, it used to be!" She laughed. "Now, I'm not sure how to describe it. School? Temple? Barracks?"

"You have a beautiful home," Clement said. But what he thought was, *You have a beautiful laugh*.

"Thank you, Clement. How kind. Won't you sit?" She gestured to a bench at the center of the courtyard.

Unconsciously, Clement fingered his earlobe and felt the mark of the awl. "No, my lady. It would not be proper."

She studied him for a moment, then sat down herself. Gesturing to the space beside her, she said in her most imperious tone, "I insist that you sit with me." Clement sat, missing as he did the look of amusement that crossed her face. "How did you meet him?"

"Who, my lady?" though he understood then she meant Paul. "Ah! He was speaking at the forum. A few days ago. We had a remarkable conversation afterward." He looked down and away, the proper comportment for a slave to adopt when addressing his betters.

"He's a remarkable man. I've known him less than a month, and my whole life has changed. Sometimes I'm tempted to lock myself in my room to avoid him." She smiled broadly and then changed the subject.

"Well. You have come to learn more about the Christos, I presume." She raised her eyebrows at him and he nodded. "You have indeed come to the right house. And you are very welcome, Clement. I'll take you on a tour in a moment. But before I do, there are a few house rules we need to go over. Fair enough?" He nodded again. She made him nervous.

"First. You are welcome to anything in my home." She pointed in quick succession to various portions of the house. "If you are hungry, my cook will be glad to fix you something to eat. The latrine is over there. If you need to lie down or have a quiet place to think, make yourself at home in any room. However, my private quarters are there and I would ask you to respect them." She paused to invite questions. Clement simply nodded. It was becoming habit.

"Second." She gestured toward his ear. He touched it again self-consciously. "You are a slave. I am a freewoman. For that reason, there are certain rules of conduct we must obey when we meet each other in the street." Clement immediately stood and lowered his eyes again, misunderstanding. She drew him down to the bench. "But in this house, Clement, there are no slaves. And there are no freeborn. Do you understand?"

"But, my lady—" Clement began to protest.

Lydia held up a restraining hand. "No, Clement. I am not 'my lady.' I am Lydia. While in this house, our social status, our backgrounds, our genders, our different circumstances mean nothing. It's one of the principles Paul seems quite committed to." She offered Clement a wry smile, inviting him to join her in humoring the little Jew and his odd convictions. "I confess it's not an easy thing. But Paul preaches a God who humbled himself to befriend us. He says the least we can do is humble ourselves with each other. There are no distinctions here." She raised her chin—point made, no discussion allowed.

And then she reached over and placed her hand on his. He stared awkwardly at her slender fingers. "Besides, Clement, there are many kinds of slavery. All of us have been slaves to something. You carry the mark of it on your ear. Others carry the mark in more hidden places. But we are all marked." She spoke so softly and with such feeling, Clement was afraid to move his eyes from her hand.

She broke the moment. "The third rule. Hmm. Come to think of it, there is no third rule." She smiled at him brightly and stood. "Well. I guess it's time for the tour."

He rose to follow as she crossed the courtyard and stood in front of an open door. She gestured for him to stand beside her. Inside the small room, eight people crowded together on the floor, focusing intently on a figure seated against the far wall. Before him was a narrow table crowded with parchments and candles. Oil lamps, hanging from each wall, threw a fitful light across the entire assembly, highlighting shoulders and heads and the profile of a face or two.

Silas looked up to acknowledge Lydia and her guest, but continued his teaching without pause. He raised three fingers and pointed to them one at a time. "The books of Moses. The Writings. The Prophets. Say that, please." His students repeated the lines dutifully. "These are the major divisions of the Jewish Scriptures. And each, in its own way, points to Jesus. Moses, for instance, promised that someone like himself, full of the Holy Spirit and the words of God, would be sent to Israel. He was talking about Jesus Messiah."

A hand went up and a young woman posed a question. "Silas, was Moses a prophet?"

He beamed at the question. "Certainly he was."

"Then why aren't his books listed with the Prophets? Why are they treated separately?"

The smile faded ever so slightly. "The books of Moses are so basic, and contain so much besides prophecy, that my people have always treated them in a special and honored way." He paused, slightly, and then moved on. "In the Writings, we learn about David, one of Israel's first kings and the forefather of Jesus Messiah. He and his son

Solomon were writers themselves and foretold the coming of the Christos."

Another hand went up. A massive soldier spoke. "How many books did they contribute to the Prophets?"

A look of concern crossed Silas's face. "No, no. All of their books are contained in the Writings. Psalms. Proverbs. Ecclesiastes."

"But didn't you just say that they foretold the coming of the Christos? I thought looking into the future was what prophets did." The student was trying to get everything straight.

Silas closed his eyes. "Well, yes and no, Marcion. The books of David and Solomon belong in the Writings. Yes, there are prophecies in their books. But mostly they wrote songs and proverbs and advice about living. Do you see?" Silas opened one eye narrowly, hoping Marcion would ask no more questions.

"Now about the Prophets—"

Lydia touched Clement's arm and they backed away from the door and out into the courtyard once again. "That was Silas, one of the men who came with Paul from Jerusalem. He is a very learned man and teaches us about the Scriptures of his people. He says that if we want to know and understand who Jesus is, we have to know and understand what God did to prepare the way for him."

She shook her head in frustration. "There is so much to learn. Some of the passages he reads to us are beautiful. And some are exciting. But much of it seems very old and very Jewish. It's hard to understand what it says to us today." She smiled encouragement at Clement. "You will make more sense of it than I, no doubt! Shall we move on?"

They moved to another open door and peered inside. Five people sat on a rug in the center of the room. A young man was talking so softly that Clement strained to hear.

"The hard part about praying isn't the words. It's the attitude. If you can understand that God loves you, that he wants to talk to you, the words will come."

"We usually leave praying to the priests," an older man interrupted skeptically. "They've memorized the prayers. They know which prayers go with which sacrifices. That's what we pay them for!

Although"—he looked around at the others—"I've never gotten my money's worth!" And he laughed—a hard, disappointed laugh that showed bad teeth.

Timothy looked pained. "Yes, I have heard that most of your praying is done in temples, by priests. I've also heard that you pray like you're trying to strike a deal with the gods. 'Do this for me, and I will do that for you.'" His audience looked at him blankly. Of course that's how they prayed. What else was prayer for? Timothy blew out a breath in exasperation. "The true God doesn't want to barter with you. He wants to converse. So talk to him. Tell him what you're feeling. Tell him what you need. He loves you. You don't have to buy his blessings with promises. Yes, Syntyche?" He turned to the small, bird-like woman on his right.

"Would you pray?" she asked. "Out loud, I mean. Show us what your prayers are like."

"Certainly." He raised his hands and then, becoming self-conscious, lowered them again. "My people usually look up and raise their hands when they pray," he explained. "You could do that. But I don't think it's the posture that matters to God. It's the heart." He paused for a moment to look at each of his students. "Let me teach you a prayer that our Lord taught his first disciples."

Once again, Timothy raised his eyes toward the ceiling. "Our Father in heaven, help us to honor your name. Come and set up your kingdom, so that everyone on earth will obey you, as you are obeyed in heaven. Give us our food for today. Forgive us for doing wrong, as we forgive others. Keep us from being tempted and protect us from evil. The kingdom, the power, and the glory are yours forever. Amen."

The room was still and silent. At last, Euodia spoke, a hint of scorn in her voice. "That's it? That's a prayer?" She looked bewildered. "Our priests pray better than that! Their prayers are longer and much more elaborate." She looked around at the others, who nodded in agreement. "I'm sorry, Timothy, but they wouldn't think much of that prayer."

Timothy smiled and shook his head. "We don't pray for the ears of priests, Euodia. We pray for the ears of God. And what God wants from us are prayers that are simple and heartfelt and genuine. That's the way Jesus Messiah spoke to God. Oh my friends," he said fondly, looking around at his little group. "God can understand us when all we can do is groan. He doesn't want fancy phrases. He wants *us*, plain and simple."

The women stared at the ceiling, pondering that for a while. Syntyche glanced over at Euodia, who took her hand, knowing what she was thinking. "Could I talk to God about my husband, Timothy? About missing him, being afraid without him. Is that the kind of thing God would listen to?"

Timothy looked down quickly and examined his hands. "Yes, Syntyche, that is exactly what God wants to hear about. If you talk to him, he will give you comfort. Do you want to try?"

Hesitantly, in imitation of Timothy, Syntyche looked up and began to speak. "Our Father in heaven—"

Again, Lydia touched Clement's arm and they backed away, both of them uncomfortable eavesdropping on so private a moment. This time, it was Clement who spoke first, in a whisper.

"Is that true, what he was saying in there? Is that how these men talk to God?" Clement was not so much opposed to what he'd overheard as he was perplexed by the logic involved. He shook his head. "It doesn't seem very . . . respectful. Why should a god care about my struggles? We praise the gods because gods love to hear us speak well of them. But to talk about ourselves? To burden God with my daily needs and all my old wounds? Why would a god want to hear that?"

Lydia smiled and shrugged. "It's a bit overwhelming, isn't it? I asked the same questions." She caught his eye. "You must try to be patient, Clement. The more you learn, the more your questions will be answered. Don't expect it to come easy. It's more complicated than that."

She considered briefly whether to say more. "You might think about something Paul told me. For him, everything goes back to the story of the Cross. He's told you about the Cross, I guess?" Clement nodded and Lydia continued. "Paul said the hard part is accepting that God loved me enough to die for me. After that, the idea that he loves me enough to listen isn't so hard. It made sense to me. Maybe it will help you."

They stood for a while, wrapped in thought, until Lydia shook herself. "Well. One more room to show you. Luke is teaching in there. I rather like Luke." She flashed an impish smile. "He's Greek, like us. He understands us better than the others. And, besides, he's telling us all about the life of Jesus. He says he wants to write a book about it one day."

She led Clement to yet another doorway, where they stood together and peered inside. This room was larger, with fifteen people sitting on the floor and leaning against the walls. Like Silas, Luke sat before a low table. On it, along with some candles and a table lamp, lay an open leather binder holding pages of closely lettered writing. As he talked, Luke sifted through the papers, reading a fragment from one, a paragraph from another, verifying facts, quoting words.

"After he had battled the Devil in the wilderness, Jesus went home to Nazareth. I'm sure it was good for him to see his mother and brothers again. But the one thing people tell me about this homecoming has nothing to do with family. It's what happened at the synagogue." Luke stopped and looked around. Though quiet, even shy in most social settings, Luke came alive in teaching situations. He had something of the actor in him, with an actor's understanding of the dramatic pause.

"When the time for the reading came—by the way, every synagogue service involves several readings from the Jewish Scriptures—they asked Jesus to read from the Prophets. He chose a passage from a prophet named Isaiah. Now, what's interesting about this—"

Lydia whispered to Clement, "He gets so excited when he teaches. You can barely get two words out of him at suppertime. But he'll teach all night if you let him."

"What are those papers?" Clement asked, pointing to the binder.

"Those are his notes. Every time he meets people who were actually there, who saw what happened with their own eyes, he interviews them. Writes down every story they tell. Checks and cross-checks that story against the memories of others. That's what he hopes to base his book on. He says he wants it to be an orderly account."

"That's why the passage from Isaiah is so important," Luke told his listeners. "Jesus was defining his ministry with these words. He was announcing to his hometown, 'This is what I'm about. This is what I've come to do. I am here to preach to the poor, to free prisoners, to open blind eyes, to speak up for the underdog.' That is not what they expected from the Messiah, let me tell you!" Luke became even more animated, waving his bony arms, looking for all the world like an elongated, emaciated Paul.

But again, Lydia drew Clement back into the courtyard.

"Does this go on every night, my lady?" Clement marveled at how completely she'd surrendered her home to Paul and to the ragbag assortment of humanity he attracted.

"Every night." She laughed. "And often through the day. I'm not sure where they find the energy. But as long as people knock at the gate wanting to learn more, there is always someone here to teach them." She stopped and a shadow crossed her face. "There's a restlessness about the four of them. Especially Paul. I get the sense he won't be here forever." But then she brightened. "The way people are responding, though, he's got enough work to keep him busy for a long time."

"I'd like to come back if I could. I want to learn more."

"Clement, you are welcome in my home anytime. I've enjoyed your company. Come to think of it, tomorrow morning is the first day of the week. It's a holy day for Paul and the others. Why don't you join us then?" She motioned to the space around them and laughed. "My courtyard becomes a temple! We sing and pray. And Paul will speak. Oh, he is marvelous! What you heard in the forum is nothing. He has to be so careful what he says there. Here, he can really let go. And when he does, my, how he can talk!"

Clement thought for a moment and then shook his head sadly. "I'm sorry, my lady. But I have duties to attend to on the morrow."

Lydia brushed away the objection. "We meet very early, Clement. Before daybreak. There will be others like yourself." She nodded at his earlobe. "We'll be finished in time for you to attend to your master's household."

He thought for a moment, then saw the plea in her face. "Very well, my lady. I'll return in the morning."

Lydia ushered him through the gate, and then called after him, "Clement! My name is Lydia, not 'my lady.'" And her laughter followed him through the streets all the way home.

~

Lanterns ringed the courtyard, playing their flickering light off walls and faces. Some sixty people had gathered in the predawn darkness, making their way from sleeping households through deserted streets to the glow radiating from Lydia's home.

Though most of the group were seated on cloaks and cushions, Clement kept to his feet at the back of the courtyard. He felt awkward, an observer rather than a participant, curious but detached. He wasn't sure he should be there. He wasn't sure he could have stayed away.

At a nod from Paul, Silas stood before the group. "God be with you." Everyone fell silent. "And may the peace of Jesus the Messiah descend upon this place and rest upon each one here. I am called Silas." He surveyed the group and smiled. "Since some of you are attending our worship for the first time, let me explain a few things. Whatever you may have heard about the worship of the Jews, we won't do anything too strange this morning." A couple of the newcomers laughed nervously. "We'll sing a few songs and speak some prayers. Our brother Paul has some words to share with us. And we will break bread together in memory of Jesus."

Silas closed his eyes and pressed his hands together, gathering himself for the act of worship. After a moment, he looked up. "Today is the first day of the week. As you may know, my people have revered the seventh day for centuries. We consider it a holy day, a day dedicated to God. But for those of my people who have accepted Jesus as the Messiah, this first day of the week is also holy. For it was on this day, early on a morning like this, that Jesus rose from the dead. We are gathered here to celebrate his resurrection and to worship the God of new life." He nodded to Timothy seated on the ground in front of him, and the two of them exchanged places.

"Good morning. I am called Timothy. Join me in singing." He raised his hands, threw back his head, and began to sing in a high, lilting chant. "Praise the Lord, all you nations."

Others in the group, familiar with the routine, picked up the melody and repeated the words back to Timothy. To Clement, the tune was new and vaguely exotic. He listened as the assembly followed Timothy's lead.

Extol him all you peoples,
For great is his love toward us.
And the faithfulness of the Lord endures forever.
Praise the Lord.

Timothy paused, eyes shining in the torchlight, then launched into another hymn. "Give thanks to the Lord for he is good."

Only this time, instead of repeating Timothy's words, the assembly chanted back, "His love endures forever."

"Give thanks to the God of gods," sang Timothy. And, again, the congregation responded, "His love endures forever."

At first, Timothy seemed to quote from a source unknown to Clement but obviously familiar to the young Jew. "To him who alone does great wonders . . . he made the great lights . . . he freed us from our enemies." Gradually, however, Timothy's chanting grew more spontaneous, the lines heartfelt rather than memorized. "God sent us his Messiah . . . he washed away all our sins . . . he teaches us to live like him." And, after each line, members of the audience supplied the chorus: "His love endures forever."

The interchange between leader and worshipers went on for some time, waxing and waning according to the mood of the words. When Timothy sang of sin or death, his voice would lower and the audience would almost whisper its reply. But then Timothy would shift to thoughts of resurrection, and the song would grow boisterous and joyful.

They sang a few more hymns as dawn began to redden the sky. Luke rose to lead the group in a simple prayer. He prayed confession and gratitude. He prayed for God's presence and for God's pleasure in their worship. He prayed that those gathered might find strength and healing in the morning's devotions.

Clement kept his place, finding himself both confused and attracted. This was unlike any other worship he had ever experienced. He'd come expecting the usual mix of ritual, mystery, and emotional manipulation. He'd come expecting the cynic in himself to see through the liturgy to the superstition and gullibility that lay beneath. As he watched, he realized that he'd come expecting to be disappointed.

But there was little ritual involved in what he witnessed. There was nothing rote or perfunctory in what he saw. Though he watched for it, Clement could discern no boredom or distraction in the worshipers, no attempts on the part of those who led to position themselves as the keepers of secret mysteries.

It was obvious that these people believed something that made a profound difference for them. He was surprised to discover that they meant what they sang and prayed. Sincerity was something he rarely associated with religious expressions.

And then Paul stood to speak. "Let me tell you a story that begins with an ending . . . and ends with a beginning." With that one sentence, he had the full attention of everyone in the courtyard. "You have heard me tell the story of Jesus of Nazareth. You know that Jesus lived a holy life, that the leaders of our people hated him anyway and turned him over to the Roman authorities to be executed. You know the ugly facts about his crucifixion. In many ways, the story of Jesus begins with his death on the Cross.

"And all of you have heard me tell the story of his resurrection, that God did not leave his body in the tomb but raised him back to life again. Silas here"—Paul nodded at his companion—"saw Jesus and spoke with him after the resurrection. I am also a witness. I saw Jesus alive. We testify to you that a dead man lives!" Paul looked around at his listeners, fixing each with a penetrating look, letting them see the conviction burning in his eyes.

"But that isn't the story I want to tell you about this morning. Instead, I want to talk to you about . . . you." A half-smile played on his lips. "Your story begins this morning with an ending. You are at the end of yourselves. Some of you are eaten up with guilt and remorse. Some of you have lost hope. Some of you are addicted, caught by the power of a vice you cannot escape. Some of you stumble through each day, numb with the sense that life has no point." At each sentence, Paul searched out members of his audience, painting their lives with his words. His gaze was met with nods, silent assents to the truth of what he said. When he spoke the last sentence, Paul looked squarely at Clement. And, in spite of himself, Clement nodded.

"Like Jesus, our stories begin with an ending. We are dead. Oh, we still walk around and exchange greetings in the street and go about our work. But we do so with dead hearts and dead hopes. We are at the end of ourselves. We're just waiting for our bodies to experience what we have already endured in our souls."

Clement stood rooted to his spot against the back wall. How could Paul know? How was he able to reach into Clement's chest and put his finger so neatly on the pain and disappointment hidden there? He blinked and crossed his arms in unconscious self-protection. He wasn't sure whether to feel angry or relieved.

"The question for all of us is whether our stories, like the story of Jesus, might also end with a beginning. Is it possible for something new to happen in us? Is there forgiveness? Is there fresh hope? Is there power for better living? Is there a purpose to life?" Paul stared so intensely at his audience now that few would meet his eyes. "Every one of us needs a chance to start over, to begin again! Every one of us needs resurrection!" Paul almost shouted the words, conviction and need and longing welling up inside him to spill out on his listeners. A long, silent moment stretched over the group.

He began again quietly. "That's why the story of Jesus is so important. If God can raise Jesus back to life again, maybe he can give new life to me . . . and to you. If death is not an obstacle to God, how much less guilt and failure and scars." Paul looked around his audience, the pleading palpable in his eyes. "O my friends. I want you to believe that Jesus lives again. Not just because it happens to be true . . . but because of what it means. I'm asking you to accept that we live in a world where resurrection is possible, where endings can become beginnings. I'm asking you to have faith that, by God's power, you can live again."

He stood before them a moment longer, arms outstretched in mute invitation. Then, quickly, he turned to a table set against the wall and took up a loaf of flatbread. "My friends and I—all of us who have accepted Jesus as Messiah—eat a symbolic feast each first day. We take bread"—he held up the loaf for them to see—"and eat it together. In a moment, we will share wine. But there is more to this feast than food and drink. There is meaning and memory that lies within these simple elements. And there is connection to what we've just talked about.

"We call this the 'Supper of the Lord.' Jesus himself gave us this memorial and asked us to think about his death and resurrection every time we eat it. The bread"—again he held it before them—"symbolizes his body. The wine"—he gestured to the flask on the table—"symbolizes his blood. In the Supper, we remember Jesus' love for us—that he laid down his life. And in the Supper, we celebrate God's power—that he made the dead live again. And one thing more—" Paul stopped and looked at his traveling companions, at Lydia, at other members of the group who had already announced their commitment to Jesus. "As we eat this Supper, we pledge to lay down our own lives. And we appeal to God to raise us, like Jesus, back to life again."

A murmured "Amen" rose from the assembly.

Lifting the bread high, Paul blessed it and tore it in half. He handed one half of the loaf to Luke, and the two of them began making their way through the seated worshipers, tearing off pieces and dropping them into outstretched hands. Each paused on occasion to whisper a blessing, or to bestow some word of personal encouragement. It was a quiet and reverent moment, made holy not by pomp and ceremony but by remembrance and commitment.

And then Paul stood before Clement—the Jew and the Greek, the rabbi and the slave, a man who had found meaning for his life and a man who needed meaning so desperately. "What about you, Clement?" And Paul held out the bread.

"I don't know." Clement felt the blood rising to his face. "I'm not sure."

Paul smiled. "Yes, you are, my friend. You have much to learn. But you know this is where it begins. You know you have nowhere else to turn."

Clement stared into the calm face of the Apostle. His eyes filled. "That's true enough." He reached out a shaking hand to take the proffered bread. Holding it up, he spoke loudly enough for the assembly to hear, "I believe that God raised Jesus from the dead. And I beg him to give new life to me."

His hand came to his mouth, and Clement—the student-turned-slave, the resentful son, the disappointed skeptic—ate resurrection just as the sun rose to the east, announcing that a new day had arrived for Philippi.

Chapter Twelve

THESE JEWS ARE UPSETTING OUR CITY!

(EARLY FALL, A.D. 49)

WHEN THE END CAME, IT WAS MERCIFULLY QUICK—ALTHOUGH CLEMENT, who witnessed most of the events of that last day, doubted that Paul would describe it as "merciful."

Years later, thinking about those events and with the benefit of hindsight and a more mature perspective, Clement could see the hand of God in it all . . . even the hard necessity of it. But at the time, it felt like a death. Worse. It was as though some malevolent surgeon had cut inside Clement and torn away a vital part of him, leaving a gaping wound he feared might never heal.

It is not as though the end had come without warning. The seasons themselves seemed to predict that a change was at hand. Summer had given way to fall. The nights grew frigid, warning of colder days ahead.

And with the changing of seasons, Clement marked a decided change in Paul's mood. A sense of urgency pervaded his activities now. He grew even more serious, even more intense—as though time were a luxury and Paul foresaw an economic downturn in the near future.

Even the evenings at Lydia's house took on the frantic feel of a city preparing to evacuate before an invading army. Silas, Timothy, and Luke stepped up their teaching, packing away a knowledge of

Scripture and Christos and practical Christian living into the heads of their willing but overwhelmed students. For all his years of study, Clement had never learned so much in so little time.

And, in small increments, Paul began to withdraw from the nightly rounds of disciple training. While the others were teaching, he would excuse himself to walk through the city with his cloak wrapped tightly against the chill. He seemed to be saving himself for something—gathering his strength for the draining demands of his forays into the agora, Clement thought at the time—though, again in hindsight, Clement saw it was more than that.

What time he did spend teaching his new flock was invested more and more in a few. Clement was pleased (and flattered) that Paul began to spend so much personal time with him. He thought it was because the two of them shared much in common—their love of learning, their age, their feelings for the little congregation of believers. It did not dawn on him at the time that Paul might be grooming a replacement.

Had he been perceptive enough, Clement could have read the signs in Paul's daily trips to the agora. Success is its own worst enemy. As Paul won more converts to the faith, a palpable antagonism began to surface in the crowd's interaction with the street preacher. Husbands resented that their wives were spending so much time in pursuit of this newfound faith. Parents worried about their sons and daughters. Masters sensed a divided loyalty in previously trusted servants. And Philippians from all walks of life knew that something different and oddly threatening was occurring in their fair city.

As a result, the banter and good-humored heckling of earlier trips to the agora gave way to hard charges and bitter denunciations. "What have you done to my partner?" one businessman demanded to know. "How can we make any money when he neglects his work to spend all his time with you!"

"And what about my daughter?" a red-faced father shouted at Paul. "You keep your dirty Jewish hands off my girl, hear?"

It didn't matter how Paul responded to such interruptions. The damage was done as soon as the charges were made. His audiences thinned as people decided, no matter how curious they might be about his message, something was dangerous and divisive about the man.

Above all, Clement should have recognized trouble in the slave girl.

Deeply disturbed and equally disturbing, she provoked in Clement a mixture of pity and anger—pity for the poor child so obviously suffering, and anger at her owners who used her suffering for personal gain. They claimed that she could divine the future, but Clement suspected she was forced to do so astride the laps of lecherous customers. She was just a girl, and already her life was used up.

So when she took to following Paul, interrupting him in the forum and the agora with her shrill shouts and unsettling presence, Clement should have foreseen the inevitable. It wasn't that Paul would resent how his crowds melted away after each confrontation with the girl. And it wasn't even that he would object to what she said, for she was neither argumentative nor obscene. In fact, her message was consistent—and as consistently supportive as the witness of such a tortured soul could be: "These men are servants of the Most High God, who are telling you the way to be saved."

What he should have guessed was that Paul would react to the girl as Clement himself did . . . that, in the end, it would be Paul's pity or Paul's anger that would prove his undoing.

As it happened, it proved to be Paul's pity.

~

Once again, they were spending the morning at the forum. Once again, a crowd had gathered, albeit smaller than in earlier days. Again Paul was deep in dialogue with his listeners, talking philosophy and religion and the meaning of life. And suddenly, there she was, appearing from nowhere, turning and crying and shouting.

Perhaps Paul was more fatigued than in previous encounters. Maybe the stresses of past days had worn away his patience and clouded his judgment. Or perhaps he simply could stand the girl's suffering no longer. For one of those reasons, or for them all, this day would be different.

The people, as in every one of these encounters, stepped away from the girl, distancing themselves from her madness as though it were contagious. As before, she made her winding way to Paul, ceasing her shouts as she neared his presence, and, finally, standing still before him. The two of them engaged in their customary staring contest, the silent battle of wills each had come to anticipate, as the crowd held its breath and watched.

And then Paul did something he had not done before. Quickly, he reached out and enfolded the girl into an embrace. She stiffened and tried to pull away. But Paul refused to let her go. He held her as she moaned and beat her small fists against his chest. A trickle of urine traced a line against the dirt of her bare leg. The crowd stood paralyzed, wide-eyed and gaping.

Paul placed a hand against the back of the girl's matted head and looked up to the sky. Expelling a breath, as if to empty himself, he inhaled deeply and spoke in a strong voice, "In the name of Jesus Christ, I command you to come out of her."

Had he not been holding the girl so tightly, she may well have injured herself. Her back arched in a convulsive spasm. Her head and neck wrenched against Paul's restraining hand. Her arms and legs went rigid. And an otherworldly, long-suppressed scream—a scream that sent children running in fear and caused adults to clamp their hands over their ears to protect themselves from its naked agony—boiled up from her toenails and scoured through her chest to pour in waves from her mouth.

Paul stood holding her, his face wet with tears, until she went limp in his arms. Still he held her, lips moving in silent prayer, hands moving in comforting circles against her back and head. Still he held her as the crowd backed away warily and broke into clots of twos and threes to talk about what they had just witnessed. Still he held her . . . until Clement stood before him and took the girl from his arms, carrying her through the streets to his quarters.

Paul had spoken of miracles in the ministry of Jesus. He'd intimated that, by the power of the Spirit, he also could perform miracles on occasion. Clement had witnessed in himself and others the miracle of new life and the healing of old wounds. But, until this point in Paul's Philippian mission, there had been nothing so tangible, so dramatic, as an exorcism. Clement placed the unconscious girl on his bed—hovering over her like an anxious father, washing the grime from her face with a cloth, marveling at the peace he read in her sleeping frame—and wondered what he'd gotten himself into.

~

It didn't take long for word of the girl to spread through the city, making its way from streets to homes to gutters—which is where the girl's owners happened to hear what had transpired with their property.

By noon, they were banging at Clement's doorway, barging into his room and demanding to know what Paul had done to their slave. Their threatening and odorous bulk filled his quarters, the greed so rank on them that Clement felt physically ill. While the girl cowered on a corner of the bed, blanket clutched to her chin, throwing pleading and heartrending looks at Clement, he tried his best to ward them off or, at least, calm them down.

But they would have none of that. They could tell at a glance something had changed in the girl. She was terrified, but clear-eyed. Her silent pleadings to Clement, in stark contrast to the usual rantings and disturbing tics with which she held strangers at a safe distance, spoke volumes to the men. She seemed too normal. Something was wrong. Pushing Clement aside, they grabbed the girl by the hair and dragged her from the room, intent on protecting their investment . . . or recouping their loss.

By mid-afternoon, they were stalking the streets and marketplaces, looking for Paul and spoiling for a fight. The girl was useless. All the anger, all the demonic dementia had been drained from her frail body. She was just a used, pitiable waif now. And what profit was there in that? They dragged her behind them—small, dirty feet scrambling to keep balance—the portable and prime evidence of the wrong perpetrated on them by this meddling Jew.

Paul was where he usually was in the afternoon—in the agora, trolling for people whose interests might run deeper than the state of the Philippian economy or the latest gossip from Rome. He and Silas were standing in front of a carpenter's stall, talking wood and tools and "Oh-by-the-way-I-knew-another-carpenter," when rough hands grabbed them from behind and spun them around to face their accusers.

"What do you think you're doing?" one of them demanded, shoving his brutal face at Paul and pointing to the girl held at arm's length by one of his companions. Paul could smell the wine on the man's breath. He could see the utter lack of compassion in his eyes. *So the time has come,* he thought to himself.

He smiled at the girl, though she was too frightened to look up. Then, turning his full attention to his accuser, Paul even smiled at him. "Good afternoon. May I help you?" Politeness, he'd found, always drove this sort to distraction.

"Help me? You scurvy Jew. I don't want your help. What I want is for you to leave me alone!" He underscored each word by poking a single, aggressive finger into Paul's chest. "What have you done to my girl?" His voice grew louder, more threatening. A crowd began to gather.

"Oh, is this your daughter?" Paul inquired, bestowing on the man a smile of radiant innocence.

The drunk grabbed Paul's tunic with both fists and pulled him closer. "You know this ain't my daughter," he hissed and bestowed a curse. "She's my slave. I own her. And you done something to her. You ruined her!" In his anger, flecks of spittle flew.

"Really?" Paul asked, keeping his tone calm and reasonable. "And how did I do that?"

"That's what we wanna know! People told us that you grabbed her and said some words over her. And now, she ain't the same, I tell you. She's spoiled."

"Really?" Paul asked again. "In what way?"

"She used to be able to see the future! She used to"—he looked warily at his partners—"to do other stuff too. Now she just sits around and whimpers. She won't do none of what we tell her. And it's your fault, Jew!" He lifted Paul off the ground and shook him like a rag doll. "Now put her back the way she was!"

Paul looked at the man before him and felt the anger boiling up inside. Put her back? Reinsert a demon? Reinstate her torture so this man could continue wringing coin from her suffering? What kind of animal was this? What kind of man could fall this low?

And then Paul remembered how low he had once fallen. He recalled what sort of man he had once been. And the anger drained from him, leaving in its place pools of pity . . . stagnant eddies of sadness and regret.

"No," was all he said. He said it quietly, just between the two of them. But he said it in such a way that the man, sober or drunk, could not mistake his refusal.

The brute threw back his head and roared. Paul thought for a moment he might be in for an immediate thrashing. But he felt a huge hand clutch the back of his tunic, heard an order to "Get the other one," and found himself and Silas being propelled through the market and streets to the forum. Eager to see the show, the crowd followed, growing with each step as word passed that the Jews were about to get theirs. Angry parents, injured spouses, jealous priests, bested philosophers were drawn to the throng by the smell of blood in the air. Everyone with a grudge against the gods, or a prejudice against the Jews . . . anyone who feared change and liked Philippi just the way it had been . . . those whose financial interests or social status or tidy boundaries had been threatened in any way by the new religion . . . they all poured from storefronts and houses and spas and temples to join the crowd and vent their spleens.

And, somewhere between the agora and the forum—as the anger built and the resentments boiled to the surface—the spark that set the forest burning (that pitiful girl and her lowlife owners) was forgotten. Along the way, the mob was abducted by other, more respectable people with other, more important axes to grind. By the time they arrived at the courthouse, the girl and her contemptible handlers had been shoved aside, replaced by aggrieved citizens who had come, out of civic concern, to address a grave danger facing their city.

The two magistrates were already waiting for them, alerted by a nervous sentry who burst into their chambers with news that something was afoot. They stood calmly on the steps of the courthouse, surrounded by the symbols of their authority—the courthouse itself with its marble-columned facade; the robes of their office, white togas trimmed in judicial blue; and the ever-present Lictors, who stood at attention beside them and carried the *fasces* (the bundles of rods and axes that declared a magistrate's power to mete out both corporal and capital punishment). They looked at the crowd grimly enough, although each was secretly delighted by the unexpected turn of events. This was not a mob; it was an audience! Before it, the two of them would play out their most pressing business—demonstrating how competent and powerful and wise they were.

When they had quieted the crowd, the younger (and more ambitious) magistrate stepped forward. "Well?" he inquired. "What's all this about? Why this disturbance of the peace?"

A tall man wearing expensive robes spoke up. "Tertullus! Forgive our little commotion. We mean no harm—to you, that is, or to our fair city. But we are concerned about these two men." As if on cue, Paul and Silas were thrust forward for the magistrates to inspect. "These men," the speaker continued, "are foreigners. Jews. They have been welcomed into our city, freely permitted to walk our streets and speak to our citizens. And they have repaid that liberty by advocating strange customs and proselytizing for a foreign god. They are teaching things not even lawful for Roman citizens to practice!"

Clement arrived on the scene at that moment, craning from the back of the crowd to see what was happening. Since noon, he had consulted a lawyer. (Could the girl be legally removed from her owners? Doubtful.) He'd seen his master about the possibility of a loan. (Perhaps he could purchase the girl from them? Expensive.) And then, frustrated, he'd gone in search of Paul. When Clement overheard word on the street that a mob had seized "the Jews" and dragged them to the forum, he groaned and ran toward the courthouse.

By the time he got there, the crowd had its mind made up. Clement could smell the fear and hatred in the air. People were shouting to be heard, eager to add their accusations to the indictment. "They've alienated my wife!" "They've subverted our children!" "They deny the deity of Caesar!"

Tertullus motioned for silence. He surveyed the crowd, reading instantly what his verdict would be, then fixed Paul and Silas with a stony glare. "My, my. You *have* been busy, haven't you? What do you say for yourselves?"

Paul knew what was coming. Already he felt the disconnect starting, that strange here-but-not-here sensation that came over him when the time for suffering arrived. It was left to Silas to answer for them both. "Your Honor, there is no truth to these charges!"

"No truth? So these good citizens are lying? Is that your position?"

Tertullus was enjoying himself, playing to the crowd, building the suspense. It wasn't often that a man in his position was handed a case so ripe with opportunity. An agitated band of taxpaying (and voting!) citizens. Expendable strangers. (Jews, at that!) And he, Tertullus—protector of the people and guardian of public order—possessed the power to give the crowd what it wanted. He glanced at his fellow magistrate and almost laughed out loud.

Clement tried to work his way through the crowd, though he knew a slave could do nothing to turn the course of events. But by now, everyone was jostling and elbowing their way toward a better view. They smelled blood and wanted to see it as well. From the corner of his eye, he caught sight of Lydia—standing white and still on the edge of the mob—and managed to fight his way to her side.

"Shall we expel them from our great city?" Tertullus tapped his finger against his lips, seeming to give this action due consideration. The vocal reaction of the crowd told him that expulsion was good, but not good enough. He and his fellow magistrate conferred momentarily.

"It is our judgment that these two miscreants should be shown that Philippians do not tolerate un-Roman ideas and activities. Let other outsiders take warning!" The crowd shouted its agreement, working itself into a frenzy of anticipation.

Turning to the Lictors, Tertullus ordered—loudly enough for the crowd to overhear—"Beat them. Throw them in prison for the night. And then evict them from the city on the morrow." The mob did not disappoint him. It howled and clapped and stomped its approval at this wise decision. Tertullus smiled and waved, drinking in their applause and already calculating how to capitalize on this latest rise in his popularity. He and his companion turned and walked back to their offices, leaving the sentence to be carried out by their assistants.

A band of soldiers had rushed to the forum when their sharp-eared sergeant caught the shouts and trampling of the crowd moving through the city streets. They stood in front of the courthouse steps, forming a loose barrier between the mob and the building. Now the Lictors motioned to them, indicating they should get on with the punishment. Being old hands at the business of soldiering, they knew what to do.

Two soldiers brought a heavy beam from the courthouse and dropped it into a socket on the pavement. The remainder of the squad closed ranks to keep the crowd back as everyone shoved and jockeyed for a better vantage point from which to view the beating. The Lictors busied themselves untying the *fasces* and selecting the stoutest, most supple rods for the brutal work ahead. Putting together two small bundles of four or five rods each, they wrapped leather straps tightly around one end, forming handles.

Solid citizens, all, Clement thought bitterly to himself. *But even solid citizens love a good beating in the afternoon.* He put his arm around Lydia and whispered that she should leave. He could feel her trembling, and feared her reaction to the ugly business about to take place. But she shook her head and grabbed fistfuls of his toga, determined to see this out for Paul's sake.

When all was ready, the soldiers walked the guilty parties to the post and ordered them to strip. Paul and Silas looked at each other, willing courage. Then, throwing off their outer garments, they stood before the crowd in loincloth and sandals.

A hush fell over the forum. Clement thought at first it was the crowd holding its breath until the blows began to fall. But then he heard the whispers and saw the pointed fingers and understood what had silenced the group.

It was Paul. He stood still and nearly naked beside the stake. Yet his body seemed to be crawling with scars and wounds and disfiguring marks. There were gashes and cuts on his chest and shoulders. And his back was a purple mass of crosshatched lines, evidence of prior and repeated beatings. Even the soldiers blanched and fell silent as they stared at that living record of punishment and pain.

Instinctively, Clement covered Lydia's eyes with his hand—she did not need to see this. But he himself could not take his eyes off Paul's back. He stared and tried to imagine the suffering Paul had endured. At first, the sight turned his stomach—no one could look at those scars and not suffer a little vicariously. But then he found himself marveling at Paul's stubbornness, his courage. Finally, his eyes filled and the scars swam and Clement felt something break deep inside. Whatever doubts, whatever reservations he had harbored to this point vanished with one look at Paul's back. Paul should have shown him that back sooner. It was his trump card, a livid validation of the depth of his faith.

"Philippi is not the first place he's made trouble!" someone called from the crowd, breaking the spell. "Let's add some Philippian scars!" another shouted.

Soldiers stepped in front of Paul and Silas and bound their wrists with thick leather straps. Leading them to the post, they threaded the tag ends through a ring near the top and hauled both men up until their arms were stretched above their heads and their feet barely touched the ground. There they swung, on opposite sides of the pillar, muttering prayers and encouragement to each other.

The sergeant pointed gruffly to two of his men—burly, hardened men who would not shrink from the task—and handed the Lictors' rods to them. Grasping the handles with both hands and each moving to his victim, they stood with legs apart, measuring the distance with feigned strokes to the backs splayed before them.

Clement had seen public beatings before—Rome believed in discipline, and corporal punishments were common in Roman Philippi. He'd seen enough to know that a beating with rods differed from one with whips. The whip was designed to cut and slice. There was a great deal of blood and often, by the end of the beating, the skin hung in ribbons from the back of the victim. But the injuries were largely surface and relatively superficial. Someone skilled with the cat-o'-nine-tails could use its embedded glass and nails to fillet a man, lashing the back muscles to the bone. Clement knew that most soldiers called on to administer punishment were neither that skilled nor that sadistic.

But rods were a different matter, and Clement shuddered as he watched the soldiers preparing to do their terrible duty. A beating with rods was intended not to cut but to brutalize. The rods were brought down swiftly against the back, breaking blood vessels deep in the muscle. As the blows rained down, the muscles pulverized and fell away from the ribs and spine. The bleeding was profuse but contained within the muscle until, by the end of the beating, as the skin split and broke, it poured in clotted streams from the victim and spattered on his tormentors. Clement had seen it before. Someone skilled with the rods might break a man's ribs . . . even his spine. But a soldier did not have to be very skilled with the rods to do real damage to a man.

But, for Clement, the greatest difference in the two kinds of beatings was noted by the ear. With both, the victim screamed and pleaded and cursed. With both, the soldiers grunted and panted. But the whip made a slapping, viscous sound against the back. With the rods, there was a deep thud—felt as much as heard.

Stepping back, the sergeant nodded to his men. They took a firmer grasp on the handles and began laying into their work, bringing the rods over their shoulders and then across their bodies and onto the backs of the offenders . . . like they were loggers felling trees . . . like the rods were axes . . . like the backs before them were bark and wood, not skin and bone.

By the fifth blow, both Paul and Silas were screaming. By the tenth, they had lost control of their bladders and bowels. By the fifteenth, they slumped unconscious against the post and the soldiers paused to wipe blood and sweat from their faces. They administered five more blows for good measure, until the sergeant stepped in and called a halt, fearing that further punishment would kill the men.

The crowd grew still and quiet as the beatings progressed. Like drunks, they had been eager for the intoxicating violence, the heady sight of blood, the rush of public reprisal. But the stark brutality of the beating sobered them and left them to stare dully at the results of their self-indulgent binge, the taste of retaliation sour in their mouths. By the time it was over, the mob had dissolved into a gathering of strangers. Within moments, they had dribbled away, one by one, ashamed of themselves.

In the end, only Lydia and Clement remained, the two of them locked in miserable embrace. She had buried her face in his tunic and clamped both hands over her ears. Her body shook with spastic sobs and her head beat rhythmically against Clement's chest—like the repetitive and self-pacifying motions of a retarded child. "Why? Why? Why?" she questioned over and over.

Clement held her and watched the soldiers finish their dirty business. Pails of water were brought from a nearby fountain and dashed against the unconscious bodies. Blood and feces dribbled down the steps of the courthouse and one of the soldiers fetched a broom to sweep away the stains. Paul and Silas struggled to consciousness, standing unsteadily on tiptoe while their leather bindings were released, and then slumping to the ground. More water was poured over them, reviving the two sufficiently for them to stand and put on their clothing. They leaned together, swaying and supporting one another, until the soldiers were ready to escort them to prison. At an order, the soldiers formed a box around the prisoners and marched away, half-pushing, half-carrying the traumatized men.

Clement watched them out of sight, and then half-led, half-carried Lydia to her home.

~

When she had recovered sufficiently, Clement rose to leave. He'd been gone from home most of the day and knew he would have to account for his absence to his master. But Lydia begged him to stay for the evening meal and, under the circumstances (frankly, under *any* circumstance), he found it impossible to refuse her.

So they reclined at the table, picking at the food, breaking silence to wonder aloud where Timothy and Luke might be, thinking but not speaking of the two men suffering in the bowels of the Philippian jail. Neither of them was very good company, but they drew comfort from each other's presence and reflected privately on the strange fate that had bound together a wealthy woman and a domestic slave.

When supper was finished, Clement again tried to excuse himself, but Lydia fixed him with a tearful look and her friend agreed to stay a while longer. Since it was the evening, members of the congregation began to arrive as usual for their nightly sessions. Some appeared at the gate with the stunned looks of people who'd just learned of the day's events. Others came smiling and eager to resume their studies—oblivious to what had transpired that afternoon. They sat, crammed together in the dining hall (it felt too exposed to remain in the courtyard), and rehashed each sordid detail of the day. And as they worried about Paul and Silas, they tried to come to terms with the fact that tomorrow their teachers would be gone.

Mostly, though, they peered anxiously into an uncertain future. Someone wondered aloud whether the authorities might also arrest them, and for the rest of the evening they all listened with one ear for a knock at the gate. They questioned how the church could survive without Paul's presence. They even talked, briefly, about the wisdom of disbanding.

It went on this way for hours, long past the time they normally broke up. They were frightened to be together, but more frightened to leave the company of their trusted companions to go home alone in the dark. And so they huddled in Lydia's house, putting off the inevitable, unwilling to bring the evening to an end for fear that, in the morning, it might never be the same.

Clement listened to their worried questions and offered what comfort a man with no answers could give. He heard their doubts and tried to give reassurance. He weighed the notion of not meeting for a few weeks, but announced quietly that he would continue on. Lydia was quick to support him. But as the evening wore on, he realized that such morbid fretting was doing them no good. They needed someone to guide them, to help them get their arms around ugly realities and prepare for what might happen tomorrow.

Studying the faces in the room, Clement was surprised to discover they were looking to him.

It was at that moment that he first felt the weight descend on him. It settled on his shoulders and made breathing difficult for a time. It seeped into his back, tightening his neck muscles and causing his temples to pound. He saw, with sudden, painful clarity, what Paul had been doing these past weeks—preparing Clement to take on the role he would soon vacate. He wanted to shout his refusal. He wanted to laugh at Paul's cunning. He wanted to sink under the burden of it all.

But then he looked at the faces. He saw the eyes fixed on him, hungry for direction. He knew the hopes that were at stake, the souls that were hanging in the balance. He looked at the trusting expressions of Lydia and Euodia and Syntyche and Marcion. He thought of the girl.

God, help me, he prayed as he surveyed his flock.

And then he stood. He raised his hands, as he had seen Paul do so often. He looked up to heaven, just as Paul did. And he spoke his first public prayer.

"Lord God, you made the heaven and the earth and the sea. You sent your Son to save your creation from the sins of men. You sent your servants to Philippi to preach Jesus Christ and announce resurrection power. And you have given each one here new life through our faith in the Savior.

"Now the people of our city have arrested your servants, beaten them, and thrown them into prison. Tomorrow, they may come to do the same to us. We are afraid, O Lord. We are uncertain. We don't know what will happen."

A chorus of "Amens" greeted this confession.

"But we believe you are Lord of all, and that your power is at work to accomplish your will. And so we plead with you tonight, O God . . . not that you protect us from harm, but that we might be bold whatever tomorrow brings . . . not that you keep us safe, but that you keep us faithful . . . not that we might avoid suffering, but that you would grant us the grace to avoid turning our backs on what we have confessed and what we believe!

"Send us from this place tonight, Lord God, with confidence that we are your true children. Fill us with boldness to speak of your Son, whatever the consequences. Stretch out your powerful hand to change lives and cast out demons and overcome the powers of the Evil One. Through the name of your holy servant Jesus, we pray."

"Amen!" Lydia exulted, eyes shining and spirits revived.

"Amen!" exclaimed Syntyche and Euodia together.

"Amen!" agreed soldiers and slaves and merchants and housewives.

At that moment, the earth shook and the walls of Lydia's house heaved. They looked at each other for an instant in terror and then jumped to their feet and took to the door. In the courtyard, the ground rolled and lifted, and Clement expected the house to crumble around them at any time. They clung to each other, trying to keep their balance and survive their fear.

And then it was over. The ground stilled and the house stood, leaving the group to look around in relief . . . and in sheepish embarrassment. A youth joked he had never seen Marcion move so quickly. The old soldier laughed and noted that the young man had beaten him to the door.

Lydia just arched an eyebrow at Clement and said, "That was some prayer!"

Chapter Thirteen

THEN THEY LEFT

(EARLY FALL, A.D. 49)

TERTULLUS WALKED RAPIDLY IN THE DIRECTION OF THE PHILIPPIAN JAIL. His lips were pursed in anger, but behind his eyes floated a cloud of fear. "What do you mean they are Roman citizens?" he hissed at the Lictor. "Why didn't they say so yesterday afternoon? We could have avoided all this unpleasantness!" Whether Tertullus meant the unpleasantness of their beating or his humiliating journey to the jail, the Lictor could not tell.

"They insist they *did* claim citizenship, Magistrate, but their claim went unheeded in the noise of the disturbance." The officer of the court had served with Tertullus long enough to see him savor the difficult circumstances others found themselves in. It was peculiarly satisfying to watch him now suffer difficult circumstances of his own. If word of this got back to Rome—for that matter, if word got out at Philippi—Tertullus could kiss his political ambitions goodbye. He'd be lucky to keep his head. The Lictor cared nothing for Paul and Silas, but he dearly loved seeing self-important bombasts like Tertullus get tripped in the mud and have to wallow for a while with the *hoi polloi*. Looking up at the clear sky, he decided it was going to be a very good day.

Tertullus rubbed his temples nervously, thinking aloud as his feet carried him along. "There has to be a way out of this. I've worked too long and too hard to be ruined by a mere oversight, a slip of the ear." He was already making his case before a tribunal. He paused and turned to face his attendant. "You know how hard I've worked. You could testify to my impartiality, my sense of justice."

The Lictor kept a straight face. "It's not me you have to convince, sir. It's the Jews." Oh, this was delicious.

"Yes, yes! Of course, you're right." Tertullus started walking toward the prison again. "Perhaps they would be amenable to a small sum of money. Not a bribe, of course, but compensation for their pain and suffering. How much coin do you think it might require?"

"Well . . . there was the shame of public arrest—by a mob—without a warrant or formal charges of any kind. Then there is the matter of conviction without due process. And we shouldn't forget the punishment itself. Too bad we used the rods, isn't it, sir? It would have been so easy to simply throw them out of town. How much pain and suffering would you say is involved with twenty strokes of the rods? Your Honor?"

Tertullus felt sick to his stomach. "You're not being very helpful, Lictor."

"My apologies, Magistrate. I will try to do better in the future." They walked in silence the rest of the way.

The jailer was waiting for them on the steps of the prison. "Your Excellency!" He saluted. "We have been expecting your arrival. This way, please."

Tertullus passed through the gate, hissing at his Lictor once again. "How many people know about this? Too many leaks! Too many wagging tongues and eager ears!"

They were led into the prison courtyard, where Paul and Silas sat stiffly on a bench, unfettered and—Tertullus was glad to see—not in immediate danger of expiring. *Let me just get them out of town alive,* the magistrate thought to himself. *Then they can die. Indeed, I hope they do. Slowly.* He was a sour man.

"Gentlemen!" Up came the smile. Out stretched the arms. On went the look of concern and, yes, shock at this miscarriage of justice. "I understand that a grave mistake has been made. Is it true that you are Roman citizens?"

Paul could hardly bear to look at the toady, but there were other purposes to serve this morning, more important matters to address. So he fixed Tertullus with a level gaze and spoke quietly. "I was born a Roman citizen, in the province of Cilicia, in the city of Tarsus. Shall I fetch the official papers? They are in my pack . . . where I'm staying."

Tertullus died a little inside. "No, no. Of course that will not be necessary."

Paul continued. "You have arrested us without charges. You have beaten us publicly without the benefit of a proper trial. And you have thrown us into prison. We are citizens of Rome and you have treated us like common criminals or barbarians. You have disdained our rights and held Roman justice up to ridicule. You have pandered to a mob when you are charged to enforce the law!" Paul's voice rose with each sentence. He knew how to speak the language of power when it was necessary.

The magistrate felt as though he were falling from some high cliff. He could sense the rocks rushing up to meet him. *Think!* he ordered himself. Should he bluff and bluster and try to bully this little Jew? One look told him better. Should he take his medicine like a good little magistrate and hope things would not go too severely for him? Too many of his peers hated him, were jealous of him, would pounce at the least sign of impropriety. In spite of the early hour, Tertullus felt a desperate need for a drink.

"Paul. May I call you Paul? This is a most unfortunate situation. I am simply devastated by the suffering you have wrongly endured. I assure you, had I known your status as citizen, I would have tried even harder to change my fellow magistrate's mind. Alas"—Tertullus shook his head sadly—"he is so prejudiced against Jews that he was blinded to the true facts of the case." He opened his hands to Paul, one frustrated man to another. "We are, all of us, limited by those with whom we must work.

"Now surely there must be some . . . accommodation we can make to secure an outcome that is in—"

"There is," Paul interrupted. He could stand the man no longer and simply wanted out of his presence and out of this prison. "I want two things. First, a private word with you, Tertullus. Second, an immediate release. Silas and I will leave the city before sundown. But we have business to attend to before going. Agreed?"

Tertullus could not believe his good fortune. The man could be bought after all! All that remained was to haggle over the price. "Certainly, Paul! Those are very acceptable and very generous terms. Jailer!" He summoned the keeper of the prison. "Clear this courtyard!"

When they were alone, Tertullus cocked a worldly eye at Paul. "Well? How much?"

Paul kept his face passive and tried to swallow his distaste for the man. "You can keep your money. What I want from you won't cost you a denarius. Give me what I want and your conduct yesterday will stay our secret. Do you understand?" Tertullus nodded. "Are you interested?" Tertullus nodded again, more vigorously.

"Then listen carefully. There may be times during your tenure as magistrate when charges will be brought against people who are called 'Christians.' A mob may bring these people to you, as they did me. Or they may come to you through regular channels. Here is what I want from you. If, after hearing the evidence, it is clear they are guilty of some crime—stealing, say, or assault—pronounce them guilty and punish them. But if the charges are brought primarily because they are Christians, because someone doesn't like Christians, because Christians make people nervous, you will recognize that. And you will do everything—and I do mean *everything in your power,* Tertullus—to protect them and see that their rights are honored. Do you understand?"

Tertullus nodded quickly, trying to memorize the terms of the deal. "If they're guilty, condemn them. If they are innocent, protect them. That sounds easy enough."

"Not for you, Tertullus." Paul's voice grew hard and he stepped closer to the magistrate. "Let me make this simple for you. Think about what happened yesterday. Do you remember that, Tertullus?" The Roman nodded glumly. Paul continued. "I am a Christian. Those people drummed up charges against me because I make them nervous. And you did *nothing* to protect me." His voice was like granite now. "The next time that happens, think about what you would ordinarily do—and then do the opposite."

Paul turned to leave, but paused momentarily. With his back to the Roman, he said, "I will be watching the situation here in Philippi very closely, Tertullus. If I hear that any of my fellow believers have suffered unjustly under your watch, I will return and bring charges against you and break you like a twig. Do you believe me, Magistrate?"

Tertullus felt his bowels turn to water. Oh, yes. He believed him.

"Well then. Have a pleasant day. I hope we will not be seeing each other again."

And Tertullus thought, *Never will be too soon.*

~

Paul lay on his stomach on one of Lydia's dining couches, stripped naked to the waist except for the bandages swathing his wounds. Lydia stood over him, bathing the cloth strips in warm water, trying to loosen the clotted blood that fastened them to his back, and doing her best to keep her tears from falling on the open lacerations.

"Someone did a good job with these bandages," she said for something to say, surprised that he had received any medical attention at all.

"The jailer was quite kind to me, Lydia." He raised to his elbow with a groan and looked her in the eye. "He and his family will be calling on you in a few days. You are to welcome them."

She met his gaze for a moment and then gently pushed him down to the couch. "As you wish, Paul."

Paul closed his eyes and tried not to think about the throbbing of his back. He knew from experience that weeks of healing lay ahead, and that, today or tomorrow, the fevers would set in. It happened every time. There was so much to do while he was still clearheaded. "Lydia, please call Luke and Clement in. We'll talk while you tend to my back."

Lydia continued to pour warm water on the bandages and gently, carefully unwrap them. "I will send for them in a while, Paul. First, there is something you and I should speak of."

"Please, Lydia. Just send for the men."

"I told you I will, Paul. But now that I have you as a captive audience, I have something to say to you."

Paul closed his eyes. He reached for that here-but-not-here feeling again, that safe place he could crawl to when the time for suffering arrived. He feared this would be worse than the beating.

~

Clement sat in the kitchen, the door closed between the dining room and himself. Having seen the beating from the edge of the crowd yesterday, he had no stomach to see the results of it up close. He could hear through the door the indistinct murmurings of their conversation, and thought he detected on occasion Lydia's quiet weeping. Paul's wounds must be worse than he imagined.

He sat and thought about the previous night, about the goodbye he would speak today, about the days that were yet to come without Paul. He recognized the role he would be required to play . . . and recognized also that, though he was willing, he was not capable. There was too much he didn't know. There were so many things he had yet to learn. The depth of his faith, his love for these people—all that was well and good. But it did not make up for his ignorance of the Scriptures or his inexperience in Christian living. Add up all the time he and his fellow Philippians had spent in their new lives and it could be measured in weeks. It was not enough.

Paul would have to leave someone behind. There was no other way. Clement would have to persuade him to part with Luke . . . or, at least, Timothy.

The door to the dining hall opened and Lydia appeared. "He wants to see you and Luke," she said. In her hands, she carried a bowl containing the bloody remnants of Paul's bandages.

"How is he?" Clement asked. She grimaced, and he noted the puffiness around her eyes, the redness of her nose.

"He'll live. But he needs someone to look after him, to keep his bandages changed and make sure he doesn't push too hard." Her eyes filled. "I guess I'll have to show Timothy how to do that." She set the bowl down on a table and left the room to look for Luke.

Clement moved to the dining hall and found Paul seated on a bench, eyes closed and mouth set against the pain. "Ah, Clement," he said as he looked up. "Come in. We have much to talk about, you and I."

"Yes we do." Clement sat opposite him and, in spite of all that needed to be said, the two were silent for a moment. "I've been thinking about the future, Paul, how we will survive without you here."

Paul spoke softly. "I've been thinking of little else for weeks now, my friend. A great deal depends on you."

There it was again. The burden. The sense of a world bearing down upon him. "I'm ready to do what I can, Paul. But there are some things—"

At that moment, Luke and Lydia entered the room. Luke took a seat beside Clement while Lydia stood, arms crossed, against the wall.

"How do you feel, Paul?" Luke took a physician's interest in his condition, noting the color of his skin, the slight tremble in his hands. "I just attended to Silas. He's having a rough time of it, I'm afraid. Diarrhea. Vomiting. Is it really necessary for us to travel today?"

"Yes. That was part of the deal." Paul closed his eyes for a moment, managing the pain. He did not look forward to the road . . . or to sleeping on the ground that night. He looked at Luke. "But you will not be going with us. Your place is here, Luke. I'm leaving you behind."

Luke came to his feet. "That's crazy, Paul. Those brutes did their best to kill you yesterday. You'll need medical attention for weeks. I won't let you—" But Paul waved away his objections and motioned for him to sit down again.

"I appreciate your concern for our condition, Doctor. But I know the routine. Timothy can do what is needed. *My* concern is for the condition of this church. We have too much invested here, too many people are counting on us, to leave them on their own. So here's what we're going to do."

Luke hated it when Paul used that tone of voice. With that tone, there was no discussion, no changing his mind. Luke had learned long ago to stop pushing and bow to the inevitable when Paul got like this.

"Silas, Timothy, and I will leave this evening, heading west. I think we'll see what doors God opens in Thessalonica. You, Luke, will remain here. I don't know for how long. If I need you, I will send for you. But this is where I need you for now." Luke nodded his reluctant agreement.

"Lydia and Clement." Paul looked at them both with deep affection, although she would not meet his eyes. "The two of you have become the backbone of this church. These people look to you. They depend on you. If you are strong, if you can step up and provide leadership for them, they will do just fine. Luke will support you with teaching and advice. But he cannot lead these people. It is not his gift." Paul smiled at his coworker. "And, even if it were, it is not his place."

The slave and the woman looked at one another. She thought of a Sabbath spent on the banks of the river. He recalled an afternoon in his room, talking with Paul about the Cross and about his father. Both of them recognized that God had been moving in their lives to bring them to this moment. They smiled at each other, a silent seal on their partnership, and nodded their agreement to Paul.

He called the two of them over and had them kneel side by side before him. Placing a hand on each of their heads, he raised his face to the ceiling and prayed. "God and Father, look with mercy on these your children. Pour out your Holy Spirit on them to guide and strengthen them. Give them always, Father, a sense of your presence. Fill them with confidence that they are not alone. Into their hands, I commit this church. Prepare them for the task ahead. In the name of your Son, I pray this."

His hands still on their heads, Paul tilted their faces up to look at his. "Love these people. Be servants to them. Keep yourselves pure. Let there be no hint of greed or ambition in what you do. Be willing to suffer, if it comes to that. Do you understand?" They nodded, overwhelmed.

"Although," Paul told them—and an odd smile came over him—"I don't think the magistrates will cause you any trouble."

~

Word spread to members of the Philippian church throughout the morning. Masters dispatched slaves to carry the news across town. Shopkeepers closed their shutters for a brief time to run to the other end of the agora and alert fellow businessmen. Women, dragging along reluctant children, made the rounds to homes and guard posts and market, looking for fellow believers who needed to know. "Paul must leave Philippi by sundown. He wants to meet with us at Lydia's house before he goes."

They came from all reaches of the city. They gathered from fields and storefronts and stables. Slaves slipped away by remembering errands they needed to run and taking longer than expected at their tasks. Wives asked older children or neighbors to watch the young ones for a couple of hours and stole away. They made excuses. They mumbled hasty pretexts. They found ways to disengage from normal life and run through the crowded streets to Lydia's house.

When they arrived, they found Paul seated in her courtyard—pale, but smiling and quick to address a word of welcome to each of them. They gathered around him in relief . . . touching him . . . offering words of sympathy . . . eager with questions. "Are you all right?" "Where is Silas?" "Where will you go?" "What's to become of us?"

He responded quietly, answering some questions, deferring others until everyone gathered, saving himself to address the group. Slowly the courtyard filled. And though so many questions hung in the air, it was enough for them to see Paul, to hear his voice, and to know that their fellow citizens had failed to break the part of Paul they'd come to love and depend on. They could not take their eyes off him. They strained to hear every word he spoke. They sat on the ground at his feet, content to wait with him for the church to assemble.

When the time came, he stood up on shaking legs and raised his voice to be heard. "My brothers and sisters. My partners in the gospel. My children in the faith." Paul paused to clear his throat and took a deep breath. "Today is a day I have dreaded for many weeks. I knew this day would come eventually but I have not looked forward to it. Today I must leave you. And my heart is breaking."

The crowd was still and hushed. Only a few sniffles and the rustle of fabric wiping faces broke the silence.

"Yet, at the same time, I feel a great joy. For I look at you"—and his smile beamed over them—"and I know that my work is finished. All of you have believed our message." Paul ticked off the basics on his fingers. "Jesus died for sinners. God raised him from the dead. And new life is now possible for those who have faith in the Lord."

He paused to look around at members of the assembly. "This is the message I traveled so far to tell you. This is the reason we came preaching. If I spent another year at Philippi, the story wouldn't change. You already know the most important thing I have to teach you."

He faltered and Luke moved to his side, taking an elbow to hold him up.

"Silas and Timothy and I will be moving on toward Thessalonica in a few moments. Luke has agreed to stay behind and continue your teaching. I have asked Clement and Lydia"—he nodded at the pair who stood together off to his left—"to provide leadership over the next few months. You trust them. You know their character and their hearts." The church looked from Paul to the slave and the woman, nodding their agreement and silently pledging their support.

Paul stood to his full height and passed a trembling hand over his bald pate. He seemed to be gathering himself, channeling his grief into the intensity of his final words. "There are some last things I want to leave with you. Listen carefully and hide them deep in your hearts. Take them out and dust them off on occasion. Remind yourselves of what I tell you now.

"First. You should expect times of trouble in the future. I don't know what that trouble will look like. Persecution. Immorality or apathy among yourselves. False teachers. The trouble could take many forms. But you should expect it. Remember that even our Lord suffered. And if the Master suffered, so will the students."

The group was somber, trying to imagine that future, wondering which trouble would be theirs.

"But brothers and sisters, it is in those times of trouble that a disciple is measured . . . that the character of a church is confirmed. Trouble is never the problem for people of faith. It's how we *handle* trouble. Persecution won't destroy what God is doing here in Philippi. False teaching, even your own weaknesses, can't defeat God's purposes in this place . . . if you hold on to Jesus and to each other." Paul barbed each word, hoping they would hit and catch.

"So when the trouble comes, remember this. Pain tempts you to let go of what you believe. Pain tempts you to let go of your love for each other." He hoped they were thinking at that moment of his own pain. He hoped they could see that his faith in Jesus and his love for them had not been beaten out of him. He marveled at how God could use even a bleeding back to teach his ways. "Especially when trouble comes, you've got to hang on to the Lord and to each other. That's when your new life and your new family matter most. If you can keep the mind of Christ when you are hurting, if you can stand together and love each other in the hard times, nothing Satan will throw against you can destroy what God is doing in this church."

He paused and took in the faces of each of them. He thought about the miracle that had occurred in these lives, the forgiveness and healing they had experienced, the hope they'd found, the life they had been given. And his soul rose up and poured out in gratitude to God. Between the throbbing of his back and the faces of these people, he felt more alive, more useful to God, than he could possibly express. He stood silently before them, savoring the moment of private worship, hating to bring his stay at Philippi to an end.

But it was time. "Finally, I want you to know that, though I am leaving, I will always be with you in spirit. One of the advantages of a broken heart is that I am able to leave pieces of it here . . . with you." The tears started now, as he looked from one to another and let his eyes rest briefly on Lydia. "You will never be far from my thoughts and prayers. Wherever my travels take me, you will go with me and I will remain with you. I have you in my heart. I will remember you. I beg you to remember me."

And then he could say no more. Paul slumped into the arms of Luke, weak from pain and exhaustion and heartache. Luke held him awkwardly, careful of his back and uncertain how to comfort the Apostle. The church gathered around, gently touching him, whispering their goodbyes. He touched them back, smiling through the tears, giving them last words of blessing and encouragement.

Finally, Paul nodded to Timothy, who stepped into a room and whispered, "Silas. It's time." Groaning, his face ashen, Silas sat up on the edge of the bed. With Timothy's help, he stood and, finding his balance, edged painfully through the doorway into the waiting crowd.

The three of them passed slowly through the group, stopping to touch, whispering words of affection, offering to some a blessing and to others a quiet smile. They came to the courtyard gate where Clement and Lydia waited for them. Timothy and Silas said a brief goodbye—as much as Silas had strength to give—and then walked out of the courtyard, down the road toward the city walls, Silas leaning heavily on the arm of his young companion.

Paul stepped through the gate and then turned to face the two people on whom so much depended. He looked from one face to another and offered a silent prayer for each, overwhelmed by how hard it was to leave them. Reaching up, he placed his hands on their wet cheeks. "Don't let them follow me," he said, inclining his head toward the crowd in the courtyard. "Let's finish this now. I don't think I can stand to prolong it." He looked again at each of them. "I will be back. Do you hear me?" He said it with a fierceness. "I don't know when. But I will be back. In the meantime—" He stopped and shrugged and left the rest unspoken. Everything had already been said.

He turned and took two steps away before facing them again. He needed the separation. He needed the distance. "I love you both. I'm counting on you." The two of them held each other and nodded mutely. They were beyond words now. "God be with you."

He turned and followed Timothy and Silas down the road. He did not look back. He could not have seen anything if he had. His weak eyes were so full of tears he could barely make out the cobblestones at his feet.

Clement watched him go, wanting to run after him, wanting to run away. Only his numbness and the woman clinging to his side kept him rooted in the gateway of Lydia's courtyard. He watched Paul's back until it disappeared around a bend in the road. And then he watched that spot for a while longer.

Finally he looked to Lydia and saw a grim determination already at war with her grief. He saw her faith and her sense of duty, her love and stubbornness, bubbling up into her face. He knew she would be all right. And he wondered what wounds had made this woman so resilient, so strong.

He turned his head to study the people milling about the courtyard and knew that, though he should go in and try to comfort them, he would not. There would be time enough for that later. Putting on his best face for Lydia, and whispering to her his need to be alone, Clement set off down the road in the other direction.

He had to find the girl.

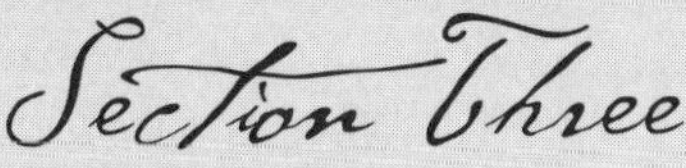

THE LETTER

WINTER/SPRING, A.D. 62

Chapter Fourteen

THE GIFTS YOU SENT

(LATE JANUARY, A.D. 62)

THIRTEEN DAYS AFTER LEAVING PHILIPPI, EPAPHRODITUS CLIMBED THE Portuensis Way to the brow of a hill. As he topped the knoll, Rome suddenly sprawled in panoramic splendor before him, spilling over the seven hills and filling up the valleys between. The sight of it stopped him in his tracks. He stood, mouth agape, trying to take in the impossible vista, feeling small and far from home.

At that moment, an unspeakable exhaustion settled over him like a wet fog. He'd pushed himself relentlessly on the journey, sleeping little and eating less. The long days of walking, and the longer nights shivering under a blanket on the frozen ground, had taken a toll. His constant sickness during the sea voyage used up whatever reserves of strength he had left. Only the thought of being so near Paul kept him walking from the boat to the city.

Now, confronted with his destination, stunned by a Rome vast beyond imagining, Epaphroditus felt something break inside him. He sank to his knees, shrugged his knapsack to the ground, and tried to let the dam give way. He wanted to laugh out of weariness and relief and joy and hope. He tried to weep for the fears of the journey and the pain that prompted it. He longed for some release from the pent-up anxieties, to shout away his doubts and his anger. He felt the knots in his shoulders, the clench of his jaw, the oiliness in his stomach, the ache in his head, and wished devoutly he could let it all go in one wrenching catharsis of tears, one hard bout of mirthless laughter. But nothing came. He was too weary.

So he simply knelt there in the middle of the road, oblivious to the carts and horses and laden pedestrians flowing around him. A wagon driver cursed him. A man on horseback almost trampled him. But Epaphroditus ignored them, filled with the single thought that soon he could unburden himself to Paul.

Trembling and dry-mouthed, Epaphroditus groped his way to a tree by the roadside and leaned against its trunk. His bowels ached and he feared he would have yet another bout of the diarrhea that had dogged him since leaving the boat. He sat there, still and quiet, while the cold ground and rough bark at his back slowly revived him. And as he sat, to keep his mind off his stomach, he focused on the city.

The sheer size of it was unnerving. Massive walls stretched for miles in a vain attempt to embrace all of Rome. Yet even their vast length could not contain the explosion of people and buildings. The city spilled over on every side, spawning *suburbae* outside the walls—any one of which was large enough to swallow pitiful Philippi. It was reported that the city sheltered over a million-and-a-half inhabitants—an absurd, ludicrous number Epaphroditus had scoffed. Until he saw the city for himself.

Even from his distant vantage point, Epaphroditus could see the buildings piled on top of each other in unruly heaps, hanging from hillsides, perched on the most unlikely sites. Apartment complexes, markets, public monuments and buildings, all were crammed together in a random and precarious mix—like the toys of some untidy giant. And when Roman engineers ran out of ground, they simply built up. All over the city, structures rose four, five, even six stories.

In the heart of Rome, a vast construction project was under way. Work crews had filled in a portion of the valley separating the Palatine Hill from its neighbor, forming a large, level space on which the outlines of buildings and porticos and fountains were taking shape. Epaphroditus guessed this was one of Nero's huge (and obscenely expensive) projects. They had become both a joke and a curse across the empire—a joke most of the year and a curse when it came time to pay taxes. Like working men everywhere, Epaphroditus resented the burden of Roman taxes. But at that moment, looking down on the majesty of the city, even a resentful taxpayer could acknowledge that greedy Rome made a grand impression.

But none of this caught Epaphroditus quite like the tangle of roads and aqueducts feeding into Rome.

Philippi had temples and government buildings of its own, if not so large and splendid. Epaphroditus had seen monuments and marble before. But never had he witnessed anything like the network of roads that snaked in and out of the city—from the coast, from the mountains, from the plains to the north and south—dozens of them, stretching as far as the eye could see. For the first time, he realized the truth of the saying, "All roads lead to Rome." Apparently, they did.

And the aqueducts! Nine bright, straight ribbons of marble, resting on gracefully arched arcades, bringing rivers of water into the city every day. They came from high ground to the north and east and south, carrying their liquid treasure in gently sloping channels from beyond the horizon. Epaphroditus reeled at the thought of such massive engineering projects. The expense! The manpower!

Studying the city through half-closed eyes, he imagined Rome as a great spider, sitting at the center of a web of roads and shipping lanes and commercial enterprises and military command lines that stretched across the far-flung empire. There she patiently waited for the wealth of the world—the fear-offerings of a thousand provinces—to flow her way. And then, just as deliberately, she consumed those riches in lavish style. She fed on the labor of distant men as they built or fought or worked their hands bloody. She was beautiful and she was ruthless. She was powerful and she was selfish. She dreamed great dreams and used any means to accomplish them.

No wonder she was called the "Great Whore." Epaphroditus felt a chill go through him, torn between admiration for the city and loathing of it.

Unsteadily, the potter rose to his feet, slung on his knapsack, and began the last leg of his journey. The road climbed gently, following the course of the River Tiber for the final few miles. As he neared the city, he passed first a smattering of outlying shops and hovels. Then came a heavier concentration of docks and warehouses fronting the river. Finally, the buildings grew denser still—a sea of concrete, wood, and brick that surged all the way up to the gray cliffs of the city walls.

From a distance, Rome had appeared shimmering and clean. But Epaphroditus soon discovered that was an illusion. As he crossed the Tiber on the Aemilius Bridge, just to the north of the Circus Maximus, the smell of open sewers and tanning factories assaulted his nose. He saw that the river was black and polluted, covered in an oily sheen. A film of gray ash had settled on every surface. Rotting garbage lay strewn and unswept in the streets.

No city that boasted this many people could stay clean. They were everywhere—teeming and pressing and moving in tides. The farther Epaphroditus walked into the city, the more they filled the streets and alleys. Prostitutes or beggars seemed to populate every corner. Squads of soldiers pushed their way roughly through the crowds. Groups gathered before food stalls and wine vendors, blocking the path and slowing progress to a crawl. His ears rang from shouting people and braying animals and carts crunching over cobblestone streets.

Epaphroditus allowed himself to be carried along with the flow of humanity, changing streams on occasion to make his way toward the Forum Romanum. Once there, he paused to fish directions to Paul's apartment from his knapsack—directions Onesiphorus had carefully sketched out the night he brought news of Paul to the Philippians.

"Rome is a maze, my friend," Onesiphorus had warned. "There are thousands of streets, few of them named. So pay attention." He stabbed his quill at a rough diagram of the city. "You are looking for the Subura, the armpit of Rome. It's a lovely little slum squeezed between the Esquiline and Viminal hills." He noted on the map the location of each. He looked up at Epaphroditus. "They have a saying in Rome. 'The hills belong to the rich, the valleys belong to the poor, and the Subura belongs to the Devil himself!'"

He turned his attention once more to the map. "You can get to the forum easily enough. Look for a plaza there named after Augustus. Directly behind that plaza is a street that heads due east. Follow it for about six hundred paces until you come to . . . "

Epaphroditus remembered the instructions well. They seemed simple and straightforward at the time. But now, overwhelmed by the city, turned around, a complete stranger to these surroundings, the potter from Philippi wondered if he would ever find Paul. Folding the directions into his tunic, he whispered a prayer for guidance and began the search for the plaza of Augustus.

All through the afternoon he wandered the narrow streets of the Subura. Apartment buildings rose up to dizzy heights on every side, almost touching at the top floors and cutting off much of the sunlight at street level. Occasionally, a voice above would shout a warning, and the contents of a chamber pot or scraps from a just-eaten meal would rain down into the street. Epaphroditus discovered that merely walking in Rome was a dangerous activity requiring constant vigilance.

His directions (which he now deemed absolutely useless) indicated an apartment on the southwest corner of the fourth floor. Epaphroditus had climbed the stairs to the fourth floor of a score of apartment buildings, pounding on doors and describing Paul. When he wasn't met with outright abuse, he faced blank looks and apathetic shrugs. No one had heard of a Jewish prisoner, and nobody cared that a provincial from Philippi was looking for him.

So Epaphroditus trudged from one apartment building to the next, retracing his steps, recounting the buildings, trying to decipher his directions. Several times he entered an apartment block twice, climbing the same indistinguishable stairs, knocking on the same faceless door, receiving for his troubles the same cursing, only amplified by the second disturbance. In spite of the winter cold, he was sweating.

As the afternoon wore on, Epaphroditus looked more and more anxiously at the slivers of sky above. "Whatever you do," Onesiphorus had cautioned him, "don't get caught in the streets of Rome after dark. Someone will gladly relieve you of your money belt and slit your throat for thanks."

Two more buildings and I'll find an inn for the night, Epaphroditus instructed himself. He pushed his way through the human tide to the next apartment block and climbed wearily to the fourth floor. He was not even sure where "southwest" was anymore, so he simply knocked on the door of each corner apartment.

At the third door, a Roman soldier filled the threshold and gruffly demanded his business. Epaphroditus, heart pounding, answered, "I am looking for a prisoner named Paul. I understand he is under house arrest in one of these buildings."

The soldier looked him up and down, determining whether this stranger might pose any threat, searching for the bulge of a hidden weapon. Then, throwing the door back, he called over his shoulder, "Hey, old man! Someone here to see you."

The soldier was huge. He was scarred and ugly. Standing there with his sword and a scowl, he was the picture of menace. And Epaphroditus was sorely tempted to kiss him on the mouth.

~

Paul stepped out of the back room and squinted toward the doorway. He could make out the figure of a man silhouetted against the late afternoon light, but the face was lost in blurry shadow. He and Rufus had not yet lit the lamps for the evening.

The old man took a few more steps toward his visitor, wondering who this could be, thinking it was time for Luke and Timothy to arrive but knowing this was not them. "Thank you, Rufus." He nodded at the soldier. "Yes? May I help you?" he queried the shadow at the door.

Epaphroditus drank in the approaching figure like a tonic—one that promised quick relief but that also went down bitter. He was so grateful to see Paul, to realize the end of his journey. He wanted to rush into the room and embrace the old man. But it had been six years since Epaphroditus had seen him last, and the potter noted sadly that time had not been kind to Paul. The Apostle had shrunk since his last stop at Philippi. He seemed shorter to Epaphroditus. The wattle under his chin hung in a loose, fatless flap and his scalp clung so tightly to his skull that every bump and depression showed in hard relief. He looked to Epaphroditus as though he would blow away in a modest gust.

"Brother Paul," he found the voice to say. "It's me, Epaphroditus. I've just arrived from Philippi." He moved into the room and the two men stood before each other. Paul stared and raised his hand to touch Epaphroditus's face, as if to remind himself of a past life and test that this was no vision. And then he broke into a broad grin and enveloped the younger man with an embrace and a joyful shout. They clung to one another and laughed—Paul so glad to be holding this lifeline back to happier times and beloved friends; Epaphroditus so glad to see Paul and to feel in the strength of his embrace an assurance that the old man was sturdier than he appeared.

They finally collapsed onto stools to stare at each other. Both men felt the press of the years of separation, a burning curiosity to hear and tell recent history. The stories crowded so thick about them, neither knew where to begin.

"What are you doing here, Epaphroditus?" Paul said at last.

"We just found out where you were, Paul." He took off his knapsack and let it fall to the floor. "We didn't know how to reach you. We weren't even sure if you were alive or dead! Do you remember an Ephesian named Onesiphorus?" Paul recognized the name at once. "He brought us news that you were in Rome." Epaphroditus shot a look at the Roman guard to see how closely he was paying attention and lowered his voice. "I've brought you a few things from Philippi"—he patted the money belt at his waist—"some news . . . and some help."

Paul only nodded in acknowledgment, refusing to take his eyes from Epaphroditus's face. He could almost smell Philippi on the young man. It was like heady perfume to the prisoner. "Tell me, how is Clement? And Lydia and the others?"

"They are well, Paul. They send their love. They all gave me letters for you." And again, he patted his waist.

They sat and talked as the light died, swapping stories of the near past, each trying to protect the other from the uglier parts, which, for now, would have to wait. Rufus finally growled at Paul to light the lamps, and Epaphroditus helped him take a flame from the stove to the lamps and candles spread throughout the apartment. They returned to their stools and their stories, until a knock came at the door and a voice called out, "Rufus, you old pagan! Open up. We've got your supper." Epaphroditus looked at the soldier in time to see a quickly suppressed grin.

Rufus gathered his bulk from the bed and went to the door. Flinging it open, he bellowed at Timothy, "You show more respect for your betters, young man. And so help me! If you haven't brought meat this time, I'll skewer you on my sword and roast you over the stove." Timothy entered laughing, not the least intimidated by Rufus's size or his bark. Behind him, Luke carried the meal they had just purchased from a street vendor. They moved past the soldier and into the room to find Paul seated with Epaphroditus.

At the sight of the potter, Timothy almost choked on his laughter. And Luke nearly dropped their supper.

~

They'd eaten and talked and caught up and reminisced. Until Paul's eyes began to wander to the belt at Epaphroditus's waist. Until the curiosity began to gnaw at him and make him visibly restless. When he could stand it no longer, Paul asked Rufus for permission to take his friends into his room. The soldier waved his consent and then ordered, "Don't be late tonight. I need to sleep."

They carried candles and stools into the inner room, moving the small table away from the wall, and sitting around it in eager anticipation. Epaphroditus lifted his tunic and untied the belt, slipping it from his waist for the first time since leaving Philippi. The stale odor of sweat and dead skin rose up and Epaphroditus wrinkled his nose, counting how long it had been since he'd visited the baths.

He held the belt before him, hesitant to hand it to Paul, knowing that now the time had come to prepare Paul for what he was about to read. He'd rehearsed this moment a hundred times on the journey. "Paul, I have come as the church's messenger. There are purses of money in this belt, gifts from your friends to help with your expenses." Paul looked down, embarrassed. "And there are letters in this belt, messages from people who love you and want to tell you that." Paul looked up at Epaphroditus again, beaming and eager. "But Paul, some of what you read in the letters will be difficult. We have some problems at Philippi. Frankly, that's the biggest reason I'm here." The smile left Paul's face, replaced by a look of concern and the weight of responsibility.

"I guess the best thing to do is let you read the letters and then we can talk. I'm not feeling very well just now anyway." He cast a covetous eye at the straw pallet in the corner. A soft bed and a little rest was what he needed. "I'm sorry, Paul. I wish we didn't have to worry you right now." Epaphroditus shrugged his apology and searched the Apostle's face. He needed some sign from Paul that it was all right, that he was forgiven for adding one more burden to the list of things clamoring for Paul's anxiety. But Paul had no absolution to offer just then. He didn't know what kind of burden he was being asked to forgive.

Paul reached for the belt and held it gently in his lap. His eyes closed for a long moment as the memories of Philippi gathered around him, as he prayed for strength and wisdom to deal with whatever problem was contained inside. And then, with a glance at Luke and Timothy, he untied the compartments of the belt and spilled out the purses of coin and packets of letters onto the table.

~

Epaphroditus lay on the straw mattress, numb with exhaustion, the strain of the journey hitting him with full force. He was so tired, and trembling and feverish.

The other three sat around the table, passing the letters back and forth, reading and pausing and staring into the distance, hearing familiar voices behind the written words.

Paul hunched over the table, his bald head cradled in his left hand, his right holding up a letter to catch the candlelight. He squinted hard as he read, holding the words close to his face. Even then, he could not decipher everything and frequently passed a letter to Luke, who obliged by reading aloud a sentence or paragraph. He treated each note as a fragile thing, worthy of special handling. One by one, he picked them up, studied the name for a time, then carefully broke the seal and gave himself completely to the reading—as if the letter might contain some coded message that only intense concentration could make plain.

At times as he read to himself, he chuckled or laughed out loud. Or his eyes filled and he smiled a sad smile of remembrance. But often, he grew still, barely breathing, focusing total energy on the black markings on white paper. When he finished a letter, he refolded it, placed it on the table, and observed a moment of silence—a ritual of memory, perhaps, in which the writer's face was called to mind; or a brief period of prayer. Only then did he let the letter go, passing it on to Luke or Timothy.

Two of the letters, marked *From Clement* and *From Lydia,* he held unopened to the candle, examining the seals and the signatures. He tapped them against the fingers of his left hand while he stared at the wall, lost in thought. Finally, he tucked them inside his tunic. He would save them for later.

For their parts, Luke and Timothy devoured the letters. Though they might not feel an apostle's burden for the Philippian church, they were certainly conscious of a burden all their own. Luke, after all, had spent over six years with these people, teaching them and growing to love them long after Paul and the others had been forced to move on. He had more time invested in the Philippian church than anyone.

Timothy also harbored a special affection for the Philippians. They were his "first fruits," the people who submitted to his earliest, bumbling efforts to share the gospel. Ever since, he'd been grateful to the Christians of Philippi—for their openness to the gospel and their patience with him. He had returned to Philippi several times over the years and was always eager to hear how they were doing. He felt an ownership in them—as if, in their progress, he found affirmation of his work. To have this trove of letters from Philippi was like finding treasure.

When they finished reading all the letters, they sat quietly. The three of them had been together so long, knew each other so well, there was no need for words just then. They were content to sit together and silently sift through the details of what they'd just read. Their eyes fixed on different objects around the room—a candle, the stack of letters, a spot on the wall. But their thoughts were focused on the same thing. They were all back in Philippi, trying to piece together what had gone wrong and how it could be addressed.

Suddenly, their reverie was broken by a loud, desperate voice, "No! Please, no!" and they turned to see Epaphroditus sitting up in bed, hands clenched to his mouth and eyes wide with terror. Even from across the room, they saw the beads of perspiration, the wet lock of hair plastered to his forehead. Luke was already at his bedside, hand to the potter's head, when Rufus burst in—sword drawn—to investigate the noise.

"It's all right, Rufus." Paul held up his hands, calming the guard.

"Nothing to worry about." He glanced at Luke and read the alarm in his face. "I'm afraid our visitor may have a fever."

Instinctively, the soldier stepped back into the doorway, distancing himself from the man on the pallet. Rufus feared no foe he could meet in a fair fight. But he feared fevers. He'd seen too many companions sweat away their lives, shaking and delirious. His eyes grew wide. "I want him out of here! Right now!"

"Of course!" Paul agreed quickly, sensing the dread in the soldier. "Timothy and Luke can take him with them." He lifted an eyebrow at Luke, who agreed that would be best.

"Right now, Paul." Rufus leveled a no-nonsense gaze at his prisoner and then escaped the room.

Paul turned to Luke, who said simply, "He's burning up. We need to go."

The three of them stood Epaphroditus on his feet, Timothy slipping under one arm and Luke the other. Epaphroditus's head lolled to one side and he mumbled incoherently. Quickly, Paul emptied the young man's knapsack, blankets and cups and grain scattering across the floor, and placed the coin purses inside.

"You better take the money," Paul said quietly, helping Timothy shrug on the pack. "I'm afraid some of my friends"—he nodded at the other room—"might help themselves if we leave it here." They staggered Epaphroditus through the door, across the front room, and out onto the landing.

"Take care of him, Doctor."

"I will, Paul. Let us get him cleaned up and cooled down, and we'll see where we stand. Timothy can come back tomorrow evening with a report."

"Good. God go with you, brothers."

"And with you, Paul."

He watched them half-walk, half-carry Epaphroditus to the head of the stairs and down one flight, until they turned out of sight at the next landing. Paul stood praying in the dark for the potter's safety, and then returned to his rooms. He found Rufus pouring a cup of wine and watched him consume it in one gulp.

"Are you afraid of dying, Rufus?" he asked.

The soldier looked at him for a moment and then, for once, answered seriously. "'Course I'm afraid of dyin'. What kind of question is that? But there's dyin' and there's dyin', you know?" He reached for the wine bottle again. "If I gotta go, let it be for a cause or a comrade. But I don't want to go with my teeth chattering and my brain scrambled." He winced as the cries of delirious soldiers, sick with plague on some distant campaign, replayed in his ears. "Dyin's bad enough. But I don't want to die for nothin'." And he drank deeply from the cup.

Paul watched him closely and kept silent for a while. Finally, he asked, "What do you think happens after you die, Rufus? What then?"

The soldier snorted. "Then it's the worms, old man. The worms and the maggots. That's all there is."

"I see," Paul said quietly. "You know I don't believe that."

"Yeah, I know. You believe in pretty stories about resurrection and eternal life." His voice grew louder, though Paul knew it was mostly the wine. "So what? What difference does it make? So I wake up and find out there really is something after death. Or maybe *you* die and never wake up! Who cares! What difference does it make here and now?"

"Oh, Rufus, it makes a great deal of difference. It makes all the difference in the world!"

"Humph!" Rufus scoffed. "Name one!"

"All right, my friend. For one thing, I'm not afraid of the fever."

Rufus glared at him and then reached for the bottle again.

~

He sat at the table and pulled the two letters from his tunic, laying them side by side in front of him. Picking up Lydia's letter, he raised it to his nose and smiled at the whiff of her perfume. She never had made it easy on him.

But he decided to read the letter from Clement first. Breaking the seal, and holding the pages to the light, he let the words flow out and over him . . . knowing it had been a hard letter for Clement to write . . . measuring by its length how worried his friend was for the church. He needed to talk to Epaphroditus, to fill in the gaps. He wanted to know more about Simeon. For now, he could only read through the letter again and try to imagine Clement as he wrote it.

"O God," Paul prayed, holding up the letter in outstretched hands. "Clement is a good man. He loves your Son and he loves your people. Grant him peace of mind tonight. Let him know I've received his letter and share his concern. Give him wisdom to lead the church through these trials. Give him strength to sustain him." He prayed on, pouring out his yearnings for these people and his worries over their turmoil.

He remembered all the work, the days spent under the summer sun in the agora, the teaching sessions in the evenings, the beating at the end—and he appealed to God not to let it all be in vain. He confessed how much he depended on Philippi—on the one church in all his missionary effort that hadn't hurt him or wandered off after some strange teaching or lapsed into apathy. "Philippi is my safe haven, Lord. My port in the storm. Don't let it be taken away from me."

The tears pooled in his eyes and spilled over his cheeks. He kept his hands lifted up, beseeching God, till the blood drained from his arms and his fingers started to tingle. He prayed long after Rufus blew out the candles in the other room, until his own candles started to sputter and drown.

Before he lost all his light, Paul picked up Lydia's letter and began to read. He read with speed, passing lightly over the particulars. He would laugh and cry and worry over the particulars later. But for now, he simply wanted to hear her voice again, the rise and fall of her tones, the phrasings and sudden turns of thought. It made him smile to hear her so plainly in his mind after all the years.

And it was with that smile that Paul put down her letter, blew out the candles, and made his way to bed.

Chapter Fifteen

HE ALMOST DIED

(LATE JANUARY, A.D. 62)

TIMOTHY AND LUKE WAITED IN THE DARK GATEWAY OF PAUL'S APARTMENT block until a drunken band of revelers lurched down the street. Stepping in behind, they joined the shouting and singing mob, staggering with the rest as though they belonged. Even if their newfound companions were drunk, there was still safety in numbers. Timothy felt a hand grab for his knapsack and he pulled away sharply, moving forward.

Fortunately, the carousers were headed in the general direction of Luke's quarters—northward. They made good progress toward the Viminal Hill, until the road began to rise toward the wealthier homes and well-patrolled streets. Drunks, like water, tend to seek the lowest level, and so the group turned west, keeping to the valley and the rougher sections of town. Luke grunted at Timothy and the two of them maneuvered the potter's limp body into an alley, waiting there until the raucous sounds of the gang faded. Stepping cautiously from doorway to shadow, they struggled uphill, carrying their sick friend between them. His moans and ramblings interrupted their labored breathing on occasion and, once, they had to stop so Luke could clamp a hand over his mouth.

They topped the Viminal Hill and paused to breathe in the fresh air that blew above the fetid slums of the city. Only a short distance to go now. The two of them renewed their grip on Epaphroditus and hurried as best they could past the walls and gardens of the very wealthy to the home of Theophilus.

They entered the gate of his rambling villa, paid for by Theophilus's dabbling in manufacture and imports and real estate. He had the Midas touch, he told Luke early in their acquaintance: "Everything I put my hand to turns to gold."

Crossing the spacious courtyard to Luke's quarters, he pushed open the door and, while Timothy steadied Epaphroditus, took a flame from a low-burning lamp and lit three other lamps around the room. As the light grew, he moved back to the two men swaying in the doorway and helped Timothy lead Epaphroditus to the couch. They removed his shoes and clothing. Besides the smell of the road and the days of unwashed sweat, the potter had the stench of the fever on him—that sharp, unmistakable odor that often attends the sick. Luke took in the smell with professional interest and muttered something beneath his breath.

"What? What did you say?" Timothy asked, ears open and trying to miss nothing. Like Rufus, Timothy was not entirely comfortable being around fevered people.

"I said he's deep in the fever. Sweats. Delirium. Shaking. I'm afraid it's going to be a long night. Maybe a few long days. If you will give me a moment, Timothy, I have some preparations to make. And then I'll need your help."

Although it was already cold in his room, Luke raised the shutters on the two windows to let in the night air. He stood before a small cabinet in the corner, and Timothy could see him opening cloth pouches, mixing herbs in a bowl, and gathering various instruments.

While Luke puttered, Timothy looked around the room with curiosity. In the two years they'd been in Rome, he had never seen where Luke lived. The doctor was private in that way. He wandered to a large table that filled one wall of the room and was surprised by the sheer quantity of scrolls and codices piled in neat stacks upon it. The only scrolls Timothy had ever seen (besides the two or three moth-eaten parchments Paul carried around and let him read occasionally) were in synagogues. Timothy was raised to view scrolls as holy things, to be treated with reverence and respect. Even when a scroll did not contain Scripture, he still felt a sense of awe about the scroll itself. *There must be a fortune tied up in these books,* he thought.

Stealing a glance at Luke, who was still absorbed with his remedies, Timothy picked up the nearest scroll, worn and well read, and opened it gently to read the first words: "This is the good news about Jesus Christ, the Son of God. It began just as God had said in the book written by Isaiah the prophet." His eyes widened and his hands began to shake as he realized this must be a copy of The Gospel, a scroll about the life and death of Jesus that was just beginning to circulate among the churches. He'd heard about the book but had never seen, much less held, a copy of it.

Quickly, Timothy rolled up the scroll and set it back in place, looking again at Luke to make sure he had not seen. He told himself the doctor wouldn't mind his old friend reading his scrolls. But then he remembered that, about some things, Luke could surprise him. Now was not the time to ask. Maybe later.

Stacked beside the scroll was a sheaf of papers covered in Luke's small, neat hand. Timothy lifted the top page and read,

> *Most honorable Theophilus: Many people have written accounts about the events that took place among us. They used as their source material the reports circulating among us from the early disciples and other eyewitnesses of what God has done in fulfillment of his promises. Having carefully investigated all of these accounts from the beginning, I have decided to write a careful summary for you, to reassure you of the truth of all you were taught.*

Theophilus? Timothy thought. He blurted out, "Luke! What's this? Isn't Theophilus your patron?"

Luke looked up from his mortar and pestle to see Timothy holding out a page toward him. A look of irritation flashed briefly across his face. Those were precious pages, the product of years of careful research and late nights. Now it was done and Timothy was leafing through the only copy that existed. But at once, Luke chided himself. He'd written the thing to be read, after all. "That's a little project I've just completed, my friend. Perhaps you would like to read it sometime. For the moment, however, we have other work to do. Please attend me."

Timothy carefully returned the page to its stack, and moved with Luke to the couch. First, they sponged Epaphroditus's body with a mixture of water and aromatic oils and herbs. "The body expels humors in the sweat," Luke explained. "They must be washed away or the body will reabsorb them and prolong the sickness." Placing Epaphroditus on his back, Luke tied a compress of herbs around his ankles—"to draw the fever away from his brain," he instructed Timothy. And finally, he made a small incision in a vein of the potter's forearm, inserted a slim metal tube, and drained off a carefully measured amount of dark blood. "That will help to restore the balance of humors in his body. He should feel some relief through the night, though we'll need to repeat this in the morning." He placed a hand on Epaphroditus's forehead, felt his wrist to measure a pulse, and then sat back heavily in a chair by the bed.

"The only thing we can do now is cover him when he shivers and uncover him when he sweats." Luke looked at Timothy. "I've seen this before. He's probably had diarrhea for the past two days. That will continue. We'll give him as much water as he can drink, but no food. And we must watch his stools. If they turn bloody"—he paused, thinking of other patients he'd lost long ago—"his chances are not good."

Timothy glanced quickly at the figure on the bed. "You mean he could die?"

"Oh yes," the doctor responded. "Right now, he's a very sick young man. If he gets worse"—and Luke shrugged to indicate that only time would tell.

Timothy agreed to stay through the night. They took turns sitting in the chair or napping under a thick cloak on the floor, always one of them attending to the patient. Cold cloths on his head. Blankets up around his neck, then down at the foot of the bed, then up again. Helping him stumble to a chamber pot in the corner; leading him, delirious, to the bed again. Luke handled it with long-practiced skill.

But even Timothy, to Luke's surprise, performed his nursing duties with determined efficiency.

~

The fever led Epaphroditus for a time back to his mother, to her lonely struggle in the other room and his silent vigil at her door. He felt himself floating up and through the door, hovering over her wasted figure, asking if there were anything he could do, wanting so desperately to do something.

Then the figure in the bed became a figure seated at a table. And when the figure turned to greet him, it wore not his mother's face but the features of the Apostle. "So you are Epaphroditus," he said in greeting. "Please, sit down. Let me find a stopping place here." He turned back to his quill and continued writing for a while.

When at last he set the quill down and faced Epaphroditus, it was as though he had to travel from a great distance to be, once again, in that room. He smiled apologetically and said, "Clement has spoken about you. He has a great fondness for you, you know."

"Clement has become the only father I've ever known," Epaphroditus acknowledged. He was more than a little nervous in Paul's presence. He'd heard so much about the tough old Jew, about his ministry in Philippi almost six years before and the brutal way it had ended.

"And you are a potter by trade?" Paul asked, making conversation until they could move to something significant.

"Yes. I have a shop near the agora. Actually, that's where Clement and I met."

"Really," Paul said. "Tell me about that."

"Not much to tell, frankly. He started coming to my shop to buy pottery for his household. We fell into conversations—about family and business and hopes for the future—that kind of thing. Now that I look back"—he smiled as he thought of it—"I can see that he was leading me. Toward more important things. Steering me to talk about faith."

"I see." Paul nodded. "When did you get to that?"

"He asked me to carry some pottery to his quarters, after I'd closed up shop for the night, and offered to feed me dinner in exchange."

Epaphroditus shrugged by way of explanation. “I’m a bachelor, you know, and not very good with a stove myself.” Why was he prattling on like this? What did such a man care about his cooking skills? But he saw Paul’s steady gaze fixed on his face and found no trace of boredom there. It occurred to him that Paul listened well—a rare quality in the potter’s experience. “Anyway. Supper led to conversation, which led, eventually, to Clement telling me a story. It was a story, he said, he heard from you.”

Paul smiled and acknowledged it was so. “If you mean the story of a good man and an unjust Cross and an empty tomb.”

Epaphroditus beamed. “That’s the one! Craziest story I ever heard. And yet”—his gaze grew serious and he shook his head—“it was as if I had been waiting for that story all my life. It was like an answer that fit a question I didn’t even know I was asking.”

Paul smiled at that and said, “I know exactly what you mean, my son. What pieces of you did it fit?” And he closed his eyes to listen more carefully, storing away the young man’s testimony with those of so many others.

“I lost my father before I was born and I watched my mother die of the fever. Death had haunted me as long as I could remember. It terrified me. The idea of a God who conquers death was good news to me.”

Paul just nodded, inviting him to continue. He did, but with his voice lowered and his eyes downcast. “There was a lost period in my life,” he confessed. “A time of drink and prostitutes and mindless violence.” Paul opened his eyes to gaze at the top of the potter’s head. “I carried the shame of that time, the waste of it, for a long while. It was like a garment I put on every morning. So when Clement told me we were all broken, I knew what he was talking about. And when he told me there was healing and forgiveness, that’s all I needed to hear.” He stopped and studied his hands carefully, the clay beneath his nails, the cracking around his knuckles. “I made my confession soon afterward”—he glanced up at Paul—“and have never looked back.”

He saw the tears standing in Paul’s eyes and knew that his story had touched something inside the Apostle. He smiled awkwardly, not knowing what else to say. The silence hung between them.

It was Paul who broke the moment. “I can only stay in Philippi for a few days. I have business in Corinth that requires my immediate attention." Epaphroditus saw the faraway look come over him again as he nodded toward the pages on the table. "I have to finish this letter and then send it on ahead before I can leave, however. Perhaps we can spend some time together while I'm here. In the evenings, say? After you close up the shop?" He looked at Epaphroditus with a smile and a raised eyebrow. "Clement seems to think you are worth my investing some time in. I'm beginning to think so too."

The potter flushed with embarrassment. "I would be honored. There is so much I have to learn."

Paul laughed. "Indeed there is! But you've made a good start, Epaphroditus. You know who you were. You know what Jesus has done for you. That's a foundation I can build on." Once again, the distant look came over Paul. He reached for the letter he was writing and, as he searched for a paragraph, muttered more to himself than Epaphroditus, "I wish the Corinthians would learn as much. At least, I wish they would remember it." He looked up at his young friend. "They think being spiritual is a matter of learning secret mysteries and speaking eloquently about holy things. They're thinking like the world, not like people who have put on the mind of Christ." He fixed Epaphroditus with those intense, hypnotic eyes. "The mind of Christ is shaped by the Cross, my son! It's about dying to ourselves and living like our Lord! Listen to this:

> *Since we believe that Christ died for everyone, we also believe that we have all died to the old life we used to live. He died for everyone so that those who receive his new life will no longer live to please themselves. Instead, they will live to please Christ, who died and was raised for them.*

"*That's* what being a disciple is about, Epaphroditus. Not secrets or fancy phrases or worldly wisdom. It's about knowing you're dead and that Jesus gave you new life and that your life is now his. Do you understand that?"

Epaphroditus nodded fervently, feeling the heat of Paul's intensity, a heat so tangible that he became conscious of the sweat pouring off his forehead and chest and pooling at his back. The heat boiled over him, like an unblinking sun in the desert, searing and deadly. He tried to back away, to put some distance between himself and the sun. But it followed him, laughing at his misery, determined to burn away the last of his pride and ambition.

He felt a cool cloth on his forehead and a voice, from far away, perhaps from Corinth, telling him to be calm. A hand slipped behind his neck, raising his head slightly. And then water! He gulped it down, craving it, desperate for it. He drank and then drank again, and laid his head back on the sweat-soaked bed.

~

They watched him like that for four days and nights. They bathed him and covered him and helped him to the chamber pot. He began to show blood in his stool and Luke shook his head in worry. "He's in God's hands," was all he would say. One of them slept while the other watched and prayed. Luke slipped out on occasion to bring food from the kitchen (though he was careful not to mention the sick man in his room—the household of Theophilus would not be eager to play host to a stranger on his deathbed).

Once a day, in the evening, he or Timothy walked down the Viminal Hill, through the slums of the Subura, to Paul's apartment—carrying supper and news of Epaphroditus's condition. Each time, Paul accepted their report quietly, and then excused himself to his room for a time before returning and eating his evening meal. They knew he was praying for Epaphroditus. They knew he was very worried.

But on the fifth day, the potter began to show signs of recovery. His fever broke and he began to sleep quietly, restfully. His bowels stopped issuing urgent demands and, in a lucid moment, he whispered to Luke that he was hungry. Luke smiled broadly (this was the sign he'd been looking for) and pronounced that if he continued to improve, he could have soup tomorrow. And then, leaving Timothy to play doctor, he rushed down the hill to tell Paul the good news.

~

"Now that we've weathered one crisis, it's time to deal with the next."

Paul sat across the room from Luke, the Apostle on the stool and the doctor on the floor against the wall. Luke studied Paul's face and realized that, while he was tending to Epaphroditus, Paul had been thinking about the other patient—an ailing church in Philippi.

"How long before Epaphroditus recovers fully, Doctor? Before he's ready to travel again?"

"Well, he's young and strong. But I'd say at least a month. He's lost a great deal of weight."

Paul looked away into the distance. "That's what I was afraid of. And do you believe he's past the worst of it now? Any chance of a relapse?"

"I don't think so, Paul. He should make steady progress from this point. It's just a matter of food and rest."

Paul studied him intently for a while. "Luke, the situation in Philippi cannot wait. From what I read in the letters, they need immediate help. A little guidance now, a little practical teaching will go a long way toward fixing this mess. If we wait, I'm afraid that a 'little' won't be enough. We may be looking at major surgery—speaking as one doctor to another." He smiled at his little joke, though neither of them felt very mirthful just then. All Luke felt was weary.

"I would go—wish I *could* go. But I don't think I could convince the guard and the courts to let me make a quick trip to Macedonia just now. I could send Timothy. But he doesn't have your history with the Philippians, or the subtle touch I believe this situation demands."

Luke rubbed a hand over his face, massaging his tired eyes and wishing he were not hearing what he knew was about to come.

"I want you to leave for Philippi immediately, my friend. As you said, Epaphroditus is recovering and Timothy can watch over him for the next few days. You'll need to travel quickly, get to Philippi as soon as you can." Paul stopped and studied the doctor for a moment. "I know it's dangerous sailing this time of year, but you can pick up a ship between Brundisium and Corinth and walk the rest of the way to Philippi. You don't get seasick, do you?" And he chuckled to himself.

Luke closed his eyes and decided to let Paul have his fun. After long months of sitting in the apartment, the chance to "do something" acted like a cold drink of water on the Apostle. As worried as Luke was about the Philippian church, he knew this problem could not have come at a better time. Luke had not seen Paul this alive in many days.

"That puts you in Philippi less than three weeks from now. We'll wait until Epaphroditus recovers, and then send him after you with a letter from me. I've already been thinking and praying about some of the things I want to say. *Then,* if we can get this legal mess sorted out, and once I learn which way things will go for me, I'll send Timothy your direction. Either way, I won't need him here. If it's freedom, it's just a matter of waiting for the paperwork to clear. If it's . . . well, if it's to be an appointment with the executioner, I certainly won't need him to hold my hand through that. He'll be of more use to you in Philippi. Once I'm released, I'll get to Philippi as quickly as I can."

He stopped and mentally reviewed his plan—turning it and considering the options—like a man holding up a vase to the light to check for flaws.

Satisfied after a few moments of quiet reflection, he said, "What do you think, Luke?" and looked down at the doctor seated on the floor. But the doctor was in no condition to give an opinion on Paul's plan. His eyes were closed and his chest rose and fell in a steady rhythm. Paul took the blanket from the bed, propped it around the doctor's shoulders and over his legs, and quietly left the room.

~

Epaphroditus opened his eyes and stared at the paneled ceiling above. The craftsmanship of the beaten tin and the reds and lapis blue with which the panels were adorned made him smile. As an artisan, he could appreciate good work.

And then his eyes came full open. Where was he? Snatches of the trip to Rome flooded back—the storm, the cold nights. He remembered finding Paul, but this was certainly not Paul's poor apartment. He turned his head to the room and saw Timothy's familiar face bowed over a sheaf of paper, lost in concentration. His mouth felt dry and foul, as if he'd not washed his teeth for days, and an urgent hunger clamored at him for relief.

He tried to call Timothy's name, but his mouth was a desert. So he raised a hand to catch his eye.

"Ah! So the dead have been raised!" Timothy set aside the papers and knelt by Epaphroditus's bed. "How do you feel, my friend? You had us very worried."

Epaphroditus motioned to his mouth for a cup of water. Timothy bent to a pitcher beside the bed, poured a cup, and brought it to his lips. Oh, it tasted good.

"Where am I?" he managed to croak. "What happened?"

"You have been very ill, Potter. It's been a week since you've said a sane word. I told Luke that wasn't so unusual for you. But he insisted it was the sickness. You've had high fever. Delirious ramblings." He looked at the chamber pot with a frown. "And more diarrhea than I ever hope to see again. Did you cross the Adriatic or drink it?"

Epaphroditus motioned for more water and took another long draft. He tried to lift onto his elbow and felt ten burly soldiers sitting on his chest. "Could you help me sit up?" he whispered. Timothy put an arm around his shoulders and lifted him back to lean against the arm of the couch. Even with the help, Epaphroditus barely had the strength to keep his balance. "I've been here for a week?"

"Almost. And you're lucky to be here at all. We thought you were a dead man more than once."

Epaphroditus took in the room, the expensive furnishings, the table against the wall laden with manuscripts. "Where am I?" he asked again.

"These are Luke's quarters. Pretty fancy, huh? He has a wealthy patron here in Rome, a friend of the family from the old country. You are staying in his villa." Timothy sank into the leather covering his chair. "A fellow could get used to this."

"Where's Luke?" With concentration, Epaphroditus found he could keep his head from falling on his chest.

"Luke left this morning. Headed for Philippi. Paul thought he might be able to stop the bleeding long enough to give us time to figure out what to do next."

"I'm awfully hungry, Timothy. Do you think I might get something to eat?"

"Ah, yes. Luke said you could eat as much soup as you like today. Then some beans and bread tomorrow. And maybe, if you keep everything down, a little meat the day after." He rose from the chair and helped Epaphroditus lie back down on the couch. "I'll run over to the kitchen and bring you a bowl of hot soup. You just rest."

But Epaphroditus was already asleep by the time Timothy could suggest it.

~

Epaphroditus had never tasted such delicious soup—all three bowls of it. It was mostly broth with a little well-cooked pasta floating in it. But to Epaphroditus, it tasted like ambrosia. He oohed and aahed and moaned about its flavor so much that, finally, Timothy fetched a bowl for himself.

"Paul will want to see you as soon as possible. I'm taking him supper tonight and will let him know you're back in the land of the living. But I think it'll be a few days before you're ready to make the trek to the Subura."

Epaphroditus set his soup bowl on the floor beside the bed and pulled the covers up around his shoulders. He felt stronger already. "Timothy?" His friend smiled back at him, wondering if he needed anything. "Thank you for taking care of me. I'm sorry to have been a burden."

But Timothy waved his hand in dismissal. "Think nothing of it, Epaphroditus. You would have done the same for me. We are brothers, after all."

"Yes we are." The potter smiled. "And I am very glad for it."

Timothy glanced down at the manuscript beside him. "What can we do to pass the time? I know!" he said as if the thought had just occurred to him. "Why don't I read to you? Luke has just finished his book on the life of Jesus. In fact, I'm to take it to the *scriptorium* in the next few days. Theophilus has agreed to pay for twenty-five copies. Can you imagine the expense?"

"That would be fine, Timothy. I'd like that." And Epaphroditus settled back into the couch, stomach full and pleasantly sleepy.

"Well. I'll just pick up where I left off reading." He found his place once more and, with a glance at Epaphroditus, resumed the story.

> *One of the Pharisees asked Jesus to come to his home for a meal, so Jesus accepted the invitation and sat down to eat. A certain immoral woman heard he was there and brought a beautiful jar filled with expensive perfume. Then she knelt*

behind him at his feet, weeping. Her tears fell on his feet, and she wiped them off with her hair. Then she kept kissing his feet and putting perfume on them.

When the Pharisee who was the host saw what was happening and who the woman was, he said to himself, "This proves that Jesus is no prophet. If God had really sent him, he would know what kind of woman is touching him. She's a sinner!"

Timothy looked over the top of the manuscript to see that Epaphroditus was fast asleep again. "Well, Luke," he muttered to himself. "I hope the rest of your readers are more appreciative."

Chapter Sixteen

TO ALL OF GOD'S PEOPLE IN PHILIPPI

(FEBRUARY, A.D. 62)

WHILE LUKE MADE HIS HAZARDOUS AND UNCOMFORTABLE WAY TO Philippi . . . while Paul fretted and fumed in his anxiety for the Philippians, pacing and praying for hours on end . . . while Timothy sat by the bedside and read Luke's story of Jesus, losing himself so in the reading that he could forget about Philippi for stretches of time . . . Epaphroditus, the potter from Philippi, slowly found his strength again. Lying on the couch, bundled warmly under rich blankets, Epaphroditus slept and let his body heal. He woke on occasion to eat and attend to his toilet (an act of independence that Timothy invariably cheered), but soon pulled up the blankets again to drift off into the waiting arms of healing and strength-giving slumber.

By the third day, he began to feel restless and impatient with the confines of his couch. Leaning on Timothy's arm, Epaphroditus made his unsteady way around the room and, later, to the front gate of the villa and, later still, down the road to a point overlooking the Subura and Paul's apartment. After each expedition, he would crawl under the blankets exhausted and wake, after a few hours, with ravenous appetite.

By the fifth day, he told Timothy he was strong enough for a visit to see Paul. Timothy glanced up from his reading and fixed the potter with an amused look and a raised eyebrow. "It's not the trip there I'm worried about. It's the trip back. Be patient, Epaphroditus. A couple more days."

And so he slept and ate and walked. And by the seventh day, when God had rested from all his labors, Timothy judged Epaphroditus strong enough to resume his.

~

The three of them sat in Paul's room—Paul on the stool, Timothy and Epaphroditus side by side on the pallet with their backs to the wall.

"Tell me about Simeon," Paul began. "What is he teaching? Why is he a problem?"

And Epaphroditus commenced the unburdening. He'd waited for this so long, looked forward to it so much, that he almost faltered for a starting point when the time came. But then the story began to flow, piece piling on top of piece, and there was no more fear of faltering. He talked quietly, trying to lay out the story in clear, understandable segments. He spoke calmly, telling the story without emphasis or emotion, determined to be as factual as possible. Sometimes he closed his eyes to see a scene more clearly. Sometimes he gestured to indicate where people sat or to mimic their motions. But mostly, he just talked.

Even as his mouth moved and the words poured, a part of Epaphroditus—the watchful part—took note of how good the telling felt. Each sentence was a release for him, each word a comfort. He was breathing again after holding his breath for so long. Paul was taking the story from him, and Epaphroditus handed it over with gratitude.

For his part, Paul guided the story with careful listening and an occasional question. There were times he had to slow the telling, pausing the story to probe some detail or ask Epaphroditus to flesh out a scene more carefully. At times, he tried to speed up the pace and keep the story moving. But mostly, he sat in silence, taking the story as it came, using it to fill in the gaps left by the letters.

It went on like this for two days: Epaphroditus trotting out a piece of the story; Paul turning it over and over and asking further questions; Epaphroditus trying to explain or dig deeper to satisfy Paul's curiosity. On occasion, Paul reached into the stack of letters, found a paragraph, and read it aloud. The words often gave a different interpretation to events or even contradicted the potter's story. And Paul would watch Epaphroditus carefully as he struggled to harmonize the disagreements. It was grueling work for all of them. But they all knew what was at stake.

On the evening of the second day, Paul rose from his stool and stretched his back once again. He stood contemplating the dark square of the window overlooking his room. And then he asked Timothy and Epaphroditus not to return the next day. "In fact, don't come back for a while," he told them. He motioned toward the Philippian. "Take him to see the sights, Timothy. Introduce him to some of the other brothers in the city. But keep yourselves busy for the next few days."

He looked back at the window, and seemed to see through it to a place far away. "I need some time alone."

~

"Far away" was a place Paul went easily and for a variety of reasons. When he fought the black moods that descended unpredictably, he always experienced a certain detachment, a distance from the present and the tangible. He sometimes felt it in worship, a sense that he was "caught up"—or, more accurately, "caught away." He could not say where he went at such moments, but he knew it was somewhere other than "here." It happened when the time for suffering came, when he heard the punishment pronounced or watched the anger rise to a certain pitch. He learned to move away from the "near" at those times . . . to draw within or step to the side so the pain was bearable.

But never did this distance, this separation, come over him so strongly as when he wrote. For reasons he could not explain, the burden of being an apostle was especially acute whenever he took up a pen. The written word seemed to matter more, to weigh more, than the spoken. Perhaps he felt this because he cared so deeply about the recipients of his letters and wanted his words to be right. Perhaps he sensed that his written words were pored over and scrutinized to a degree his spoken words were not. Most of all—as a man of learning who'd lived with books all his life—Paul understood that written words took on a life of their own, that they often survived their author and found audiences never intended or imagined.

As a result, he always approached writing with great seriousness . . . and deep humility . . . and a heightened sense of God's purposes. The words he committed to paper needed to be God's words. He saw his letters as containers for the thoughts and ideas of Another.

So Paul found it necessary to withdraw himself from the press of the present whenever the time for writing arrived, to find a "far place" where he could first commune deeply with God. From his earliest apostolic writing, Paul observed a ritual for his writing that served him well over the years.

It was to this ritual that Paul turned now.

First came the fasting. For three days, Paul practiced physically what he hoped to achieve in spirit—the body playing schoolmaster to the soul. He limited what went into his stomach (only water) even as his focus narrowed and he deliberately constricted the range of thoughts permitted to enter his heart and mind. He purged his bowels—emptying himself, cleansing himself—to demonstrate physically his readiness, his room, for a spiritual filling. As the time passed and his body stilled, Paul concentrated on quieting his spirit, preparing it for the meeting to come.

On the third day, he stood in the middle of his room, stripped off his clothing, and washed himself according to the ways of his people. In better circumstances, Paul would have performed this cleansing at a synagogue, in an immersion pool dedicated to such ceremonies. But, under house arrest in Rome, a basin of cold water and a sponge were the best he could do. Starting at his feet and ending with his head and hands, Paul washed every part of himself, humming the ancient purification prayers as he scrubbed.

By the time he finished, Paul was trembling. He moved to the foot of his pallet and took a clean loincloth from the meager stack of linen folded there. Wrapping it under and around himself, he moved to the corner of the room where the gifts from Philippi were stashed. He reached for the tunic sent by Syntyche, held it to his face briefly—smelling the fabric and the soap still in it—and then put it on and cinched it tight around his waist. He put on his cloak and wrapped a blanket from the bed around his shoulders and, at last, the cold began to recede.

Three days, and Paul was empty and calm and clean before the Lord. With the physical ritual completed, Paul turned fully to the more difficult, inward work. Difficult because it *was* inward. Difficult because, though very real, it lacked substance.

Judaism had always been a religion of "place." Paul reflected on the importance of burning bushes and Sinai, altars and holy ground, tabernacle and temple in the long history of his people—places where his forefathers had gone to meet with God. He envied the solidity of those places, their palpable reality. He longed for a Sinai of his own, where he could approach God's presence and bring God's word down to the people. But in the religion of Jesus, heart supplanted place as surely as grace replaced law. From long experience, Paul knew that his communion with God would happen "within," not "here" or "there."

And so, as the light faded in his window and the busy noises of the day gave way to the cries and raucous laughter of the night, Paul reached for that "far place," that quiet corner of his soul where he withdrew to meet with God. He sat on the stool, eyes closed and lips moving in silent meditations. He prayed for hours . . . no requests or pleadings or supplications . . . just reaching and seeking.

Late in the night, after the revelers had stumbled to bed and the guard in the next room had snored his way into a deep sleep, Paul opened his soul to God and began the dialogue upon which his writing depended.

As usual, the conversation began with Paul's words. He poured out his worries about Philippi, the troubles they faced, the threats he saw to the gospel and to the church. He lay before God the problem as he understood it and the remedies he thought were needed. He did this not because God required information about events in Philippi, but because Paul needed confirmation (or correction) of his own understanding of those events. He lifted up pieces of the Philippian puzzle to God and listened for the Spirit to question and probe and test what he knew. He felt like Jacob long ago, wrestling with the angel of the

Lord, straining through the night to gain a blessing. It was exhausting work.

Finally, just before morning dawned and the city awakened outside his window, Paul fell silent, passing the conversation to God and listening to be filled with his words. He approached these holy moments with anticipation, eager for the touch of God in his mind, but never quite sure what to expect. What would God give him this time?

Sometimes, words burst upon him with such force and clarity that he knew those words must appear in the letter about to be written. Often he heard not words but ideas and themes, a bare melody the Apostle was expected to support with harmonies of his own. And there were times—like this morning—when all he received was an overwhelming sense of peace, a divine endorsement of the words and ideas that had already formed in his thoughts.

He looked at the lightening window and greeted the day in his usual manner. "In the morning, O Lord, you hear my voice. In the morning I lay my requests before you and wait in expectation." And a broad smile chased away the fatigue of the night and the weight of the past few days.

~

Once again, the three of them gathered in Paul's quarters—Timothy and Epaphroditus in their usual places on the pallet, Paul perched on his stool or pacing in manic fashion around the room. To the secret delight of the two seated on the floor, Paul was displaying the full range of idiosyncrasies that made up the Apostle's legend—the tilted walk, the waving hands, the voice that started low but rose in volume and pitch as he grew more excited, the pauses to straighten his back, the open palm resting on his bald pate. Each of them had seen friends of Paul mimic these mannerisms, to the howling delight of audiences who knew Paul well.

But never when Paul was present. Now all the two of them could do was watch with glowing eyes while hiding smiles behind their hands.

"Later this afternoon, we will get to the actual writing. Timothy, I want you to be my *amanuensis*. We'll use this fancy pen and paper

Epaphroditus hauled all the way from Philippi." He paused and shook his head, and Epaphroditus almost laughed at the predictable response. "We have to find some way to put such baubles to good use. What a ridiculous waste of coin!" But even as he said it, he picked up the writing pouch from the table and fondled its soft leather.

He resumed his pacing. "Epaphroditus! You'll be reading this letter to the Philippians. They will have questions for you and will depend on you for answers. So I want you here while I dictate to Timothy. And I want you to understand what I'm writing and why." His hands punched the air for emphasis. And then he paused to unkink his back. Timothy had to look away.

"Any questions?" Both of them shook "no" from behind their hands.

"Very well. Let me talk through the main ideas we need to address. Epaphroditus, you listen closely. People often get lost in the words of a letter. They can't see the ocean for the waves. Your job will be to make sure the Philippians don't miss the basic points I want to make. Although," and here Paul placed the flat of his palm on his head, as though he were preventing his head from floating away, "people have an amazing capacity to hear what they want and ignore what is actually said." He pursed his lips momentarily and then forged ahead.

"First of all, the Philippians need to know that problems and suffering are a normal part of our lives in Christ. Faith doesn't protect us from pain. In fact"—and he stretched his back again unconsciously—"it opens us to suffering we could otherwise avoid." He pulled at his lower lip as he spoke. "The pain they feel now is not a sign of God's disfavor. It is a testing, a measuring of their faith. Can they handle themselves as God's people even when they hurt?" Paul pounded a fist into his open palm, a hammer nailing fast his point. "I'll share some of my struggles with them—what it's like to be caged up in this apartment for two years, to be on trial for your life. I need to remind them of the sufferings of Jesus and how he stayed faithful through them all. I may even speak of your sickness, Epaphroditus; your suffering for the cause." And he looked at the young potter thoughtfully for a moment.

"Next, our Philippian brothers need to hear what it means to live the gospel when things get tough. And it is precisely here that they are struggling." He fixed his two listeners with a look of such seriousness, such intensity, that it burned away whatever mirth they still felt. He held his arms out to his sides, fists closed. "There are two things that pain tempts us to let go of: our commitment to Christ," and he opened one hand, "or our commitment to each other." He opened the other. "It tempts us to fall away or fall apart. Happens every time," Paul assured the two of them.

"Now, from what the letters tell me, and what you've said yourself, my son"—Paul nodded at Epaphroditus—"letting go of faith doesn't appear to be your most serious problem." Epaphroditus agreed. "Still, I think it would be helpful to debunk some of Simeon's teaching, to state flatly that nothing besides Christ and the Cross matters." He shook his head in exasperation. "So help me, there are times I think some of my countrymen care more about circumcision than salvation. They're less concerned about Gentile souls than about Gentile foreskins!" And, again, the palm pressed flat on his head, a vain attempt to contain his frustration.

"The immediate danger, however"—Paul looked at Epaphroditus for confirmation—"is the church coming unraveled. Let me see if I understand the situation correctly." He ticked off the items on his fingers. "We have people behaving selfishly and not thinking about others. We have complaining and arguing going on in the church. There is a distance growing between these brothers and sisters because they don't trust each other like they once did. The elders are being criticized for their handling of the Simeon situation. Euodia and Syntyche"—and here Paul's voice caught slightly—"are not even speaking to each other. How did I do, Epaphroditus?"

"That's about it, Paul. That, and the fact that no one is finding much joy in any of it anymore."

"Yes, yes." Paul waved at him distractedly. "I'll come to that in a moment." He paused and then took up a conversation with himself; a quieter, more reflective tone to his voice. "I really expected better of the Philippians than this. They should know that you cling to each other most when things get hard. That's what they did in the early days. Why is it so different now?"

Epaphroditus started to answer, and then saw by the look on Paul's face that the question was enough for now. It hung between them.

"I guess they'll just have to learn some basics over again. Like forgiveness and humility. Like compassion and the importance of unity. I'll need to stress those things in the letter." Paul looked down sadly, a great weight bearing on him, making his shoulders droop and his hands hang still, for once, at his side. "I thought they'd learned those lessons. Of all of my churches, I thought they understood."

And the sadness was so heavy on him, Epaphroditus felt burdened by it from across the room. He could see it etched in the lines of Paul's face and the contours of his worn body. He wanted to move to Paul, to relieve some portion of the melancholy. He realized all over again how much Philippi meant to the Apostle, how he counted on the health of this church. He felt he was forever doomed to watch loved ones suffer and be helpless to offer comfort.

But Paul would not permit the luxury of sadness for long. Not if he could help it. With a visible effort, he shrugged off his despondency and turned his attention back to the task at hand.

"They need a reminder about the attitude of Christ Jesus. They need to hear again the story of his sacrifice and selflessness." As he spoke, his head came up and his companions saw hope lighting his face. "This letter needs to call them to humility and service—Christ lived out, in the way they treat each other. That's what they need!" And the smile returned. "A good dose of the mind of Jesus."

He closed his eyes and saw the letter spread out before him—the grand themes, and the practical teachings that made the themes helpful. He saw how he would connect the ideas, how he would take suffering and tie it to the mind of Christ and use that to encourage the Philippian church in its faith and in its fellowship. There was only one other idea to talk about, one more color to weave into the fabric of this letter.

"Joy!" Paul's eyes popped open and fixed the younger men. "They *have* lost their joy, Epaphroditus. It's written all over their letters. They are anxious and afraid and wounded and confused. What they are *not* is joyful! Wouldn't you agree?" But Paul was not looking for confirmation. He rushed on before Epaphroditus could say anything. "It is one of the hardest things to learn about following Jesus. I struggle with it still after thirty years as a disciple. Listen up, men." Paul moved to the pallet and sat down on the floor in front of his companions, leaning forward in his eagerness to share a hard-won wisdom.

"Some will tell you that joy is an elusive thing, coming and going with the tides of fate. They connect joy to pleasant circumstance and good fortune. When all is well, joy breaks out. But when life turns dark, joy fades. I think our brothers in Philippi have listened to such ideas." Paul looked from one man to the other. Epaphroditus felt the hair rise on the back of his neck as a memory from the boat, a sermon he preached in a dream, came flooding back. This was his sermon! Coming out of Paul's mouth! How could that be?

"I have learned from my years in Christ that *his* joy does not vary with circumstance. It is a deep constant that transcends the troubles of the day or changes in fortune. Christ's joy grows in the soil of contentment and character and commitment. When we learn to be content, whatever our circumstances . . . when we conform our character to Christ . . . when we remember our commitment and live out our calling . . . nothing can take our joy away. Not trouble. Not disappointment. Not Satan himself." The Apostle's eyes were shining.

He sat back and smiled, a little self-conscious about the intensity of this moment. Timothy stared at him, aware that he'd just been given a precious thing, a part of Paul that others did not often see. And Epaphroditus sat stunned, realizing that in the words of the Apostle and the words of his dream, he had received a message he desperately, urgently, utterly needed.

~

Timothy sat on the stool at the table, clean white pages spread before him, and the bronze pen resting sumptuously between his fingers. He could not take his eyes off it. Epaphroditus lay on the pallet, hands behind his head, still meditating on the meaning of the dream and Paul's words. As for Paul, he hovered behind Timothy, hands on the young man's shoulders, waiting for the preparations to be finished.

"Very well, Paul." Timothy turned his head. "I'm ready now. Go slowly, please." He knew his pleadings were pointless.

"I will." And Paul patted his shoulder in reassurance. Lifting his eyes to the ceiling, he whispered a prayer and began.

"Paul and Timothy"—he squeezed Timothy's shoulders—"both of us committed servants of Christ Jesus, write this letter to all the Christians in Philippi, pastors and ministers included. We greet you with the grace and peace that comes from God our Father and our Master, Jesus Christ."

The nib of Timothy's pen flowed smoothly across the polished surface of the paper. The rich black ink stood sharp and crisp against the page, not blotting and blurring like cheaper inks on cheaper paper. He looked proudly at his penmanship. *Expensive or not,* Timothy chuckled to himself, *this makes writing a pleasure.*

But Paul was not waiting for Timothy to admire his work. "Every time I think of you, I thank my God. And whenever I mention you in my prayers, it makes me happy. This is because you have taken part with me—"

"Wait! Wait, Paul. You're going too fast! I can't keep up if you don't pause once in a while. At least take a breath," Timothy begged. They'd just begun and already he was behind.

Paul started again patiently, slower. "You have taken part with me in spreading the good news from the first day you heard about it." Pause. "God is the one who began this good work in you"—he paused once more—"and I am certain that he won't stop before it is complete on the day that Christ Jesus returns."

"That's right, you know," he spoke now to Epaphroditus. "I've never had one doubt that God was doing something very special in Philippi. And you, my son," he added fondly, "are part of what I love about God's work there."

Timothy looked up from his writing in alarm. "Did you want that in the letter, Paul?"

"No, no!" And he hurried over to read what Timothy had written, bending close to the paper and stabbing a finger at the words to be marked out. Reluctantly, mourning how clean the writing was to that point, Timothy crossed through the last few words he'd printed.

With a nod from Timothy, Paul continued. "You have a special place in my heart. So it is only natural for me to feel the way I do." He thought back to the rods, to Lydia's tender care, to the worried and heartbroken friends who told him goodbye that day. "All of you have helped in the work that God has given me, as I defend the good news and tell about it here in jail." He waited for Timothy's pen to catch up. When he spoke again, his voice was subdued, guttural. "God himself knows how much I want to see you. He knows that I care for you in the same way that Christ Jesus does."

Timothy finished the sentence and waited for Paul's next thought. But Paul seemed content to wait with him for a few moments, to savor the memories and mourn the distance that separated him from these people.

"I pray," he continued abruptly, "that your love for each other will overflow more and more, and that you will keep on growing in your knowledge and understanding." Even in dictation, Paul could not keep his hands still. They waved and poked and flexed. They seemed especially responsive to adjectives. "For I want you to understand what really matters, so that you may live pure and blameless lives until Christ returns." He stopped and let Timothy scribble. "May you always be filled with the fruit of your salvation—those good things that are produced in your life by Jesus Christ—for this will bring much glory and praise to God."

He paced until Timothy finished and then took the page from him and read it over closely. The winter light filtering through the window was weak and Paul read with his nose almost touching the paper. He squinted at the page for a moment, looked up reflectively, then dipped his head to read more. "Very good," he pronounced, handing the page back to Timothy. "Now let's tell them a little about Rome and our circumstances. I want them to hear how God has used a prison to let me preach the gospel. I want them to realize that our troubles can be useful to God."

He cocked his head for a moment, gathering the words, and then began once more. "I want to report to you, friends, that my imprisonment here has had the opposite of its intended effect. Instead of being squelched, the Message has actually prospered. All the soldiers here, and everyone else too, found out that I'm in jail because of this Messiah." Timothy lifted his left hand, holding Paul off until he got the words down. As he waited, Paul thought of Rufus, of the conversations leading the old soldier to uncertain ground, of the conversations yet to come. He smiled a mischievous smile. He had Rufus right where he wanted him.

Timothy signaled his readiness to continue. "That piqued their curiosity," Paul continued, "and now they've learned all about him. Not only that, but most of the Christians here have become far more sure of themselves in the faith than ever, speaking out fearlessly about God, about the Messiah." He put his hand on Timothy's shoulder and said, "Stop there for a moment."

He crossed the room to look down at Epaphroditus. "I'm about to touch on something in the letter you need to know about. Even here, I have people who try to wound me from one side of their mouth while they talk about Jesus with the other. Like Simeon, they preach Jesus but they also preach Moses. And they're taking advantage of my confinement to spread their version of the gospel." Paul sat on the pallet beside the potter and smiled ruefully. "My being locked up here has been the greatest incentive for evangelism in the history of this city! I can't go into all of this in the letter. You'll have to supply some of the details when you get back to Philippi. But I want the church to know that I understand what they're dealing with. I know what it's like to be excluded by people who claim Jesus as Lord."

He looked up at Timothy and motioned toward the table, ready to dictate a few more lines. "It's true that some here preach Christ because with me out of the way, they think they'll step right onto center stage. But the others do it with the best heart in the world." He paused and showed that rueful smile to Epaphroditus once again. "One group is motivated by pure love, knowing that I am here defending the Message, wanting to help." He closed his eyes, choosing his words carefully, not wanting to be too caustic in his description of his rivals but needing to leak some of his pain and disappointment to the Philippians. "The others, now that I'm out of the picture, are merely greedy, hoping to get something out of it for themselves. Their motives are bad. They see me as their competition, and so the worse it goes for me, the better—they think—for them."

He looked at Epaphroditus with a broad grin and jumped to his feet again, pacing and moving, the excitement building inside him.

He wagged his eyebrows at the potter and said under his breath, "Now comes the good part!"

"Here we go again, Timothy. Are you ready?" Timothy waved him on. "So how am I to respond? I've decided that I really don't care about their motives, whether mixed, bad, or indifferent. Every time one of them opens his mouth, Christ is proclaimed, so I just cheer them on." He looked at Epaphroditus and beamed. "Do you see it, Epaphroditus? God always takes problems and uses them for good. I go to jail and God gives me a whole new audience to tell about Jesus. God uses people who want to hurt me to spread the good news even further. I'm under house arrest and I can't think of a time I've been more productive for the kingdom!" Paul shook his head and laughed.

Catching Timothy's eye, he continued. "And I'm going to keep that celebration going because I know how it's going to turn out. Through your faithful prayers and the generous response of the Spirit of Jesus Christ, everything he wants to do in and through me will be done." He paused, both hands palm down on his head, barely able to contain the elation, the anticipation, he felt. He waited as long as he could stand it. And then the words spilled out of him, too urgent to show any regard for Timothy's tired hand. "I can hardly wait to continue on my course. I don't expect to be embarrassed in the least. On the contrary, everything happening to me in this jail only serves to make Christ more accurately known, regardless of whether I live or die. They didn't shut me up; they gave me a pulpit! To me the only important thing about living is Christ, and dying would be profit for me."

He finally caught himself and stopped while Timothy frantically scribbled. But Timothy could not get it all. "To me? What comes next?"

And Paul repeated himself more slowly, savoring the words, comforting himself as he hoped the Philippians would be comforted. "To me the only important thing about living is Christ, and dying would be profit for me." While Timothy caught up, Paul bowed his head and worshiped.

When he heard the pen's scratching stop, Paul looked up to see the light beginning to fade in his window. It was time for supper and he knew Rufus would be impatient for his evening meal. They could continue this tomorrow.

"Let's finish for the evening," he suggested. Timothy, massaging his cramping hand, heartily agreed. Paul gave him a sympathetic smile and asked, "Can you manage just a few more lines?"

Paul stared back at the window, composing himself, thinking of what he needed to say. "As long as I'm alive in this body, there is good work for me to do. If I had to choose right now, I hardly know which I'd choose. Hard choice!" He became very conscious at that moment of the ache in his back, the limits of his sight. He felt the cold and the fatigue. He went on softly. "The desire to break camp here and be with Christ is powerful. Some days I can think of nothing better." He paused once more, listening to the pen on paper, letting his thoughts turn to Clement and the others. "But most days, because of what you are going through, I am sure that it's better for me to stick it out here." He looked at Epaphroditus and shrugged. Ah, well.

"So I plan to be around for a while, companion to you as your growth and joy in this life of trusting God continues. You can start looking forward to a great reunion when I come visit you again. We'll be praising Christ, enjoying each other." And again Epaphroditus saw the faraway look come over him and knew he was back in Philippi, hugging people he loved, touching the faces of people he would die for . . . people who would die for him. Paul's eyes welled up.

"Meanwhile, live in such a way that you are a credit to the Message of Christ. Let nothing in your conduct hang on whether I come or not. Your conduct must be the same whether I show up to see things for myself or hear of it from a distance." He paused, and Epaphroditus wondered what it would be like to live with such uncertainty, to be unable to make definite plans, to be waiting and waiting, your life in the balance.

Paul began to pace again, his hands moving, an edge to his voice. "Stand united, singular in vision, contending for people's trust in the Message, the good news, not flinching or dodging in the slightest before the opposition. Your courage and unity will show them what they're up against: defeat for them, victory for you—and both because of God."

He came to a stop in front of Epaphroditus, his back to Timothy, and locked eyes with his young friend. He spoke the last words as much to Epaphroditus as to the Philippians. "There's far more to this life than trusting in Christ. There's also suffering for him. And the suffering is as much a gift as the trusting. You're involved in the same kind of struggle you saw me go through, on which you are now getting an updated report in this letter."

He raised an eyebrow at Epaphroditus, questioning. The potter looked at the old man for a long while, then nodded and said simply, "I understand."

Chapter Seventeen

I MUST SEND HIM BACK TO YOU

(MARCH, A.D. 62)

ALL HIS LIFE, IT SEEMED, HE'D BEEN HAUNTED BY THE PRESENCE OF PEOPLE no longer there.

His father, gone before Epaphroditus was born, was kept alive through his childhood by the memories and stories of his mother. She loved to tell tales at bedtime in which his father played hero and strode larger-than-life through the streets of Philippi. Looking back, he knew the stories were fables . . . knew somehow that he'd always known that. But they seemed so real to him at the time that, through them, he could hear his father's voice and see his brave smile. To a young boy growing up fatherless, an imagined father was better than none at all.

His mother, gone when he was still a child, lingered on in his own memories and in stories he told himself. He held to those when he could no longer hold to her, drawing strength and warding off fears by conjuring her presence in his mind's eye and watching her as she silently watched him. Through his youth, he found that a remembered mother, like an imagined father, was better than none at all.

In certain ways, she was hard to hang onto—the shape of her face dimming with time, the sound of her voice fading. Yet she still appeared in his dreams on occasion and would surprise him in the smile of a stranger or with a whiff of perfume in the market.

In the same way, his spiritual childhood had been haunted by the distant presence of Paul. Gone before Epaphroditus was born into Christ, Paul lingered in the memories and stories of the disciples at Philippi. He reached across the years and the miles to shape the church, his teaching and example still alive, perhaps more powerful, in his absence. Paul was talked about and quoted, remembered and remarked on, so often that Epaphroditus felt he knew the man before he actually met him.

And when they *did* meet and Epaphroditus got to spend a remarkable week with Paul—when he finally put a face to the legend and saw the scars peeking out from the neck of his tunic—it was as though the dead had been raised and a ghost had become flesh. To be able to touch the Apostle, to ask questions and hear a reply, to watch him as he preached—it all had a dreamlike feel, a hint of unreality. Epaphroditus spent those days with the certain knowledge that this could not last.

And, of course, he was right. Like all apparitions, the time came for Paul to fade once more into the mists of memory. Standing on the outskirts of Philippi, watching Paul's back as he marched off toward Achaia, Epaphroditus felt an acute sense of loss, of abandonment. He surprised himself with a hot flush of anger. Why couldn't Paul stay? What was so urgent in Corinth that he couldn't linger a little longer in Philippi? It was then that Epaphroditus, the orphan, understood that imagination and memory may indeed be better than nothing. But they weren't better than the thing itself. Not by a long shot.

Now he was in Rome, spending a part of every day with Paul, learning and growing, gaining confidence even as his body regained strength. Yet still he felt haunted by the presence of people who were not there. He found that his thoughts turned increasingly to Clement and Lydia, to Marcion and Syntyche, to Lucian and the rest. He consoled himself by dwelling on them in memory, telling stories about them, tracing their faces in his mind and hearing their voices. But such shadows were not reality. More and more, he grew impatient with the remembrance of those he loved. He wanted to hold them and laugh with them and struggle with them.

He wanted to go home.

~

They finished the letter two days later—Paul pacing, Timothy writing, Epaphroditus listening and receiving an occasional aside from Paul. Besides Paul's nervous striding and Timothy's moving hand, none of them had expended much physical energy. Yet they commented at the end how weary they felt, like they'd spent the days hauling rock.

Timothy turned on the stool with the pages in his hand. *Not many to show for so much effort,* he thought to himself. He stared at the pages, just words on paper, and thought as he stared how important words could be. Epaphroditus had risked his life to fetch these words. He would risk it again carrying them to Philippi. There the words would take on new life—changing hearts, guiding behavior, prodding and provoking and persuading. Paul would preach with these words, touching audiences who could not hear his voice. Timothy thought of it all and shook his head in amazement.

"Why don't you read back the closing part, Timothy?" Paul leaned against the wall, letting the cold numb some of the burning in his back. He closed his eyes to focus on the voice, ready to hear the words and think how they would sound to the Philippians.

Timothy looked back a page, seeking the place, and began to read. "I am very happy in the Lord that you have shown your care for me again." Timothy read carefully, giving each word its due. "You continued to care about me, but there was no way for you to show it. I am not telling you this because I need anything. I have learned to be satisfied with the things I have and with everything that happens. I know how to live when I am poor, and I know how to live when I have plenty. I have learned the secret of being happy at any time in everything that happens, when I have enough to eat and when I go hungry, when I have more than I need and when I do not have enough. I can do all things through Christ, because he gives me strength."

Paul hung on the words, weighing them, testing their sound, praying that they would prove adequate to their task.

"But it was good that you helped me when I needed it. You Philippians remember when I first preached the Good News there.

When I left Macedonia, you were the only church that gave me help. Several times you sent me things I needed when I was in Thessalonica. Really, it is not that I want to receive gifts from you, but I want you to have the good that comes from giving."

Paul's eyes opened. "Epaphroditus. You must bear down on that point. Make sure they know how grateful I am for their help, now and in the past. And make sure they understand that what means more to me than the help is their *partnership,* their willingness to stand by me." He looked away for a moment and said quietly, "I don't have many people I can count on like that."

Timothy looked at Paul. "Here's the last part: And now I have everything, and more. I have all I need, because Epaphroditus brought your gift to me. It is like a sweet-smelling sacrifice offered to God, who accepts that sacrifice and is pleased with it. My God will use his wonderful riches in Christ Jesus to give you everything you need. Glory to our God and Father forever and ever! Amen.

"Give our regards to every Christian you meet. Our friends here say hello. All the Christians here, especially the believers who work in the palace of Caesar, want to be remembered to you.

"Receive and experience the amazing grace of the Master, Jesus Christ, deep, deep within yourselves."

Paul stood against the wall a little longer, letting the last sentence echo around the room, until he pushed himself away and said, "Good!" He took the pages from Timothy's hands, leafed through them quickly, and then placed them on the table with the scrolls and letters and writing utensils. "Now we let it age for a bit. We set it aside a few days, then see how it sounds when we read it later." His eyes twinkled. "I haven't always done that. There've been a couple of letters I sent off too quickly. Too much heat!" He tapped the letter with his fingertips and looked steadily at Epaphroditus. "We'll let this sit for a while. You're not well enough to travel anyway."

~

It is one thing to put a friend on a boat during the winter season when the need is great and the cause is urgent. Paul had sent Luke by sea to Philippi without a twinge of conscience—he was needed there, immediately.

But to put Epaphroditus in the same danger, to make him face again the rigors of a winter crossing on the Adriatic, made no sense to Paul. Luke was there and, no doubt, already hard at work smoothing the church's ruffled feathers. There simply wasn't the same urgency.

And so, in spite of Epaphroditus's rising eagerness to get home, Paul held off his departure until the end of March. *Let him recover,* he thought to himself. *More time to prepare him for when he gets home.* A few more weeks and the worst of the winter weather would be over. And then he could safely follow Luke's trail—by foot to Brundisium, a ship through the Gulf of Corinth to Lechuion, and from there the long road to Philippi.

In the meantime, Timothy made a careful copy of the letter to the Philippians. "In case you end up at the bottom of the sea!" he teased Epaphroditus. "Of course, if that happens, I'll have to rewrite the part about welcoming you home."

And Paul had the potter read the letter, out loud, over and over. "The first time they hear this will be when you read it to them, my son. So read it well. Speak out! Say it like you mean it!"

Epaphroditus walked with Timothy around the city. He met with some of the house churches on the Lord's Day. He went with Timothy to deliver Luke's manuscript to the *scriptorium*. He ate and slept and gathered strength for the journey.

But mostly he passed the days in Paul's room. Talking. About anything and everything. About people and places, the past and the future. They talked about the gospel of grace and Roman politics and Greek philosophers. Paul told stories of the early days and of his ongoing battle with his own countrymen. He spoke quietly of men he'd teamed with through the years: Barnabas and Silas, Titus and Tychicus.

Every once in a while—late of an afternoon, perhaps, and almost casually—Paul would pause from his storytelling long enough to reveal something so intimate, so personal, it stilled Timothy and Epaphroditus into silence. Like a door opening onto some private chamber, Paul would speak frankly of regrets and disappointments. He confessed struggles and sins. He talked of loneliness as if it were an intimate companion. He wondered whether his work would matter ten years after his death.

And then the door would close, and Paul would change the subject, and the two of them would be left to ponder what they'd just heard.

It took Epaphroditus a while to understand what was happening. Only near the end did he realize that Paul was talking "in case." In case the trial did not go well. In case his scarred body refused to keep going. In case, at some future time, a ship foundered beneath him and he slipped beneath the waves. Paul needed to share his story, to take his worries and ideas and experiences and place them for safekeeping in the minds of younger men. And so he talked and said things few others had ever heard him say.

Epaphroditus was reminded of something Lydia once told him. "We are all two people. The public and the private. The person we share with others and the one we keep to ourselves." She'd asked him to listen for the private man.

So he did.

~

They packed the pages of the letter into the leather writing case. Paul even made Timothy tie the bronze pen back into its pouch and include it with the ink bottles and blank paper. He took the case from Timothy and helped Epaphroditus find a safe place for it in his knapsack. "Give the writing supplies to Clement when you get home. And tell him I never want to see another stained mess like his last letter again!" He paused and smiled. "After you embrace him for me, of course. After you tell him how much he is missed."

Paul seemed nervous, awkward. Letting Epaphroditus go was hard. Not going himself was hard. "Do you have plenty of coin? Are you taking a blanket?" Epaphroditus tied his knapsack closed, letting Paul fuss and worry, knowing he found some comfort in it.

"Timothy will guide you through the city and make sure you find the right road. Do we need to go over your route again?" The potter just shook his head "no" and shouldered the bag.

The three of them stood in the room, tongue-tied and ill at ease. There was nothing more to say, yet each of them felt the press of too much left unsaid. They stood together, staring at the floor, embarrassed by the moment.

Finally, Paul stepped forward and placed a hand on Epaphroditus's head. "Father of Mercies. We commit our brother into your hands. We ask that you speed his journey, protect his life, and bring him safely to Philippi. May the letter he carries work peace among your people there. In all things, your will be done." Timothy and Epaphroditus spoke the "Amen."

Paul kissed Epaphroditus on the cheek, eyes brimming, chin trembling. "Go with God, my son."

The three of them crowded into the next room, where Rufus sat impassively on the bed. "Goodbye, Rufus," Epaphroditus said. "Take care of Paul."

"Take care of Paul?" The old soldier laughed. "Paul has someone higher up than me looking out for him!"

"Do you think so, Rufus?" Paul was never one to miss an opportunity.

Rufus growled, "Don't start with me, old man." But he wished Epaphroditus a safe trip all the same. And he promised to do what he could to watch over Paul.

They piled onto the landing and Paul watched the two of them descend the stairs, exchanging one more farewell with Epaphroditus for good measure. He stared at the empty landing below him and thought of other empty places, of so many other people he'd said goodbye to over the years.

All his life, it seemed, he'd been haunted by the absence of people he wished were there.

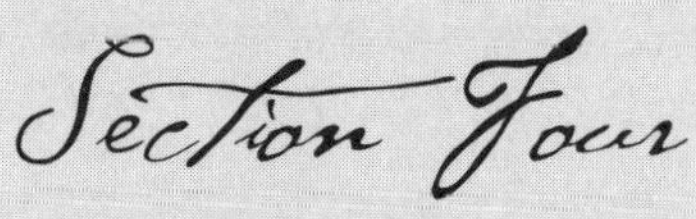

THE RESPONSE

SPRING, A.D. 62

Chapter Eighteen

GIVE HIM A GRAND WELCOME

(LATE APRIL, A.D. 62)

IT WAS LONG PAST SUNSET BY THE TIME EPAPHRODITUS TOPPED THE FINAL rise above his hometown once more. The city stretched out beneath him, becalmed in a dark sea of fields and forest. The lights of Philippi—lanterns and candles brightening her windows, fires flickering in her courtyards—blinked like muted stars against the black mass of buildings and roads. Low clouds scudded across the moonless sky, obscuring and then revealing the great swath of stars that looked down on the Datos Plain. The mountains to the north formed a solid ebony band between the sparkles of the city and the intermittent twinkling of the sky. Yet even the dark mountains glimmered from time to time, the high snow taking up the light from above and below and reflecting it back toward the cold traveler standing above the city.

It was a moment to be savored.

Briefly, of course. Already the cold was seeping through Epaphroditus's boots and sending tremors down his legs and arms. Movement was warmth, and he could not afford to stand still on this rise, relishing this moment, for long.

Nor did he *want* to remain there long, isolated above the city, separated from the people he'd journeyed so far to rejoin. The urging that for many weeks simmered just below the surface now boiled up within him and spilled over into an insistent, pressing need to run to Philippi, knock on familiar doors, and throw arms around the first brother or sister to answer.

But Epaphroditus resisted the urge, choosing instead to stand suspended there between the journey and the destination, between the loneliness of the way and the welcome of friends, between the memories of Paul and the anticipation of homecoming. He felt the knapsack pressing between his shoulder blades and thought of the letter carried there. He realized, in some certain but undefined way, that things could not be the same now. The journey had changed him, had changed him in the eyes of this church if in no other way. He was no longer just Epaphroditus the potter, the student of Clement. He had traveled to Rome and kept company with Paul. He'd risked his life for the cause. Now he was more than their messenger to Paul . . . he was Paul's messenger to them.

Epaphroditus guessed what that meant, had reflected on it throughout the return journey. It meant greater responsibilities, more opportunity to teach and lead, the chance to shape the Philippian church and guide it into the future. It meant he would be permitted a role that had not been proper for him before.

At first, as all of this dawned on him, a flush of pride surfaced. But pride quickly gave way to that heaviness he shared with Clement, the sense that something was being asked of him he was not big enough to give. Now he stood above Philippi, trembling as much from the weight of expectations as from the cold.

It was time to go home. He looked to the south quadrant of the city, trying to pick out Clement's household, to see movement in the street. He thought, if he went carefully, he might avoid running into anyone he knew long enough to reach Clement. And then, together, they could figure out what to do next.

With a wash of relief, it dawned on Epaphroditus that whatever his responsibilities in the future, he would not bear them alone. At least he wasn't sitting by himself in an apartment in Rome—cut off and remote. At least he didn't have the weight of the world and its teeming millions piled up on his lonely shoulders. Just this church. Just these people. And even with them, Epaphroditus knew he had companions he could count on to share the burden.

~

Clement could not keep the silly grin from his face. Crouched on his stool, staring down at Epaphroditus sprawled on the bed, he'd tried to wipe the smile away several times already. But it proved to be a persistent thing, in spite of Clement's best efforts. It kept creeping back onto his face as he watched and listened to his young friend. It took advantage of Clement's relief. It found opportunity in his joy to have Epaphroditus back where he belonged. Clement would discover it beaming from his eyes and mouth and, embarrassed, replace it with a frown of concentration and concern. Then he would forget himself again, lost in Epaphroditus's story or the simple joy of being near the potter once more, and the grin would reappear.

"Rome was amazing," Epaphroditus was saying. "The buildings. The Circus Maximus. The crowds. I've never seen anything like it." The words tumbled out, impressions and reactions piling up like the apartment blocks of the city itself. Epaphroditus spoke with the awe of the tourist, the wonder of the simple provincial who had seen sights he could not have imagined before. He shook his head. "Aristias warned me it would be overwhelming, but I had no idea."

He looked up at Clement and smiled. "But I'm glad to be home again, Clement; to see you and this room again." He looked around at the familiar walls and furnishings. "Rome was amazing, but I don't belong in Rome. I belong here, in this place, with these people. With you." And he fixed Clement with a look of unembarrassed affection.

Clement wiped the grin from his face one more time and said, "It took me a long time to realize that for myself, Epaphroditus, to find a place where I belonged. You're fortunate to discover it so young. And you are right. This is where you belong. Welcome home, my friend."

And they sat quietly for a few moments, basking in the warmth of being exactly where they wanted to be, of being together once more.

"Now tell me about Paul." Clement set his jaw and dragged them to the pressing issue. "He is healthy? Things are going well for him in Rome?" A pained look darkened his face. "How did he react to our difficulties here in Philippi?"

"He speaks to all those things in his letter." Epaphroditus nodded at his knapsack. "I'd rather he talk for himself."

"Yes, I understand that," Clement pushed impatiently. "But there are things Paul would never share in a letter, things he would not write about. What did you see in him, Epaphroditus? How did he seem to you?"

Epaphroditus pulled away for a moment, seeking Paul in his memory, trying to organize his thoughts. He sat up on the bed, put his feet on the floor, and rested his elbows on his knees. "He's getting old, Clement. And tired. He's not the same man he was when I first met him. He still gets excited. And he still has that intensity about him. But it's not constant like it used to be. He's pacing himself now, saving himself for when it really matters." Epaphroditus stared at his hands and then looked up into the face of his mentor. "That fellow from Ephesus—the one who first brought news about Paul—he was right. These last years have taken a toll on Paul."

Clement absorbed the report, saddened but not surprised. He knew that all men had limits. He knew from personal experience how age and injury wore away at the soul. And he knew that time respected no man, not even an apostle.

"The news about Philippi hit him hard for some reason." Epaphroditus spoke softly now, still trying to work out something he'd puzzled over on the long journey home. "I think he's come to expect problems with his other churches. Immorality. Wrongheaded ideas. But Philippi is different for him. He counts on us."

Epaphroditus paused again, finding it difficult to put into words something he did not fully understand. "You'll see it in his letter—his affection for us, his fond memories. He knows we're not perfect. But I think he wants us to be. I think he hopes we will be. It's like he needs one church, just one church, to feel confident about—to point to and say, 'See!'"

He glanced at Clement and wondered if this was making any sense. But Clement was looking past him and gave no indication, except for his utter stillness, that he was listening at all. The potter continued, "I didn't get the impression that Paul was all that worried about our problems. He didn't seem upset when I told him about Simeon and the rest. When you read the letter, you'll find that he expects us to recover, to get on our feet again quickly.

"But the fact that there were any problems here, that we might not be as mature and Christlike as we should be, seemed hard for him." He shook his head again. "When we talked over what was happening at Philippi, I can't say that he was hurt or angry. He just seemed very, very tired."

They sat quietly for a while, with the candle sputtering on the table and the oil lamp sending up a smoky plume toward the ceiling. They sat considering Paul's reaction and weighing how much damage the news had done him. Clement's thoughts turned to the letter, and he wondered bitterly if it had cost Paul anything like what his own letter had cost him. He felt ashamed.

"We need to get the letter to Lydia and Luke. As much as I want to open it right now, I think it might be best for all of us to read it together." Clement cocked his head to the stillness of the street outside his door. "It's late. They'll be asleep. But I don't think they'll mind getting up for this. Or to see you!" Clement leaned forward and slapped Epaphroditus on the knee. "Ever since Luke brought news you were ill, we've been so worried about you."

Epaphroditus stood and spread his arms for Clement's examination. "Well, as you can see, I've survived the sea and Rome and even Timothy's nursing. But right now, I'm about to die of hunger. Do you think Lydia might have something for me to eat?"

He paused, struck by something he'd not thought about before. "Strangest thing. Ever since leaving Paul, I've been hungry as a horse."

~

After all the teary hugs, after the laughter of relief, after the rush of story and the frenzied catching-up and a hasty meal served by a sleepy cook, the four of them lounged around Lydia's dining chamber staring at Epaphroditus's knapsack and thinking of the letter inside.

Epaphroditus looked from one to the next, beaming. This was a delicious moment for him, a moment he'd anticipated from the time he left Philippi. He'd left with questions; he'd returned with answers. He'd left carrying problems; in his knapsack were solutions. The letter was the reason for his journey. And now the time had come to bring the journey to its end. As he reached into his knapsack, he felt an odd sadness, the inevitable disappointment that snaps at the heels of every accomplishment. But, looking at their faces, the sadness quickly passed.

They were staring at him with the fixed concentration of the hungry. What he held in his hands was food for them, and they could barely contain their appetite. They were tired and this was rest. He drew the writing case out and, in that moment, knew it had been worth everything.

"Paul wanted the three of you to read the letter first. He thought you might have questions I could answer, things we might want to talk about before taking this to the church." Their eyes shifted from the writing case to Epaphroditus and back again. He opened the case and withdrew the precious pages, glad to see they had weathered the journey well, holding them up for the others to view. "How do you want to do this? Do you want to read this yourselves, or shall I read it for you?"

Lydia reached for the pages in silent answer to his question. Luke and Clement gathered close around her, each holding up a candle for light. Together, as Lydia turned the pages, they read what Paul had to say to them.

Epaphroditus watched their eyes as they read. He saw that Clement scanned each page quickly and then went back to read more carefully. Lydia latched onto one feature of each page—a sentence, a word—as if she were looking only for certain information and was impatient with the rest. Luke, as in so many other things, was methodical in his reading. His eyes started at the top of each page and made their orderly way to the bottom.

But often, the three of them would stop together, arrested by a particular thought or the wording of a sentence. Their eyes would fix on the same spot on the page—musing and probing, interrogating the letter mutely, squeezing the words for every ounce of meaning—until they broke away to stare off into the distance. Eventually, one of them would reach to turn a page in Lydia's hand. The reverie would break. And the reading would continue.

They read through the news of Paul and his tentative plans for the future. They read the admonition to "stand united" and Paul's pleading for love and selfless behavior. They read Paul's warnings against the "dogs" and "those wicked men and their evil deeds"—at which point the three of them stopped to stare off for a long while.

When they got to the part about Euodia and Syntyche, Lydia began to read out loud, sensing that, for all of them, the subject was too sensitive to be borne alone or in silence.

"And now I want to plead with those two women, Euodia and Syntyche. Please, because you belong to the Lord, settle your disagreement. And I ask you, my true teammate, to help these women, for they worked hard with me in telling others the Good News." Lydia paused long enough to glance sympathetically at Luke, knowing the words were addressed to him and feeling the weight of his responsibility to bring these two stubborn women together.

Her eyes returned to the page. "And they worked with Clement and the rest of my coworkers, whose names are written in the Book of Life." Lydia interrupted her reading again, wanting to think about Paul's words, trying to remind herself that, as much as she might disagree with Euodia, they were still sisters in the Lord, companions in the faith. Clement seemed to be thinking along the same lines. Luke, still chewing on Paul's words to him, wore the pained expression of a man who'd just been given a job he did not want to do, was not sure could be done.

"Shall I finish?" Lydia looked around at the others and received their nodded encouragement.

She began reading again, her voice stronger now, her mood rising the more she read. In her mind, she could almost see Paul and his waving hands. Every phrase suggested some gesture. Every thought spoke volumes about the nature of the man who wrote. "Always be glad because of the Lord! I will say it again: Be glad. Always be gentle with others. The Lord will soon be here. Don't worry about anything, but pray about everything. With thankful hearts offer up your prayers and requests to God. Then, because you belong to Christ Jesus, God will bless you with peace that no one can completely understand. And this peace will control the way you think and feel."

Lydia stopped again, eyes shining, and looked up at her companions. Together, they laughed and shook their heads at Paul's ability to affect them, to lift them, from a jail cell so far away. They'd said similar things themselves over the past months: "Don't worry" and "Pray" and "God will bless us." But, somehow, the words did not sing and dance, they did not live like they did when Paul spoke them. As always, Paul was the consummate salesman. Words were his tools. But what he peddled was hope.

Lydia continued. "Finally, my friends, keep your minds on whatever is true, pure, right, holy, friendly, and proper. Don't ever stop thinking about what is truly worthwhile and worthy of praise. You know the teachings I gave you, and you know what you heard me say and saw me do. So follow my example. And God, who gives peace, will be with you."

She read on as Paul acknowledged the gifts they'd sent. She read of his irritating contentment ("I have learned to be satisfied with whatever I have"), thinking to herself, *He cannot take a gift in one hand without pushing it back with the other.* She thought he redeemed himself a bit with his gracious closing words—his love of the Philippian church, his sense of partnership. She heard her own voice intone the final blessing, "Receive and experience the amazing grace of the Master, Jesus Christ, deep, deep within yourselves."

She turned the last page over, hoping for more on the back, knowing full well that those words ended the letter just as Paul would want to—testifying to the grace of Jesus, praying for an experience of that grace in the lives of those who read the letter. She realized she'd been hoping Paul would direct some word to her, offer a passing acknowledgment of her friendship or, at least, of her existence. But no.

The reading was finished, yet the letter remained the focus of their attention. They stared at it and leafed through it again, studying a passage here, trying to understand better a paragraph there. They did it all in silence, Luke and Clement holding the candles high, Epaphroditus (who knew the letter by heart) watching them and gauging their reactions, Lydia juggling the pages.

They studied the letter until they exhausted themselves, until they grew weary of their own thoughts and eager for the reactions of the others. Only then did the letter fall to Lydia's lap, allowing Clement and Luke to set their candles on the table and massage their aching arms.

"Well?" They turned to each other.

"He's worried about how things will go in Rome," Lydia said, looking reproachfully at Luke. "You told us it was merely a formality, just a matter of time until his release. But it's more than that, isn't it?" She watched him through narrowed eyes.

Luke spread his hands and pleaded for understanding. "There's nothing we can do. Is his situation serious? Yes. But it's not desperate. Not yet. I keep telling him that Rome cares nothing about an old man who tells strange stories. But as he keeps telling me"—and he shrugged—"Rome is not the most rational place these days."

Clement was mulling over something else. He interrupted quietly. "I thought what Paul said about standing united, about thinking of ourselves like Jesus did, was helpful." He glanced at Epaphroditus. "That part about being united, about humbling ourselves and leaving it to God to lift us up—that would make a pretty good sermon for someone to preach." And, to make sure the young man got the hint, Clement raised his eyebrow.

Epaphroditus laughed and lifted his hands in surrender. "I've already been thinking about that, Clement. It's my favorite part of the letter."

Lydia sorted through the pages until she came to the paragraphs directed at Simeon and his spiritual kin. "I was reading these words—'dogs,' 'mutilators,' 'worthless,'" she hunted through the letter with her finger, "um, 'garbage'—and I was wondering how Euodia will hear this letter. It seems awfully strong. I don't think this will make her feel any better about Paul."

Epaphroditus nodded, remembering that he'd said as much to the Apostle. But Paul had been unbending. "No, Epaphroditus!" He shook his head side to side. "We do no one any favors, least of all Euodia, by pretending this is less serious than it is. This Simeon, or someone just like him, has dogged me my whole ministry. Mostly, they are good, sincere, conscientious men who happen to believe that Jesus needs a little help from Moses. Just a pinch of circumcision. Just a measure of the right foods. Just a bit of Sabbath-keeping. And *then* the Cross will be effective. *Then* God can work his will in our lives. *Then* we'll be as spiritual as they are!" Paul's eyes burned and his breathing grew labored. He stood so close to press his point that the potter felt uncomfortable, smothered.

"They're wrong, Epaphroditus. And they are wrong at the one place where being wrong is deadly." Paul stepped back and moved to the center of the room, turning his back on his companion. Epaphroditus watched him carefully, relieved to have some distance between them but still keenly aware of Paul's intensity, the depth of his feeling about this matter. "They miss the meaning of the Cross. They overlook the work of the Spirit. They think God smiles on them because of what they do." Epaphroditus could see the back of his head shake slowly. And then Paul wheeled to face Epaphroditus. "But God approves of us because of what Jesus did on the cross. When we crawl up on that cross with Jesus, when we die with him, that's when God smiles on us. And changes us. But it is his work, not ours. It is his power, not ours." And, once again, his hands punched the air and his elbows flailed to keep up.

"The people of God can recover from sins of the flesh. They can endure mistaken ideas and broken relationships. What they cannot survive is spiritual self-reliance, the notion that we can accomplish for ourselves what Jesus died to achieve. That kind of thinking makes a joke of the Cross. Why did Jesus have to die if a knife and a little self-discipline can accomplish the same thing?"

Epaphroditus smiled at the memory and at how vividly it returned to him now. He described it for Lydia. "He wouldn't change a word. He just kept saying that, if you're going to perform surgery, you use a sharp knife."

But Lydia was seeing Euodia's face and imagining how the words would affect her. "I still think she'll be hurt by what Paul says. I can't imagine this helping Euodia and Syntyche get back together again."

"Euodia's got to make a choice," Clement broke in. "She has to stand with Paul or throw him over entirely. Paul's helping her, pushing her." He chuckled to himself, though there was nothing particularly funny about the matter. "He chose those words deliberately. They don't allow Euodia any middle ground."

They sat and contemplated that for a few moments longer.

Finally, Epaphroditus broke the silence with an observation of his own on the letter. "I've had longer with this letter than you have. And there's one part of it that's grown on me the longer I've thought about it." He reached for the letter in Lydia's lap, turned to a page near the end, and read a sentence aloud. "Finally, my friends, keep your minds on whatever is true, pure, right, holy, friendly, and proper. Don't ever stop thinking about what is truly worthwhile and worthy of praise."

He lowered the letter and looked intently at his companions. "The more I think about that sentence, the more I am convinced it defines where we went wrong. As a church, I mean. On the trip back, it dawned on me that we've spent a considerable amount of time around here filling our minds with just the opposite of what Paul recommends." His three companions stared at him as he spoke. "I mean, think about it. When you're hurting, when you're disappointed with people, what do you focus on?" His eyes moved back and forth from the letter to the faces of his companions. "You focus on what's false and inferior, what's disgraceful and fake, what's arguable and unkind. We've done exactly what Paul tells us not to." He held up the indicting pages. "We've looked for the worst, not the best; the ugly instead of the beautiful; what needs to be fixed rather than what remains strong and healthy in this church."

He paused to see whether they were following, whether he was making sense to them. "Don't you see? No wonder we've been discouraged. All we've thought about is how bad things are, what problems we have. And we've overlooked the good things God has been doing among us even in our troubles."

Lydia and Clement blinked at Epaphroditus, trying to follow his point. They had the look of someone who'd just been hit on the chin—dazed and glassy and uncertain whether to cry or get angry. Lydia opened her mouth to respond, then closed it again.

It was Clement who put the question to words. "What are you saying, Epaphroditus? That Simeon wasn't the problem; it was the way we were thinking about him? That if we'd just had a better attitude, he would have gone away?" Perhaps it was the late hour or the tenderness of the subject. But there was an edge to his voice.

"Of course not, Clement." Epaphroditus did not intend to minimize the church's struggles or the pain Clement had endured. But he did want to make a point. And it struck Epaphroditus as he did so that something had changed in his relationship with Clement. He would always be Clement's son in the faith. But the son was now grown up. The son could teach the father.

"Simeon was a very real problem. He was a splinter in the foot of this church, so to speak. But Clement," Epaphroditus appealed, "sometimes we make matters worse when we go digging for the splinter. We cut and gouge and pick to the point that we wind up wounding ourselves more than the splinter could. We get so focused on the splinter that we can't think about anything else."

Epaphroditus paused and frowned at the letter in his hands. "Paul has to deal with splinters like Simeon all the time. There are always aches and pains somewhere in the body of Christ. Do they have to be doctored? Yes. But Paul has found a way to deal with those problems without amputating a leg. He still manages to find joy in the church, in the good things God is doing. He's learned to look for what is right in people and in churches, not what's wrong."

He felt suddenly embarrassed, unaccustomed to playing this role with these people, all too conscious of the gap between his own behavior and the words he'd just spoken. "Simeon has been painful for all of us. I know we're hurting for Euodia." He looked around at each of them. "But, all along, we've had each other. God is still using us to touch our neighbors and tell good news. The church here keeps growing and maturing even in our struggles, maybe *because* of our struggles. I lost sight of that for a while." He stared down at the floor. "I was looking so hard at Simeon, I forgot to see God's hand on this church."

He fell silent. The others looked at each other and then back to Epaphroditus and then away. Clement thought back over the preceding months, counting the ways he'd let Simeon consume his attentions, how his feelings for Marcion and Jason had been governed by his fears and worries. He remembered words he'd spoken, impatient words, fueled by his concerns for the church and, now that he could see it, by his lack of faith that God was still at work among them. He glanced at Lydia, remembering all those feverish meetings held at her house or his, trying to figure out what to do. He realized that he'd allowed himself to wallow in worry, fearing the worst of other people, doubting their commitment and questioning their motives.

He felt the conviction come over him, gripping at his heart like a cold hand, and lowered his head. Of course, Epaphroditus was right. It was so obvious, he had not seen it. There would always be problems in the church. Moral failures. Misunderstandings. Rifts in relationships. A cooling of spiritual fervor. If Clement allowed every problem to steal his joy, if he permitted his pain to overwhelm his confidence and his ability to lead, he would himself become a problem, an impediment to the greater good of the church.

He reached for the pages in Epaphroditus's hand and stared for a long while at Paul's words. *Next time,* he thought to himself, *I have to keep my eyes on what God is doing, not how we're messing things up. I have to remember that this is his church and he will take care of it.* He closed his eyes and offered up a silent prayer, a confession of failure and a plea for more faith. He prayed for the church and, for the first time in months, listed with gratitude the good things God had been doing in their midst. The faces of his fellow Christians floated in front of Clement's closed eyes and he recalled forgotten acts of kindness, overlooked words of encouragement and support. The more he prayed, the more he realized how soured he'd grown in recent months, how oblivious to the signs of God at work and people reaching to do what was right.

He'd had eyes only for Simeon and the trouble he was causing. He'd not been able to see beyond Euodia's pain and the fear of losing her. But all along, God had been sending him subtle signs that he was still at work in the lives of these people, that he had not abandoned this church. Now that he could see it, Clement poured out his thanksgiving and joy.

How long he prayed, he didn't know, lost as he was in a kind of communion he rarely experienced. When at last he raised his eyes again, he found Epaphroditus watching him. The look on the potter's face, in that unguarded moment, was so patient, so profoundly trusting, it warmed Clement like a blanket. He looked over to see

Lydia kneeling across the room, hands clasped in her lap, locked in her own silent communion with God. He noticed that Luke, overcome by the hour, was stretched out on a dining couch, fast asleep.

His eyes were drawn to the window, and he saw with surprise that dawn had come. He realized that he should be tired, that old men and sleepless nights do not make good companions. But he did not feel tired. He felt . . . what? He searched his own heart, trying to sort through the mix of emotions he'd experienced through the night. What was he feeling now?

And then he knew. Clement felt relief. Sweet and liberating relief. He experienced a sense of lightness—as if the burden he carried for the church had been stolen away by a stronger and more capable hand. Looking back to Epaphroditus, Clement smiled a vast and contented smile, and thought to himself, *It's going to be all right.*

Chapter Nineteen

STAY ON TRACK, STEADY IN GOD

(LATE APRIL, A.D. 62)

IT WAS NOT UNTIL THE NEXT EVENING THAT THEY COULD GATHER THE church together. That morning Lydia and Luke, Clement and Epaphroditus divided the city among themselves—making their sleepy way through the forum and the agora, up to the acropolis and out to the fields beyond the city walls, to stables and shops and villas and hovels, spreading the news that the potter had returned bringing a letter from Paul. By midafternoon, Epaphroditus was worn out. The rigors of the journey were catching up. The all-but-sleepless night just passed made him feel numb and slow. But mostly he was worn out from returning the exuberant hugs of brothers and sisters who missed him, were worried about him, and were overjoyed to see him again. His neck was sore from their relief.

Gradually, as the afternoon wore on into evening, the people of God at Philippi closed up shops and gulped down the last of the evening meal and tucked children to bed so they could run to Lydia's house and be with the family of believers when the letter was read. They met in the streets, groups of twos and threes moving briskly in the same direction. They came in the dying light of the spring sunshine, picking their way carefully through the shadows. Those who arrived later came with torches stretched before them to light the dark roads, talking loudly to warn off lurking scoundrels. They banged on the gate and called into the courtyard and entered to find Epaphroditus and wrap him, groaning, into an enveloping embrace.

Lydia had her servants light every torch, taper, lamp, and candle in the house. The courtyard was ablaze with their flames. An open fire had been set in the middle of the courtyard—the single source of heat in the rapidly chilling night. While waiting for the meeting to begin, people gathered around the fire, extending cold fingers to its warmth, turning their backs to the flames when their faces grew uncomfortably hot. As more people arrived, they joined the ring around the fire, drawn to the warmth and to the fellowship. There was a buzzing about the crowd, a barely suppressed excitement. They were eager for the letter.

Epaphroditus stood against the wall, Clement at his side, watching the church assemble, praying about the reading of the letter, hoping that God would use these words from Paul to bring healing and hope to those huddled around the fire. His eyes traveled from one person to another, catching familiar faces, weighing the impact of the letter on this personality, that situation. He was interrupted frequently by yet another friend wanting to welcome him home. But he managed to avoid extended conversations ("The letter will explain everything") so he could concentrate on the group as a whole and on his prayers.

Finally, Lydia stepped forward and held up her hands to welcome the church to her home. She asked Marcion to speak a word of blessing on their time together. And then, turning to Epaphroditus, she gestured an invitation to stand beside her. The potter stepped forward, pulled the letter from his tunic, smiled at his brothers and sisters, and began to read.

~

The reading went well at first, after Epaphroditus got over his nervousness and settled into the rhythms of Paul's words. He read as Paul had instructed him, punching this phrase, pausing after that one. Though he knew the letter by heart, he was careful to read rather than recite. This was too important. He could not afford to drop a sentence or leave out a word.

Yet he could not stand to read the letter and not read his audience as well. He was desperate to know how they were receiving this, what they were thinking. And so, between sentences, as he took a breath or paused for emphasis, he took in the faces spread before him, trying to gauge their responses.

But they were hard to read. Their concentration was so fierce, it looked at first like disapproval. Going through the opening segment of the letter, where Paul spoke of his fondness for them and his prayers for the Philippian church, Epaphroditus looked up to see frowning faces, sober and seemingly unmoved by the Apostle's affectionate language. His heart sank, and he shot a worried glance at Clement, until it dawned on him that they were simply consumed with the hard work of listening. But then they laughed about Paul tormenting his guards with the gospel. They groaned over the people using Paul's arrest for their own purposes. They stood like statues as Paul confessed his desire to go on and be with Christ. And Epaphroditus understood then that they were with him and began to relax and give himself fully to the reading.

He worked through the heart of the letter, Paul's plea for unity and unselfish living, the call to put on the attitude of Christ. *Listen!* he kept praying with that part of himself not involved in the reading. *Hear and understand!* He wanted to shout every word. He wanted to jump up and down to emphasize important phrases. Instead, as Paul instructed, he read slowly, enunciated carefully, and trusted the words to do what was needed in the lives of these people he loved.

While he read, his audience stood around the courtyard in various listening poses—leaning against walls or shifting from foot to foot, arms crossed against the cool of the night, eyes closed or fixed on Epaphroditus or staring off into the dark. Some of the women held each other, partly for warmth and partly for courage. And there was a continual movement in the crowd as people cycled from the warmth of the fire to the cold of the courtyard perimeter and back to the fire again. Occasionally, a hand would raise as listening transformed into worship. Epaphroditus could hear an "Amen" now and then, an audible agreement with the words of the Apostle.

His own fingers were cold holding the letter. He could see his breath as he read.

As he spoke Paul's words about Christ's humiliation and honoring, about the obedience of the Son serving as a model for them all, Lydia stood behind him, studying the group. She looked from one person to another, willing them to receive what Paul had to offer. And she knew, as Epaphroditus read, that they all needed to hear this simple message again. Somehow, they had forgotten this lesson—all of them. Clement and the elders. Euodia and Syntyche. Herself. All of them. They'd forgotten that selflessness and service, humility and obedience were the essential attitudes of a disciple. They had forgotten that these attitudes were especially important when times got hard—when a cross loomed on the horizon, when conflict threatened. They had forgotten that their job was to keep loving and giving and forgiving. They had forgotten that God would take care of how things worked out in the end and who would be honored or shamed. In all the worry and anguish over the difficulties in their church, these people had forgotten to be Christlike and leave to God the matter of who won and who lost. Lydia recognized that lapse and silently confessed and repented.

Syntyche did not dare look around. She kept her eyes fixed on Epaphroditus, afraid that otherwise she might see Euodia and dissolve into tears. She listened with the abandon of one who had used up all the ready answers. For months, she'd racked her mind for some compromise, some middle ground. She'd spent sleepless nights trying to envision a meeting place where she and Euodia could find truce, if not reconciliation. The distance between them weighed on her in ways she could not express. It was not simply the loss of the long friendship or the surprising hostility that seemed to bubble so close to the surface of them both. It was the realization that—whether through sin or stubbornness—not all differences could be reconciled, not all relationships could be mended even among disciples of Christ. It was a limit to her faith that disappointed her and made her reflect on the depth of human failure—of her own failure.

So now she latched onto Paul's words and what he had to say about a new attitude, about the example of Christ and the work of God among his people. She found that the words brought an abrupt release, a softening, the welcome conviction that a surer hand than hers was guiding the affairs of the Philippian church. The letter contained healing for her. And for that, she felt a flood of gratitude.

Almost halfway through, just as Paul touched on the subject of bickering and arguing in the church and Epaphroditus could feel his listeners tensing, the letter turned abruptly to the Apostle's future plans. "Whatever you do, don't feel sorry for me. I plan (according to Jesus' plan) to send Timothy to you very soon so he can bring back all the news of you he can gather. Oh, how that will do my heart good! I have no one quite like Timothy. He is loyal, and genuinely concerned for you. Most people around here are looking out for themselves, with little concern for the things of Jesus. But you know yourselves that Timothy's the real thing. He's been a devoted son to me as together we've delivered the Message. As soon as I see how things are going to fall out for me here, I plan to send him off. And then I'm hoping and praying to be right on his heels."

Epaphroditus could feel the crowd relax, smiling at the news that Timothy would be coming soon. Those who had been there from the beginning remembered the young man with great affection. Many of them had learned to pray through his patient instructions. They recalled his unlined face and the surprise they felt when this beardless boy spoke with such maturity and learning about the Scriptures. The Christians of Philippi had taken Timothy to their hearts, adopted him as one of their own, and followed the news of his work over the years with the pride parents feel for a precocious child.

But when they heard that Paul was also planning to visit, their excited murmurs threatened to overwhelm the reading of the letter. They turned to each other with wide grins and bright eyes. "Did you hear that?" "I wonder when he will come?" "I hope he can stay longer this time."

Epaphroditus paused a moment to let the excitement die down. And as he waited, he scanned ahead.

Since leaving Rome, he'd wondered how to handle the next part of Paul's letter. On the one hand, he was Paul's messenger and Paul fully expected him to read the letter—in its entirety—to the Christians of Philippi. But, on the other hand, the thought of reading what Paul said about him personally prompted a discomfort that was nearly paralyzing. His hands turned clammy in the cold and an acute modesty threatened to turn his mouth into a desert. As the crowd quieted, he panicked, looked to Lydia in desperation, and shoved the letter toward her.

Lydia turned to Epaphroditus in surprise, found where his shaking finger was pointing, and then tried without great success to suppress the smile that came to her lips. She glanced over the letter toward the crowd and explained, "I think our favorite potter is embarrassed about this next part. So, if you will permit"—she bent her head to the pages, took a breath, and began to read.

"But for right now, I'm dispatching Epaphroditus, my good friend and companion in my work. You sent him to help me out; now I'm sending him to help you out. He has been wanting in the worst way to get back with you. Especially since recovering from the illness you heard about, he's been wanting to get back and reassure you that he is just fine. He nearly died, as you know, but God had mercy on him. And not only on him—he had mercy on me, too. His death would have been one huge grief piled on top of all the others."

Epaphroditus stood to the side and tried to find a place to put his conflicting emotions. He felt a bewildering mix of pride and embarrassment, humility and guilty pleasure, gratitude and self-consciousness. As the words were read, he flushed and looked down at his hands, feeling the eyes of the congregation on him, wishing he could be somewhere else. It was true, of course—the part about his illness and his desire to get home. But at the same time, it was too much. He did not feel particularly brave or deserving of such praise. He'd begged Paul to leave this part out. Paul had simply fixed him with an appraising stare for a long moment, and then continued to dictate. It was the last they spoke of the matter.

Lydia kept reading. "So you see why I'm so delighted to send him on to you. When you see him again, hale and hearty, how you'll rejoice and how relieved I'll be. Give him a grand welcome, a joyful embrace! People like him deserve the best you can give. Remember the ministry to me that you started but weren't able to complete? Well, in the process of finishing up that work, he put his life on the line and nearly died doing it."

She stopped reading and placed her hand on Epaphroditus's shoulder. "We do owe Epaphroditus a great debt. I know he is embarrassed by Paul's words. But because of his courage and sacrifice, we have this." And she held up the pages of the letter for everyone to see before handing them back to Epaphroditus.

He stepped forward again, the letter in his hands, and immediately moved from self-conscious nervousness to a nervousness prompted by how the words to come would be received. He knew suddenly, and with a certainty he had not felt before, that this would be difficult, that this part would not go down well. His eyes found Euodia before lowering to the letter and reading the hardest part of Paul's message to the Philippians.

"And that's about it, friends. Be glad in God! I don't mind repeating what I have written in earlier letters, and I hope you don't mind hearing it again. Better safe than sorry—so here goes."

He took a deep breath, said a quick prayer, and soldiered on. "Watch out for those dogs, those wicked men and their evil deeds, those mutilators who say you must be circumcised to be saved. For we who worship God in the Spirit are the only ones who are truly circumcised. We put no confidence in human effort. Instead, we boast about what Christ Jesus has done for us.

"Yet I could have confidence in myself if anyone could. If others have reason for confidence in their own efforts, I have even more! For I was circumcised when I was eight days old, having been born into a pure-blooded Jewish family that is a branch of the tribe of Benjamin. So I am a real Jew if there ever was one! What's more, I was a member of the Pharisees, who demand the strictest obedience to the Jewish law. And zealous? Yes, in fact, I harshly persecuted the church. And I obeyed the Jewish law so carefully that I was never accused of any fault."

The chill of the evening grew perceptibly colder as he read these words. Every movement in the courtyard froze as people winced at Paul's language, all of them thinking together of Euodia.

She winced at his words as well. Pushing away from the far wall, from the spot she'd found to distance herself from the others, Euodia stared defiantly at Epaphroditus, waiting proudly in her isolation for the rest of what Paul had to say. She knew Paul would have to say something, that he could not avoid the matter of Simeon and his teachings. And she was well aware that he would not approve of Simeon's attempt to harmonize the demands of the Cross with the requirements of Sinai.

But she'd come this night determined to hear how Paul would react, to give him one last chance to make his case. She did not expect to be swayed by his arguments, but she was curious to hear the tone he used in making them. She was curious to know if he would extend his hand or a sword, if it was to be peace or estrangement.

She sensed the way things would go early in the letter when Epaphroditus read the words "opposition" and "defeat for them, victory for you." She tensed at those martial words and phrases, thinking—hoping—that perhaps Paul would soften his tone when he addressed Simeon's teaching directly.

She should have known better.

Dogs? Mutilators? This was not the language of a man who wanted to compromise, to settle on some accommodation that would allow them all to live in peace! Euodia recoiled physically as each epithet jumped from the letter to Epaphroditus's mouth and then struck her frontally. The phrases cut her and deepened the wound opened when Simeon had been forced to leave the church. Paul spoke of those "who worship God in the Spirit" . . . as opposed to the ones who don't, no doubt. His Jewish "credentials" were a transparent attempt to belittle Simeon and his qualifications. She listened with rising anger and a deepening awareness that this would not end well.

"I once thought all these things were so very important, but now I consider them worthless because of what Christ has done. Yes, everything else is worthless when compared with the priceless gain of knowing Christ Jesus my Lord. I have discarded everything else, counting it all as garbage, so that I may have Christ and become one with him. I no longer count on my own goodness or my ability to obey God's law, but I trust Christ to save me. For God's way of making us right with himself depends on faith."

Euodia could feel her nails digging into her palms. Her breathing grew shallow and hard. She felt the flush of anger moving from her neck up her face. This was intolerable! Worthless? Garbage? How dare he! He'd never met Simeon. He knew nothing about the man's sincerity, about his consuming desire to live a righteous life. And to throw labels around like that, to dismiss a man's earnest attempt to take seriously the Law that Jesus himself observed! Euodia considered walking out of the courtyard at that moment. But then she locked eyes with Syntyche and determined to stay. She wouldn't give them the pleasure!

Syntyche did not want to look at her old friend, but her eyes would not listen to her wants. They sought out Euodia of their own will, moved by a wrenching empathy that took Syntyche by surprise. Even in the dark, even from that distance, Syntyche could tell Euodia was suffering. And no wonder. Paul was pulling no punches. In his blunt, insistent way, he was cutting away any ground for concession. Truthfully, Syntyche was not sure why Paul had to be so strident, so severe. Yet she knew that something about Simeon's message struck at the heart of Paul's gospel. Simeon had placed his heavy finger on the one part of Paul's faith he would not negotiate.

"As a result, I can really know Christ and experience the mighty power that raised him from the dead. I can learn what it means to suffer with him, sharing in his death, so that, somehow, I can experience the resurrection from the dead!"

Clement was staring at Euodia as well. He knew the confusion and pain Simeon had caused this little flock; he did not wish him back. And he knew Paul was right, that to compromise on this point was to enslave these people to a new kind of rule-keeping. But his shepherd's heart went out to Euodia nonetheless. He could see how the letter was hurting her, standing there so alone, keeping at arm's length the very people who had once been her only family. It was heartbreaking. Clement wanted to rush to her side, to invade her isolation, to drag her back physically into the embrace of the church. But he knew that would accomplish nothing. And the helplessness that rose up within him, looking across the courtyard into her tormented face, tasted like bile.

Epaphroditus kept his eyes glued to the pages in his hand. Before, he had wanted to read his listeners. Not now. He could feel Euodia's hostility. He could almost smell the embarrassment of the others. Their desire for Paul to ease up, to move on, rose like a vapor in the night. He kept reading, hoping the act itself would block out his swelling fear that Paul's passion might push them over the edge, that the disturbing presence of Euodia would overwhelm the Apostle's rebuke.

For a moment, it got better. "I don't mean to say that I have already achieved these things or that I have already reached perfection! But I keep working toward that day when I will finally be all that Christ Jesus saved me for and wants me to be. No, dear brothers and sisters, I am still not all I should be, but I am focusing all my energies on this one thing: Forgetting the past and looking forward to what lies ahead, I strain to reach the end of the race and receive the prize for which God, through Christ Jesus, is calling us up to heaven."

Epaphroditus kept reading. What else could he do? But he knew what was coming. And the dread of it gnawed at his mind like a guilty secret. Part of him marveled at how different the words had sounded in Rome than they would here, to Euodia's face. But mostly, the inevitability of what was about to occur filled him with a sadness that barely allowed him to speak.

"I hope all of you who are mature Christians will agree on these things. If you disagree on some point, I believe God will make it plain to you. But we must be sure to obey the truth we have learned already. Dear brothers and sisters, pattern your lives after mine, and learn from those who follow our example."

A voice screamed in the back of Epaphroditus's mind, *Stop there! Don't keep reading! Paul would not go on if he were here, reading the letter for himself.* Another voice shouted, *Trust Paul. Trust his words. God is in this.* Behind both voices, soft but insistent, he could hear Paul saying, *If you're going to perform surgery, use a sharp knife.*

The next voice he heard was his own. "For I have told you often before, and I say it again with tears in my eyes, that there are many whose conduct shows they are really enemies of the cross of Christ. Their future is eternal destruction. Their god is their stomach, they brag about shameful things, and all they think about is this life here on earth."

There was a collective gasp from the listeners—an audible outpouring of distress at Paul's hard words and of feeling for Euodia. A voice or two rose in objection. Several in the crowd stepped toward her, wanting somehow to soften the blow, to deflect the words rather than let them strike Euodia full force.

But words move faster than feet. Euodia rocked back as if she had been physically assaulted. Her face turned red, then ashen. A single groan escaped her. Holding up her hands to those moving toward her, she shook her head and warned them off. Now she needed her isolation, a moment alone with her shock. *So this is what it has come to. These are Paul's true colors.*

No one moved. No one made a sound. Euodia looked from face to face. She'd imagined, if the time ever came, she would blubber like a child, she would feel torn and grieved. But Paul's words had burned away those sentiments. She turned and, dry-eyed, passed through the group and out of Lydia's home.

Since she could not cry for herself, the church cried for her. Almost before she had cleared the gate, a low wail filled the courtyard. The crowd turned from watching Euodia leave to see Syntyche slumped on the ground, rocking back and forth in misery. She moaned softly and pulled at her hair, cheeks wet with despairing tears. The women moved to her in a rush and sat in the dirt beside her, joining their tears and groans with hers. Their men stood in a circle around the clot of women, awkward and choked, fighting back tears of their own, several of them losing the battle.

Epaphroditus stood staring at the offending words in his hands, wondering if he had done the right thing. He felt wretched, sick to his stomach. He told himself he was only the messenger, but the evasion did little to ease his sense of guilt. He wondered why faith had to be so hard. He wondered if it was worth it.

He felt a hand on his shoulder and looked up to see Clement beside him. And then, surprised, he looked more closely. Clement's eyes were firm and dry. There was a look of calm about him, the calm Epaphroditus could imagine on the face of a soldier who had seen the worst of battle but still believed in the cause.

They stood that way until the tears stopped and people began to compose themselves, wiping at eyes and noses. They stood there until, one by one, the faces in the crowd turned toward them, hungry for direction, needing some healing word that would make sense of what had just happened. They stood quietly together, waiting for the last of the mourners to make eye contact, waiting finally for Syntyche to drag her red-rimmed eyes from the ground to rest, pleading, on them.

Clement reached out and took the letter from Epaphroditus's hand. He cleared his throat and said, "There is more to the letter and it is important for us to hear it all." Taking up the reading where Epaphroditus had left off, ignoring the dull looks of people who had already heard more of the letter than they wanted, Clement spoke the remaining words in a clear, strong voice.

"Dear brothers and sisters, I love you and long to see you, for you are my joy and the reward for my work. So please stay true to the Lord, my dear friends." He read Paul's words to Euodia and Syntyche, that they should iron out their differences and make up. He read Paul's encouragement to Luke, to help them work things out. He read Paul's admonition to focus on the good, the noble, the praiseworthy. He read Paul's thanks for their support and generosity.

Epaphroditus listened as Clement read, to the calmness in his voice and the stubborn determination to see this through, and thought it was one of the bravest things he'd ever witnessed.

When he was finished, Clement looked around the group and said, "It's late and we are all tired. This has been a difficult evening and I know that many of you have concerns about this letter, about Euodia. There will be time to talk in the next few days, after we've rested and prayed about what happened tonight. But right now, it is time to go home."

He raised his hands above the group in benediction. "Father, guard our hearts and tongues in the days ahead. Grant us understanding of your will. Show us the way you want us to take. I pray it by your Spirit and through your Son."

A subdued "Amen" rose from the group and quickly, quietly, they made their way out of the courtyard, through the streets, to their homes. Clement and Epaphroditus stayed to watch the last of them leave. And then they too parted company in silence, each of them going to his solitary quarters to stew alone about the evening.

~

For the first time since his return, Epaphroditus opened the door to his shop and felt his way in the dark to the table where he always left a candle. Of course, it was not there. Why would anything go as it should tonight? He inched over to the counter, stumbling against a pot on the way, knocking it against the wall, where it shattered. He bit back a curse, forcing down the old habit that only surfaced when he was very tired and very angry. His hands ran over the surface of the counter, searching in vain for something to light the darkness. He slammed his fist down in frustration and sank to the floor.

Shrugging off the knapsack that had been his home for the last few months, he groped inside for a flint and took a sheet of fine parchment from the writing case. *An expensive light,* he thought wryly. But he was feeling reckless at the moment, and the waste of the paper seemed appropriate to the theme of the evening. He struck a spark and blew the parchment into flame. Holding it high, he used its flare to locate a candle and kindle its wick.

He lit three other candles around the room and looked to see how the shop had weathered his absence. He stared mutely at the disarray of the shelves, the litter on the floor. He ran a finger through the dust on the table and promised himself that he and his hired man would have a talk. *After I get some sleep, though,* he thought, rubbing at his tired eyes. *After I get over this urge to beat somebody senseless.*

He pulled up a stool and sat among the plates and pots for a while. He realized, tired as he was, he would not be able to sleep any time soon. There was too much boiling inside him. His head was too full of the letter and Euodia's ashen face.

This was pointless. He knew what he needed to do. Pinching out all but one candle and leaving it to burn on the table where it should have been in the first place, Epaphroditus left the shop and turned toward Clement's part of town. He walked quickly, unconcerned about who might be hiding in the shadows, vaguely hoping that someone might accost him in the street. He pitied the thug who tried that tonight.

Arriving at Clement's doorway, he knocked roughly and shouldered his way into the room without waiting for an invitation. He wasn't feeling particularly polite.

Clement sat on the bed, head tipped back against the wall, his eyes closed. "I thought you might come by," he said without looking, too weary to do the unnecessary, to open one eye to confirm it was Epaphroditus.

"I'm mad," Epaphroditus announced, sitting down heavily on Clement's stool. "I'm mad at Simeon for starting this mess. I'm mad at Euodia for getting sucked into it. And I'm mad at Paul for adding fuel to the fire." His voice matched his mood, echoing loudly off the close walls of the room.

Clement smiled and opened his eyes to observe his friend. "My, my. Anyone else on your list? Are you mad at me?"

Epaphroditus ignored the jab. He would not allow anything to take the edge off his anger. "Tonight was a disaster. I thought the letter would solve our problems. I thought hearing from Paul would end all this and let us get on with the healing." He shook his head in disgust. "Apparently, I thought wrong."

He took a ragged breath and let it out slowly. "Did you see them, Clement? Did you watch them during Paul's 'garbage' speech? I thought they might tear the letter from my hands and rip it to shreds. I've never seen them so upset at him. I don't think they were all that pleased with me."

Clement spoke in a low and even voice. "They listened well enough at first. And even the hard part—they may not have liked what Paul said, but they heard it."

"I was there when Paul wrote that part. I warned him it was too strong. I know he didn't mean those words for Euodia. I know he was thinking about Simeon and the others like him. He's angry about what they've done to his churches. He's tired of dealing with them all these years. But still—why did he have to be so harsh? Why didn't he think about her feelings?"

Now Clement sat forward, his own anger sparked. "Did you think it would end any different? Did you think there wouldn't be any blood on the ground when all this was over? Grow up, Epaphroditus. You're offended that you had to get your hands dirty. You're angry that you had to read something with bite, that Paul made you risk something for what you believe. Well, I'm sorry your feelings are hurt, but there it is."

The younger man's eyes grew wide and he started to say something. But Clement held up his hand. "No, wait. Just listen. One of the hard realities of believing something deeply is that we don't do faith by consensus. We can't trim our convictions here, adjust them there, just because someone sees things differently than we do. And I'm not talking about little stuff, things on the periphery of our faith. What happened tonight was at the core of what we believe. Is the Cross sufficient or not? Are we righteous because we keep the rules or because Christ is transforming us by his Spirit? Is our confidence in our religious credentials or in the resurrecting power of Jesus?"

Clement's eyes bore in on the potter. Epaphroditus discovered that his anger had evaporated and, in its place, a nervous tremor ran over him.

"Simeon chose the ground for this fight. He set the rules. He can have fifteen sons and circumcise every one of them if he wants. He can eat his kosher food to the day he chokes on it and I wouldn't care. He can live as a good Jew and still claim Jesus as Messiah and I bet he can get to heaven that way. But I'll be cursed before I let him force all that on us! And *that's* what tonight was about. Not how Simeon chooses to live his life before God, but what Simeon wants to force on us. Not how Simeon practices his own faith, but how he demands we practice ours. Paul was exactly right. He said just what he needed to say. And who do you think you are to correct a man who carries more scars for the faith than you can count?"

Clement slumped back against the wall, his anger used up in the outburst. It left behind the taste of metal in his mouth. He needed a drink but was too weary to walk across the room to the ladle and bucket. He stared at Epaphroditus, sitting with his head down on the stool, and wondered how the young man would react to the rebuke. He thought he should be sorry for his anger, but realized, at the moment, he didn't feel particularly penitent.

When Epaphroditus looked up, Clement could see the tears standing in his eyes. "I'm sorry, Clement. Please"—and he turned his hands palms-up in his lap, a silent plea for forgiveness.

Clement closed his eyes and thought how badly he needed to sleep. "It's all right, son. We're both tired. We can talk about this tomorrow."

Epaphroditus stood awkwardly. He needed to say something. He could not bear for tonight to end like this, for the two of them to be strained. He did not want to face the night with Clement's anger still sounding in his head. But he could not think of anything to say. He didn't know how to make it better.

"Well. Good night then," he finally managed. "We'll talk tomorrow."

"Yes. Good night, Epaphroditus," Clement said. He let the younger man walk to the doorway. And then, softly, "I'm worried about them too, son. But we gave them something tonight, something that will help them. You and me together."

Epaphroditus turned. "What? What did we give them?"

Clement smiled. "We gave them words. Words are powerful things. They can cut and they can heal. Tonight, they did a little of both. But words always take a while to do their work. They will not be hurried. But neither will they be ignored. Trust the words, son. Let them have their way."

Epaphroditus thought about that for a moment. And then he too smiled. Somehow, he knew he would be able to sleep now.

As he walked home in the night, he thought about fathers and sons, about Clement and himself. And he laughed softly, thinking, *The son may be grown up. But the father can still teach him a thing or two.*

Chapter Twenty

HELP THEM WORK THINGS OUT

(MAY, A.D. 62)

CLEMENT WAS RIGHT. THE WORDS NEEDED TIME. AS THE DAYS PASSED, THE pain of watching Euodia's back faded and the church found its way to a more objective view of the letter and its message. The Christians of Philippi began to touch on the letter in their conversations. Carefully, at first . . . cautiously . . . like patients who had recovered sufficiently from surgery to test the wound and see whether the stitches would hold.

Then, with rising confidence, they poked and prodded at Paul's words, finding that the more they struggled with what he said, the stronger they felt.

Lydia became the official "keeper of the letter." She devoted a room of her house to it, setting it on a table and surrounding it with benches. It attracted a steady procession of believers. Sometimes alone, often with a companion, they would sit at the table and pore over the letter. Many of them brought paper and ink and made copies for themselves. Those who could not read came anyway, trusting that Lydia would read the pages for them. Early in the morning, in the evening after the workday was done, and at all hours between, people would walk into Lydia's courtyard, enter the room, and stay until finished with their reading or interrupted by the next visitor.

Lydia tried to ignore the traffic, doing her best to carry on her daily routine. But it was not easy living in the same house as the letter. A servant would knock at her room to say she was needed by an illiterate friend. She would look up to see a familiar face coming or going across the courtyard, and often found herself drawn into an extended discussion of something Paul had written. And there were those occasions when she would interrupt herself, stealing softly to the door of the room, pushing it quietly open to watch the person huddled over the pages or to overhear groups of two or three talk about what they read.

It reminded Lydia of the early days. Somehow, it made her feel closer to Paul.

As the Christians of Philippi came to know the letter better, as the words grew familiar to them and the ideas lodged more firmly in their memory, it became the dominant topic of conversation among them. They debated it ceaselessly—worrying about Paul's situation in Rome, wondering when Timothy would arrive, reciting to each other the Christ Hymn, talking about what Luke would do with Euodia and Syntyche.

They even managed to talk calmly of Paul's hard words about Simeon. Many of them still regretted his language, wishing Paul had chosen other words to express his concerns. Yet all who knew Paul recognized that tact was not his strength. And, besides, what he said was right. Whatever quibbles they had with the way he said it, what he said about Simeon needed saying. They all agreed on that point. After all, it wasn't Paul who started this fight.

~

Clement looked around at the dozen believers who had come to read the letter and arrived at Lydia's house, quite by accident, at the same hour of the evening. Since they were there anyway, they decided to make Clement defend Paul's words.

He shook his head at them and laughed. "Let me tell you a parable. You're like the boy who was getting beat up by a bully. Every day the same bully would bloody this lad's nose and he would run home crying to his mama. It went on like this for months. Then, one day, somebody saw the bully about to hit this boy in the nose again. He walked up to the bully and hit *him* in the nose instead. 'Stop that,' he told the bully. 'Don't hit this boy anymore.' And do you know what the boy did?"

They shook their heads, not seeing yet where the story was going, but amused by it nonetheless.

"He ran home crying to his mama again. 'Mama,' he said. 'Some bully just hit my good friend.'" Now they saw the point and started to laugh with Clement.

But Clement was suddenly serious. "Don't you see? Simeon has been beating us up for months now. I think he meant well. I think he was sincere. He sincerely believed that regularly bloodying our noses was good for us." They smiled at that. "You'd run crying to Jason and Marcion and me. We'd wipe your noses and send you back to church, where, once again, Simeon would start swinging and you'd get in the way. For a while there, he'd hit you in the nose and then you'd hit each other in the nose, and *then* you'd come crying to mama." It was hard for Clement not to laugh. The parable fit so well.

"But when Paul comes along and tells Simeon 'Stop that' and bloodies his nose to make sure he gets the message, suddenly you are offended!" Clement imitated an aggrieved child. "'Mama, Paul shouldn't have said those things to poor, sincere Simeon. What a bully!' Well, Paul did say those things and no doubt they were painful. But let me ask you something." The group waited expectantly. "How does your nose feel lately?"

They rocked back on their benches to consider the question for a moment, to recognize that the letter had effectively ended Simeon's ability to cause them pain. One of the women in the group spoke up. "That still doesn't change the fact that Euodia was so hurt by what Paul said. Did she just happen to be in the wrong place when Paul was taking a poke at Simeon?"

Clement shook his head sadly. "I hurt for Euodia as well. I've been hurting for her a long time now." He looked around at each of them. "And maybe that's the point. Some of you have been critical of the way I handled the situation with Simeon." Several of his listeners interrupted to explain themselves, but Clement smiled and held up his hand. "No. It's all right. Perhaps you were right. I acted cautiously.

I didn't want to do anything rash. But in the meantime, Simeon was swinging, you were bleeding, and Euodia . . . well, Euodia was caught in the middle. Every time we'd argue with Simeon, she would feel attacked. And I imagine that every time Simeon beat on us, she felt a little wounded herself."

They thought about that for a quiet moment, realizing Clement was right, that Euodia was suffering from both sides.

"In my caution, I left Euodia hanging there in the middle . . . for months! I was trying to be compassionate, but it sure looks like cruelty now." He looked down and added softly, "I was not a very good shepherd to Euodia. I was too cautious. And you were right to criticize that.

"But now Paul comes along and speaks boldly. And you don't like that any better! You people are awfully hard to please." His words could have been offensive. But he spoke them gently and with a smile on his face. "I will say this in defense of boldness. Euodia isn't caught in the middle anymore. She's made her decision. As painful as the letter was for her to hear, it pushed her to choose. I think there may even be some relief for her in that."

He stopped speaking for a moment, rubbed his eyes, and thought how hard it was to care about people, to shape them and lead them. He looked around at the group and marveled at the energy they required. It struck him that, by the time you were wise enough to be useful to people, you lacked the stamina to do it for long. He smiled at the thought and filed it away to worry about later.

"What will happen to Euodia now?" one of them wanted to know.

Clement considered the question and answered honestly. "I don't know. Luke will go see her, now that a little time has passed. I don't think things can ever be the same. I guess we've probably lost her to Simeon." It made him sad to say it. Like writing the letter to Paul, something about putting unpleasant thoughts to words gave them a reality Clement would just as soon avoid. But Clement knew he could not afford the luxury of avoiding unpleasant realities any longer. He'd learned that from the pain his church had just endured, from the letter Paul had sent. If he was to lead these people, he must find the courage to see things as they *were,* not as he wished them to be.

Epaphroditus sat at his wheel, merrily turning plates and cups, replenishing the spaces on his shelves. It felt good to be working with the clay again. He'd missed the routine, the simple pleasure of feeling the clay and creating something useful with his own hands. He also realized there was a certain cycle to his work that he'd missed—a beginning and an end, a definite start and a definite finish. When he pulled a jar from the kiln and set it in its place on the shelf, he felt a satisfaction that eluded him when he worked with the church.

He was putting a jar on the shelf, thinking these thoughts, when Lydia came through the door. He smiled and welcomed her, and mentioned the difference between a potter's work and a preacher's.

"The trip to Rome was good for me. I've grown in ways I don't even understand yet. But I missed the clay," he confessed as they sat down together. "The clay is simple. I know what to do with it. And at the end of the day, I don't worry about what I've done or have nightmares about all my pots falling apart. Working with people isn't like that."

He shook his head and smiled again at Lydia. "Things get so complicated with people, don't they? For the last few months, all I've done is wrestle with problems and juggle wounded friends and think about things over my head. It's anything but simple. Most of the time, I don't know what to do. And I can't ever turn it off. I worry about them all the time. I dream about them at night. Getting back to the clay is a relief." He looked at her for a moment. "To tell the truth, I'm not sure I'm cut out for this."

And by "this," Lydia knew he meant matters of the kingdom.

"I'm not sure anyone comes to this naturally," she said, and then smiled and shrugged. "Well, maybe Paul." She frowned again in concentration. "The question is not what's easy to do. The question is what's worth doing." She nodded at the shelves and the shop. "Working with clay is easy. But, in the end, you make cups and bowls. That's honest work, Epaphroditus, but it's not exactly life-changing. You couldn't waste your life doing this *all* the time . . . not now . . . not after what you've learned."

Epaphroditus closed his eyes and repeated her words to himself. He wasn't sure he liked it, but he knew she was right.

"I have a story to tell you, Epaphroditus. Perhaps it will help." She took a moment to settle herself on the stool, clasping her hands in her lap so she would have something to look at as she talked.

"It's about a young woman who was born with the curse of beauty. Her looks were all she had, for her family was very poor. When she came of age, her father noticed the way men followed her with their eyes and realized that her beauty could be profitable for him.

"He sold her to the owner of a brothel. For a great deal of money, I am told. She was thirteen and the first night she ever lay with a man, she was required to service a string of them. They also were willing to pay a great deal of money, some say, because she was very beautiful.

"Her beauty, then, was her curse. But it was also her blessing. It kept her from being wasted on the streets. Her owner reserved her for his most privileged clients. She was given only to those who could pay premium prices.

"They say she was very good at her work. She studied the art of her profession and became the most desirable courtesan in the city, perhaps in the land. But just because she was required to give her body did not mean she was willing to give her soul. All through those years, she held back a part of herself, a hard kernel of self-respect and hope.

"As fate would have it, she passed a synagogue one Sabbath and heard a strange, chanting voice spilling out into the street. The voice was saying something, reading something, and for some reason the young woman stopped to listen." Lydia closed her eyes and quoted the passage from memory. "All men are like grass, and all their glory is like the flowers of the field. The grass withers and the flowers fall, because the breath of the Lord blows on them. Surely the people are grass. The grass withers and the flowers fall, but the word of the Lord stands forever.

"Perhaps it was only the beauty of the poetry that caught her. I like to think it was the contrast between what is fading and what is forever. A girl like that would worry about the future, what would happen when her beauty faded—like the grass.

"She returned to the synagogue later to speak with the rabbi. He was a kindly man, a good man, and he welcomed her. She had never met anyone like him before. He asked nothing of her. His behavior was always correct, even tender. He taught her the ways of his people and introduced her to the Law. They say he was the one who taught her to recite the *Shema*." She looked down for a moment, her face pale and set.

"Since her days were free, they spent a great deal of time together, reading through the prophets and talking about the Hope of Israel. He loved to talk about Messiah and longed for the day he would come, but there were things about Messiah he did not understand. There were rejection and suffering themes in the Scriptures that did not square with the Victorious Warrior so many thought Messiah would be. They talked of that too. But of one thing he was sure. 'Messiah will be for all nations,' he would say. 'Me being Jewish, you being Gentile—none of that will matter when Messiah comes,' he would tell the girl . . . or so the story goes.

"She had grown wealthy through the years. Clients would leave expensive gifts for her. And her master shared his profits, hoping to keep her happy and hard at work. But the tension between her nights and days, between the work on her back and the knowledge in her head, became unbearable.

"The rabbi died suddenly. A stroke, they say. And on the day he died, the young woman went to her owner and quit. 'You can't quit,' he laughed. 'I own you.' She had planned on that. Taking a sharp blade, she placed it against her cheek and pushed in the point until the blood ran down her chin. 'My only value to you is that men find this face beautiful. I want out. Refuse, and I'll make sure that no one will pay money to have me again.' Her owner looked at her and laughed nervously. 'You won't do it,' he said, and his look turned cold. She pushed the blade in farther and a fresh trickle of blood ran down her cheek and stained her garment. 'You forget I'm a whore. You force me to do worse than this every night.' And the look she returned him was colder than his.

"They drew up the papers that afternoon. The next day, she went to visit a frequent client and bought into his business. She even got a bargain price when, in their negotiations, she wondered if she might meet his wife. The day after that, she left the city and moved to a place far away."

The story had grown long and Lydia paused to glance up at Epaphroditus, thinking perhaps he was losing interest. But his eyes were fixed on her and she could tell from his face that he wanted all of it.

"Some years later, in her adopted city, she met a working man much like yourself, Epaphroditus. His hands were calloused. He also had a trade. But he practiced it little. Like you, he'd become a Christian. And what he learned about Jesus changed him. He decided he would not waste his life making tents. Tents were easy. They made no demands. They did not come back to haunt his dreams. His new work was hard. It cost him in every way imaginable." She looked off for a moment. The story was almost done.

"It was because he chose the hard thing that he traveled to her city. She met him on the banks of a river, where each of them had come to pray. He told her about Jesus. And for the first time since thirteen, she felt clean."

She looked at Epaphroditus and raised an eyebrow. "The question is not what's easy to do. The question is what's worth doing. Is the hard thing worth it? She thinks so. I believe he does too. What do you think, Epaphroditus?"

He could only look at her and nod. The story had moved him.

They sat in silence for a long while, until Lydia stood to leave. "Well . . . I should be on my way."

Epaphroditus cleared his throat and asked, "Why did you come here today?"

She tilted her head. "Oh, I had to get away from the house. People coming and going. You wouldn't want to keep the letter here for a while, would you?" And she laughed. "To be honest, I stopped by to find out more about how Paul is doing. Remember? Before you left? We talked about the two people in each of us?"

Epaphroditus nodded and walked with her to the door. "We can talk about that if you'd like."

"Not today, my friend. I've taken up enough of your time. We'll speak of it later."

Epaphroditus leaned in and kissed her on the cheek. "Thank you, Lydia."

"Pah!" She waved him away, embarrassed. "It was only a story, Epaphroditus. I've got more where that came from." And then she was out the door.

Epaphroditus stood in the doorway watching her walk down the street. When she turned a corner and was gone from view, he shut the door and returned to his stool. He sat there until late in the day, mercifully unbothered by customers, thinking about hard things and going over their conversation again.

He'd looked for it when he kissed her goodbye. And when he found it, he was not surprised, though he had never noticed it before.

A tiny scar, high up on her flawless cheek.

~

Luke and Syntyche moved through the streets with the grim faces of people who had work to do they did not relish. They walked together without speaking, each of them praying for something good but preparing themselves for something else. They had put this off as long as they could. It was time to get it over with.

They arrived at the gate to Euodia's courtyard and exchanged nervous smiles. "After you, Syntyche"—and Luke gestured gallantly toward the gate.

"Oh no. After you, Luke." And Syntyche pushed him through ahead of her. They stood together in the middle of the courtyard and called out Euodia's name, unsure where she would be, unwilling to go knocking at every room.

The door to the eating area opened and Euodia stood at the threshold looking at the two of them. She held a cloth in her hand and they saw that they had interrupted her meal. "Hello Luke . . . Syntyche." She nodded at each of them. "May I help you?" Though she knew why they had come.

"We didn't realize it was your mealtime, Euodia," Luke apologized. "Should we come back later?" All this politeness would be the death of them, he thought.

"Not at all. This is as good a time as any." She reached back and pulled the door closed. Walking into the courtyard, she gestured to a bench and sat down across from them.

They sat for an uneasy moment, saying nothing, making eye contact briefly, smiling, and then looking away.

Luke cleared his voice. "Euodia, I'm sure you know why we're here. We could make small talk and avoid what we need to talk about. But perhaps it is best to get right to the point."

Euodia nodded at him. "I appreciate that, Luke. I think that would be better."

"I know the letter was hard for you. I am deeply sorry for that. Paul did not mean to hurt you. But he is very concerned about Simeon . . . and about this church."

Again, Euodia nodded. "Different concerns, no doubt. But, yes, I realize Paul did not mean to hurt me. He probably was not thinking of me at all when he wrote those words."

"That's not true, Euodia. He read the letter you sent. He agonized over it. He thought, from its tone, you were probably beyond his reach no matter how he responded. But he cried when he told me that."

Her hands gripped each other in her lap, the knuckles white against the dark fabric of her garment. She considered for a moment. "He was probably right. I think I've known for some time how this would end, what my decision would be."

"What have you decided, Euodia?" Syntyche spoke up for the first time, though she could manage only a whisper.

"I've asked Simeon if I can worship in his home. He has agreed. There is much to learn, of course. He requires that I keep a kosher table if I am to have intimate contact with his family. I have to memorize the synagogue service and learn the purification rites. Their worship is more structured . . . formal . . . than I am accustomed to." She lifted her chin stubbornly. "But, in time, I'm sure I can perform adequately."

Luke closed his eyes at the last statement, thinking, *And that, in a few words, defines the problem.* But he said nothing. It was too late to argue.

He looked at her again. "Paul wanted me to tell you that he loves you . . . that he will always love you. He is grateful for the time you had together, in the beginning. Those days are among his fondest memories."

The smallest of cracks appeared in her rigid demeanor and she nodded again. "Those were good days," she admitted, glancing briefly at Syntyche.

"For myself, Euodia"—and Luke took a deep breath, flooded suddenly by the thought of the years he'd spent at Philippi and how many of his memories included her. "For myself, I hope you know my regard for you . . . my love for you."

She smiled slightly, knowing that small statement represented an emotional outpouring for Luke. "I know, Luke. You have been a good friend to me." And, again, she glanced quickly at Syntyche.

"If there is ever anything I can do—" he offered.

She shook her head. "It won't be necessary, but thank you."

They sat in silence again, ready to be finished with the conversation, but knowing there were still things to be said.

"I was thinking the other day about how much your comfort meant to me when our husbands died." Syntyche spoke in a whisper again. "I'm not sure I ever told you that . . . or thanked you."

Her knuckles grew whiter, and Euodia lowered her chin. "We comforted each other, Syntyche. We were *both* needy."

Syntyche looked across at her old friend. She noted with surprise that Euodia's hair was showing gray and realized that it had been a long time since the two of them had really looked at each other. They had been too busy looking away or looking past. She felt a wave of regret and knew she would live with it for a long time.

"I'm sorry, Euodia. Please forgive me."

The two of them locked eyes for a moment. "I do, Syntyche. And I am sorry. I need your forgiveness as well."

"Of course."

Luke knew that now everything had been said. It was time to go. "There will come a time, my sisters, when your friendship will be healed . . . when all your differences will be forgotten. I pray that time will come soon. But if not, there is a place we look forward to, a place where there are no tears and where all wounds are healed. If you cannot mend what is broken, our Lord can. And if not here, then there."

The two women looked at each other. They had not thought of it like that.

"I look forward to that time," said Syntyche.

"So do I," said Euodia.

And the two women smiled at each other.

On the walk home, Syntyche glanced at Luke. "You surprise me, Doctor. What you said at the end there . . . that meant a lot to Euodia . . . and to me. For a man of few words, you were quite eloquent."

Luke grinned. "I wish I could take credit for it, Syntyche. Paul knows you better than you think. He knew two women of your character and faith would get to repentance and forgiveness eventually. He told me to watch for it. And then he told me what to say when it happened. Those were his words, not mine. He made me memorize them. He thought they might help."

He walked on in silence for a moment. "He said it was the only gift he had left to give Euodia . . . the only one she might accept from him . . . a gift of hope."

Chapter Twenty-One

I RUN TOWARD THE GOAL

(MAY, A.D. 62)

"WHEN I WAS A BOY, I WANTED TO COMPETE IN THE GAMES. I LISTENED TO the stories of the great champions and attended the processions when the athletes paraded through Philippi. I imagined myself on the fields of Olympus being honored by the judges and cheered by the crowds." He smiled at his listeners. "Every night, I put myself to sleep thinking about wearing the victor's wreath."

Epaphroditus studied the faces tilted up at him, lit by the glow of lanterns and torches and the faint blush of approaching dawn. It was the third Lord's Day since his return to Philippi and this was his first time to address the church. Of course, he'd read the letter to them all. And he'd told the church about his journey, reporting on Paul and the situation in Rome. But so far, he'd managed to avoid preaching, complaining of fatigue and the need to attend to his flagging business. The truth, however, was that he wanted to give the letter time to work on the congregation. He wanted time to reenter the life of the church. And he needed time to think about what he would say.

"But I wasn't interested in wrestling. I cared nothing for the javelin or the horses. I wanted to run. I wanted to run the great marathon. I saw myself eating up the miles with long, flowing strides while the maidens lined the path and swooned as I passed by." The young girls giggled at that, and even their mothers smiled.

"I discovered early on that I was fast on my feet. My friends and I used to mark off a course through the streets of Philippi and race each other. I always won. It was easy for me. All I did was throw back my head and let my legs do the work. But I got cocky about it—as boys sometimes do. And after each race, I would crow about winning the marathon one day and being the most famous runner in all of Greece."

He could see knowing looks on the faces of many in his audience. They remembered their youth. They remembered dreams of their own and foolish, boyish boasts.

"There was a carpenter on my street who heard me boasting. I guess he heard me more than once, because one day, he came into the street and took me by the ear. He said, 'Young man, you can boast about being faster than your buddies, and I reckon that's the truth. And you can brag about winning races to the agora and back, and that's a fact too. But I'm sick of hearing you sound off about winning the marathon when you ain't never run more than a mile in your whole life.'

"And then he turned me around and pointed to Mount Pangaion and said, 'See that mountain? When you can run all the way there without stopping, then I'll build a little platform out in front of my shop and you can step up on it and crow to your heart's content, and I'll be glad to listen. But, till then, I don't want to hear no more about what a great marathoner you're gonna be.'"

The people before him chuckled to themselves. They could almost feel their own ears burning, the tight grip of a parent or neighbor compelling attention.

"I decided right then I'd show him. The very next morning, I took off running for the mountain. I ran through the streets of Philippi and out beyond the walls and through those fields to the west." He pointed in that direction. "It was easy. Until I hit the hills just beyond. I started sweating. I could feel my heart pounding in my chest. I couldn't catch my breath so I slowed down—just a little. My side started to hurt, and I slowed down a little more. By this time, my feet were aching. They started to bleed. I crossed a stream and stopped, just for a moment, to cool down and get a drink. I ran up another hill with my legs cramping and knotted, but I kept running.

"When I got to the top of that hill, I expected to see Mount Pangaion right in front of me. I thought I was almost there. But the mountain hadn't moved at all. It seemed just as far away as when I started. I stood there looking at it for the longest time, thinking about how easy it is to run fast and how hard it is to run long. And then I turned around and walked home."

He smiled and looked sideways at his audience. "I think that was the day I decided to be a potter instead." The laughter came quick and bright. His listeners caught each other's eyes as they laughed.

"Funny thing about doing what's easy," he said when the laughter tailed off. "It's easy. But what about when the easy gets hard? What happens when running—or other easy things—start to hurt?"

He let the questions sit there a moment for all to think about.

"Paul talks about Christos in his letter. You know the part." Epaphroditus looked down at the notes he held in his hands. He didn't need the notes. He knew the passage by heart. But there was a comfort in reading the words, a moment of rest from the utter concentration speaking always required of him.

"Christ was truly God. But he did not try to remain equal with God. Instead he gave up everything and became a slave, when he became like one of us. Christ was humble. He obeyed God and even died on a cross."

When he looked up between sentences, Epaphroditus could see people moving their lips, quoting the words to themselves as he read. Others bent over their own copies of Paul's letter, following the reading closely. These moments always amazed the potter—the time in a sermon when a hundred minds would be locked on the same thought, when distractions fell away and the whole church could huddle around a single idea for a short time. Such moments were precious to him, holy things to be longed for and savored.

"Then God gave Christ the highest place and honored his name above all others. So at the name of Jesus everyone will bow down, those in heaven, on earth, and under the earth. And to the glory of

God the Father everyone will openly agree, 'Jesus Christ is Lord!'"

They knew the words so well. Still, as they listened, it was as though the words were new. The thoughts were so beautiful, the phrases so haunting and melodic, that the potter's reading of them in the assembly became an act of worship in itself. Behind Epaphroditus's voice, they could hear the voice of the Apostle. And behind that, they could almost hear the voice of God.

"Paul writes here of a time when being the Anointed One was easy. Our Lord was in the presence of God. He was God. He had all the privileges and status that go with being God. Holiness, doing what was right, honoring the Father was an easy thing for Christos then. It came naturally.

"But then God asked Christos to do something hard. He asked him to be holy, to do right, to be obedient—not up there—but down here. 'Give up your status. Put aside your privileges. Become flesh. Become a slave. Obey me when I ask you to go the Cross.'

"So what happened when the easy got hard for Jesus? What happened when being obedient started to hurt?" He asked as much with his eyes as with his words. "Jesus kept running. It didn't matter that he couldn't catch his breath. It didn't matter that his side hurt and his feet bled. He lived an obedient life. He died an obedient death. He ran all the way to the tomb."

They sat like boulders, still and silent in the morning chill. Their eyes weren't fixed on Epaphroditus now. They found other things to watch—the flames of a torch, the flickering shadows playing across a wall—the better to hear his words. "What happened when the easy got hard for Jesus?" They'd been caught by that question. They needed a moment to think about it.

He gave them that moment, and then moved on. "Because Jesus was willing to do the hard thing, God exalted him and gave him the victor's wreath. It's because he obeyed when obedience wasn't easy that we bow in worship before him today and praise him as Master of all."

He could see their heads moving. He could hear murmurs of assent. They were seeing it now. The truth of it touched something in them.

It was time. They were ready.

"My brothers and sisters. Paul also writes about us in this letter. Just before he speaks of Jesus. Do you remember this part?" He glanced again at the notes in his hand.

"Does your life in Christ give you strength? Does his love comfort you? Do we share together in the Spirit? Do you have mercy and kindness? If so, make me very happy by having the same thoughts, sharing the same love, and having one mind and purpose. When you do things, do not let selfishness or pride be your guide. Instead, be humble and give more honor to others than to yourselves. Do not be interested only in your own life, but be interested in the lives of others. In your lives you must think and act like Christ Jesus."

He looked up from his notes to catch their eyes. He did not want them staring away now. He wanted them watching him for the next part.

"Paul reminds us of a time when being a family—loving each other and treating each other right—came easy for us. We felt strong. We belonged. We found companionship and tenderness and mercy in this church. We enjoyed being together. We loved loving each other.

"But then God asked us to do something hard. He asked us to be a family not when it was easy but when it hurt. How would we act when troubles came, when angry words were spoken, when we didn't agree with each other, when we didn't even like each other very much? Would we be humble then? Would we still put ourselves aside and do what was best for each other? Would we still offer tenderness and compassion to people who weren't being very tender, very compassionate, to us?"

He looked around at the upturned faces and saw that they knew where he was going, what he was reaching for. And though they also knew it would be painful, they needed him to go there, to say the words that would lance the boil and allow the wound to finally heal.

"What happened when the easy got hard for us? What happened when it hurt to do the right thing? I won't speak for you. Each of you must examine your own heart and behavior. But I can confess for myself."

He took a breath and gathered the hard, shaming convictions that had gnawed at him all the way from Rome. "There came a time when loving you got hard for me—too hard. It hurt to be humble. Turning the other cheek, forgiving people who offended me, was more than I could manage. Patience and gentleness cost me too much. So I slowed down and eventually stopped running. I acted selfishly and excused myself for it. I got angry and blamed it on the pain. When people talked about me, I talked about them, and felt justified when I did. I gave myself permission to stop loving, to cool off with a little gossip and pride and apathy. I stopped on a hill far from the mountain and told myself, 'I can't go on.'"

They stared up at him with wide, unblinking eyes. They wanted to look away, ashamed of themselves and each other, seeing the truth in the potter's confession and knowing they shared his guilt. But they did not look away. If Epaphroditus could find the courage to confess, they could find the courage to watch as he did so, and speak their own confessions back with their eyes.

"Paul wrote this letter to tell us, 'You had something good there in Philippi. You found encouragement and companionship and community and compassion. But something happened. You slowed down. You stopped running.'" Epaphroditus shook his head slowly and shared a weak smile with his family. "And, of course, Paul is right. We did.

"Brothers and sisters. We have two choices before us today. We can stand in the middle of our failure and choose to give up and go home. Or we can confess our failure, ask God for strength, and start running again." He said it boldly, without qualifications or conditions. It was time for clarity.

"It's simple to see which choice Paul wants us to make. He says, 'Do me a favor. Remember how sweet it was when loving each other was easy? Well, do what is necessary to protect that love when things get hard.'"

Epaphroditus looked at his notes again, at the words of the letter. "He's telling us to recapture what we once had. He's asking us to be one again—in what we think, in the way we love, in our spirits. He tells us we can't let ambition or pride get in our way. We have to be humble. We have to look out for each other. That's how we start running again!"

He was almost finished now. Just a few more things to say. He looked around at the group with an affection so overwhelming, he wondered for a moment if he would be able to speak. To give himself a little time, he looked at his notes once more and read a final passage from the letter.

"My dear friends, you always obeyed when I was with you. Now that I am away, you should obey even more. So work with fear and trembling to discover what it really means to be saved. God is working in you to make you willing and able to obey him. Do everything without grumbling or arguing. Then you will be the pure and innocent children of God."

He set the papers down at his feet, freeing his hands, and counted Paul's points off on his fingers. "Keep obeying God. Keep living obedient lives, no matter what. Discover what it really means to be saved. God is at work in you. Quit quarrelling."

He stared around the group, catching Lydia's eye, seeing the top of Clement's bowed head, glancing briefly at the attentive faces of Jason and Syntyche, Claudia and Marcion.

What was it Lydia had said? *The question is not what's easy to do. The question is what's worth doing.* He smiled to himself and knew again she was right. He would never be happy as a simple potter. She'd said it was because he'd learned too much to go back. Maybe. But looking around the group, Epaphroditus understood that what ruined him for an easy life, what damned him to the hard, was not just what he knew, but who. He knew these people. And with a rising knot in his throat, he recognized that he would do any hard thing for their sakes.

"When things got hard for Jesus, he didn't give up and walk back to town. And when things get hard for us, we can't give up either. It doesn't matter that sometimes we can't catch our breath. It doesn't matter that sometimes our sides hurt and our feet ache. It doesn't matter that the road seems so long and the mountain looks so far away.

"We've got to keep running. When times are easy and when times are hard. When it feels good and when it hurts. When we're in the presence of God and when we're facing a cross. We keep running until we can't run anymore. And then we ask God to fill us with fresh energy and renewed strength. And, with the same mind that Jesus had, we start running toward the mountain again."

He stopped there and thought for a moment about saying more. But as the moment lengthened and the last sentence hung suspended over them all, Epaphroditus decided that made a good place to stop . . . the mind of Jesus . . . running for the mountain. He cleared his throat and looked around at them all a last time. And then with a smile, he made his way to the back of the courtyard as the morning light strengthened and the sounds of the awakening city grew louder.

The church sat in silence for a long while after he was done. No one stood to continue the worship. No one spoke to break the moment. They sat quietly, with only a cough or the whispers of a child to disturb their meditation.

Epaphroditus stood behind them, praying for open ears and hearts, for conviction and healing. He felt a hand on his shoulder and the hot breath of Clement in his ear. "You should travel more often, Potter. It does wonders for your preaching."

Epilogue

BE GLAD IN GOD!

(JULY, A.D. 65)

THE RAILING AROUND THE DECK OF THE SMALL COASTAL GALLEY WAS OLD and well used. Apart from breaks port and starboard to permit the loading of cargo and passengers, it ran from the stern to the bow of the ship, rising waist-high above the decking planks. The wood itself had been rubbed smooth by coarse ropes and the hard hands of sailors and stevedores. Heavy posts anchored the railing to the deck. Around these hung the ropes and braces and tackle by which sailors would raise sail or tie in at dock or move cargo.

As railings go, it had its problems. In direct sunlight, the wood baked so hot it would burn the hands of careless passengers. The ceaseless cycles of wet and dry split the wood in places, raising splinters to stand, waiting, for unsuspecting fingers and palms. On rare occasions, the railing received a fresh coat of paint. But, for the most part, it faced the elements naked and defenseless.

For all its shortcomings, the railing did provide a hold for sailors awash on a stormy deck . . . and a place for weary passengers to lean and watch the setting sun.

It was setting now, the last reds and purples of dying light touching the calm sea and reflecting against the hull of the ship. Shapes on the deck began to merge into the darkness, indistinct lumps fading into the dark mass of land to the east. Only objects silhouetted against the sky retained recognizable form—the vertical sweep of the mast, the horizontal line of the railing, the diagonals of ropes and rigging.

And the solitary figure leaning against the rail. He bent over it, both hands resting on its still-warm wood. A shawl covered his head and shoulders and he swayed to the rhythm of the ship's gentle rocking. He mumbled softly, praying in Hebrew, communing with God as evening became night.

Before it did, though, the old man paused to note the last of the light and to appreciate its dying beauty.

"Where morning dawns and evening fades," he intoned, borrowing from the Psalms, "you call forth songs of joy."

He stood there at the railing, bent and tilted, watching as day faded; hearing the insects fully alive in the final moments before dark; smelling the sweet fragrance of the sea. The old man loved this time of the evening. He loved these sounds and smells.

He thought of tomorrow and the miles he would have to walk to reach Philippi. He thought of yesterday, so many years ago, when he landed at this shore for the first time. He closed his eyes and saw the vision all over again—the urgent Macedonian with his urgent message. And he smiled, thinking how that message had changed his life.

He heard a noise behind him in the dark. "God be with you, Rufus," the old man called softly.

A massive shadow detached itself from the cluster of barrels surrounding the hatch leading down into the bowels of the boat. It approached the old man, towering over him. "And God be with you, Paul," the ex-soldier growled.

The two of them stood side by side at the railing, looking into the dark, comfortable with the quiet and with each other. Rufus thought again of the walk ahead of them and smiled to himself, thinking that there was still strength in the old man. Even so, it was a long march and Rufus was not sure how many miles Paul had left.

That touched on another issue that Rufus, once so impatient with reflection, had given a great deal of thought to. It had to do with the nature of strength. He was huge. The old man was slight to the point of frailty. He was muscled. The old man was painfully thin. He could walk for weeks under full pack. The old man required a rest after each mile and could not string many together on any given day.

Yet the old man was the strongest person Rufus had ever met. Strong in his mind. Strong in his stubborn convictions. Strong in his loyalties and his faith. It had taken Rufus a while to see that strength, to recognize the fortitude of the man. He was accustomed to measuring strength in the obvious way—the size of an arm, the weight of a load. And so it had taken time for him to see in the old man another kind of power that put his own brawn to shame. It was the recognition of that strength that finally broke the soldier and allowed him to listen to the story Paul wanted to tell, to answer the questions the old man kept asking.

"Are you happy, Rufus?"

Questions! Always questions! "I am learning to be, old man." At least now he could hear the questions. At least they didn't frighten him anymore or disturb his sleep.

"And what is it that makes you happy, Rufus? What gives you joy?"

Rufus blew out an exasperated breath. "Well, at the moment, I am warm. My stomach is full. There is a breeze blowing the smells of the sea to us. And I plan to sleep well tonight." *What's not to be happy about? You don't have to be a philosopher to feel good on a night like this.*

The old man smiled and remembered the night a lifetime back, when he and Silas suffered in a dungeon, and he had surprised them both by bursting into song. He remembered how his back throbbed and his ankles chafed and they sang until they were hoarse. He remembered how it felt, how clean and sure, to know that nothing—not rods or stocks or threat of death—could steal away the joy of standing in God's will. And he remembered, most of all, why he had started singing in the first place, why the joy had welled up inside him and spilled out in psalms and praise.

There, in the dark of the dungeon, he had seen their faces. Clement and Marcion. Syntyche and Euodia. Lucian and Jason and Lydia. One by one, they hovered before him in the blackness. He thought of changed lives and new hope. He thought of strangers-become-family. He realized that a life here, a life there, added up eventually to a new world and a different future. Somehow, it made the bleeding worthwhile. It made the pain bearable.

That's when he'd started to sing.

He saw the faces again now and felt the quickening, the eagerness, to see them for real.

"I think I'll sleep on deck tonight, Rufus. Under the stars."

Far into the night, as Rufus snored quietly beside him and thoughts of Philippi kept him from sleep himself, Paul squinted up into the night sky, covering one eye and then the other, trying to resolve the blurred smudges of blue-white into the familiar constellations of his youth. After a while, his concentration slipped. His knotted shoulders relaxed. His breathing deepened.

Paul slept. And dreamt of the questions he would ask God when he met him finally, and in person.

Scripture Source Notes

Prologue
WITH A SOLDIER TO GUARD HIM

Page
8 "*In the morning*": Psalm 5:3 NIV

Chapter Three
THOSE WHO OPPOSE YOU

43 "*Rolled away*": Joshua 5:9 NIV

Chapter Seven
COME OVER TO MACEDONIA

100 "*Give thanks*": Isaiah 12:4-5 NIV

Chapter Eight
ON THE SABBATH

111 "*Bless the Lord*": Psalm 103:1-3 NIV paraphrased
111 "*Hear, O Israel:*": Deuteronomy 6:4 NIV
111 "*These commandments*": Deuteronomy 6:6 NIV
112 "*To love the Lord*": Deuteronomy 11:13 NIV
112 "*You are to make*": Numbers 15:38 NIV
113 "*I will raise up*": Deuteronomy 18:18-19 NIV
113 "*Here is my servant*": Isaiah 42:1 NIV
114 "*This is what God*": Isaiah 42:5-7 NIV
114 "*I am the Lord*": Isaiah 42:8-9 NIV
117 "*He was pierced*": Isaiah 53:5 NIV

Chapter Nine
I HAVE YOU IN MY HEART

127 "*He poured out*": Isaiah 53:12 NIV
127 "*A band of evil*": Psalm 22:16-18 NIV

Chapter Ten
THE OTHER VETERANS

135 *The Lord is my shepherd:* Psalm 23:1-4 NIV
136 *The people walking:* Isaiah 9:2 NIV

Scripture Source Notes

PAGE

136 *He will swallow up:* Isaiah 25:8 NIV
137 *The cords of death:* Psalm 116:3-4 NIV
137 *There is no god:* Deuteronomy 32:39 NIV
137 *For men are not:* Lamentations 3:31-33 NIV
139 *If the only home:* Job 17:13-15 NIV paraphrased

Chapter Eleven
THE ONE WHO BEGAN THIS GOOD WORK IN YOU

147 *"Our Father in heaven":* Matthew 6:9-13 CEV
151 *"Praise the Lord":* Psalm 117 NIV
152 *"Give thanks to the Lord":* Psalm 136 excerpt from NIV
152 *"His love endures forever":* Psalm 136 excerpt from NIV
152 *"Give thanks to the God":* Psalm 136 excerpt from NIV
152 *"His love endures forever":* Psalm 136 excerpt from NIV
152 *"To him who alone":* Psalm 136 excerpt from NIV
152 *"His love endures forever":* Psalm 136 excerpt from NIV

Chapter Twelve
THESE JEWS ARE UPSETTING OUR CITY!

159 *"These men are":* Acts 16:17 NIV
160 *"In the name":* Acts 16:18 NIV

Chapter Fifteen
HE ALMOST DIED

203 *"This is the good news":* Mark 1:1-2 CEV
203 *Most honorable:* Luke 1:1-4 NLT
207 *Since we believe:* 2 Corinthians 5:14-15 NLT
212 *One of the Pharisees:* Luke 7:36-39 NLT

Chapter Sixteen
TO ALL OF GOD'S PEOPLE IN PHILIPPI

220 *"In the morning":* Psalm 5:3 NIV
225 *"Paul and Timothy":* Philippians 1:1-2 MSG
225 *"Every time I think":* Philippians 1:3-6 CEV
225 *"You have a special":* Philippians 1:7-8 CEV
225 *"All of you have":* Philippians 1:7-8 CEV

PAGE

226 *"God himself knows":* Philippians 1:7-8 CEV
226 *"I pray":* Philippians 1:9-11 NLT
226 *"For I want you":* Philippians 1:9-11 NLT
226 *"May you always":* Philippians 1:9-11 NLT
226 *"I want to report":* Philippians 1:12-14 MSG
227 *"That piqued":* Philippians 1:12-14 NLT
227 *"It's true that some here":* Philippians 1:15-18 a slight paraphrase of MSG
227 *"One group is motivated":* Philippians 1:15-18 a slight paraphrase of MSG
227 *"The others, now that":* Philippians 1:15-18 a slight paraphrase of MSG
228 *"So how am I":* Philippians 1:15-18 a slight paraphrase of MSG
228 *"And I'm going to keep":* Philippians 1:19-20 MSG
228 *"I can hardly wait":* Philippians 1:21 NCV
229 *"As long as I'm alive":* Philippians 1:22-26 MSG
229 *"The desire to break":* Philippians 1:22-26 MSG
229 *"But most days":* Philippians 1:22-26 MSG
229 *"So I plan to be":* Philippians 1:22-26 MSG
229 *"Meanwhile, live in":* Philippians 1:27-30 MSG
229 *"Stand united":* Philippians 1:27-30 MSG
230 *"There's far more":* Philippians 1:27-30 MSG

Chapter Seventeen
I Must Send Him Back to You

233 *"I am very happy":* Philippians 4:10-17 NCV
233 *"You continued to care":* Philippians 4:10-17 NCV
233 *"But it was good":* Philippians 4:10-17 NCV
234 *"And now I have everything":* Philippians 4:18-20 NCV
234 *"Give our regards":* Philippians 4:21-23 MSG
234 *"Receive and experience":* Philippians 4:21-23 MSG

Chapter Eighteen
Give Him a Grand Welcome

247 *"And now I":* Philippians 4:2-3 NLT
247 *"And they worked":* Philippians 4:2-3 NLT

Scripture Source Notes

PAGE

247 *"Always be glad"*: Philippians 4:4-7 CEV
248 *"Finally, my friends"*: Philippians 4:8-9 CEV
248 *"Receive and experience"*: Philippians 4:23 MSG
251 *"Finally, my friends"*: Philippians 4:8 CEV

Chapter Nineteen
STAY ON TRACK, STEADY IN GOD

259 *"Whatever you do"*: Philippians 2:18-24 MSG
260 *"But for right now"*: Philippians 2:25-30 MSG
260 *"So you see why"*: Philippians 2:25-30 MSG
261 *"And that's about it"*: Philippians 3:1 MSG
261 *"Watch out for those dogs"*: Philippians 3:2-6 NLT
261 *"Yet I could have"*: Philippians 3:2-6 NLT
262 *"I once thought"*: Philippians 3:7-9 NLT
263 *"As a result"*: Philippians 3:10-11 NLT
264 *"I don't mean"*: Philippians 3:12-17 NLT
264 *"For I have told you"*: Philippians 3:18-19 NLT
266 *"Dear brothers"*: Philippians 4:1 NLT

Chapter Twenty
HELP THEM WORK THINGS OUT

276 *"All men are like grass"*: Isaiah 40:6-7 NIV

Chapter Twenty-One
I RUN TOWARD THE GOAL

285 *"Christ was truly God"*: Philippians 2:6-8 CEV
285 *"Then God gave"*: Philippians 2:9-11 CEV
287 *"Does your life"*: Philippians 2:1-5 NCV
289 *"My dear friends"*: Philippians 2:12-15 CEV

Epilogue
BE GLAD IN GOD!

292 *"Where morning dawns"*: Psalm 65:8 NIV

About the Author

TIM WOODROOF follows an almost genetic call to preach. Both his father and grandfather were in the ministry. Altogether, the three of them share over 125 years of preaching experience. Tim has served churches in Nebraska, Oregon, and Nashville, Tennessee. He has written two other books for NavPress *(Among Friends: You Can Help Make Your Church a Warmer Place* and *Walk This Way: An Interactive Guide to Following Jesus)* and is the author of numerous programs for adult education in churches.

Tim did his graduate work in psychology and theology, receiving an M.S. in clinical psychology (from Texas A&M University) and a Ph.D. in community and human resources (University of Nebraska). He narrowly avoided being awarded an M.Th. from the Harding Graduate School of Religion in Memphis by virtue of being so tired of school he could not bring himself to write yet another thesis.

Though Tim speaks for functions around the country, his primary love is the local church. In 1998, he and his family moved to Nashville to work with the Otter Creek Church. He and Julie have three (mostly) adorable children—Sarah, James, and Jonathan. Tim has notified us that he is booking speaking appointments only in places close to blue-ribbon trout streams.

Acknowledgments

It is one of the happy chores of an author to express gratitude to those who have given encouragement and comfort during the writing of a book. Though readers may find such expressions tedious, an author should at least remind his readers (and himself) that books are formed within the context of the author's life. And *this* author's life is filled with people who influence, nurture, and guide him. Without these people, writing would be impossible—or, at least, greatly impoverished.

Several people read this manuscript, made suggestions, and contributed improvements. My thanks to Ron and Kay Stump, Sandra Collins, Jim and Louine Woodroof, Dr. Larry Long, LeeAnn Rice, John Ott, and Sarah Woodroof.

As always, I am grateful to the elders of the Otter Creek Church who encourage my writing ministry by their words and by allowing me time to focus on the task of writing. Their tangible support is rare and appreciated and worthy of emulation by other church leaders who find themselves blessed (or burdened) with preachers who are called to write. My companions in full-time ministry at Otter Creek cover for me and take on additional work for my sake while I am away putting words on paper. Thanks to Kay Duncan, Corky French, Keely Hall, John Ott, Scott Owings, Emma Phillips, LeeAnn Rice, and Brandon Scott Thomas.

From time to time, people offer me a cabin or condo for writing purposes. Thanks to the Stites and the Sawyers for their generous hospitality.

In a special way, I need to acknowledge several people connected in various ways with NavPress: Sue Geiman, former editor with NavPress, who first saw the promise in this project and signed a contract; Harold Fickett, who helped me shape the narrative and taught me the difference between telling a story and reporting it; William Klein, who read through the notes, catching several grievous errors and making a number of excellent suggestions; and Greg Clouse, my current editor, who picked up this project midstream and wrestled it safely to shore. NavPress has a wonderfully competent editorial staff—thanks to Darla and Nanci in particular.

Finally, I am eager to thank Julie (my loving and longsuffering wife) and Sarah, James, and Jonathan (our sweet kids) for their support. More than a few hours have been stolen from them and given to this. I could not write without their encouragement.